DISARMING IRAQ

DISARMING IRAQ

THE SEARCH FOR WEAPONS
OF MASS DESTRUCTION

HANS BLIX

BLOOMSBURY

First published in Great Britain 2004

Copyright © by Hans Blix 2004

The right of Hans Blix to be identified as the author of this Work has been asserted by
him in accordance with the Copyright, Designs & Patents Act 1988.

Bloomsbury Publishing Plc, 38 Soho Square, London W1D 3HB

A CIP catalogue record for this book is available from the British Library

ISBN 0 7475 7354 9 Hardback edition
10 9 8 7 6 5 4 3 2 1

ISBN 0 7475 7358 1 Export paperback edition
10 9 8 7 6 5 4 3 2 1

Printed in Great Britain by Clays Ltd, St Ives plc

All papers used by Bloomsbury Publishing are natural recyclable products
made from wood grown in well-managed forests. The manufacturing
processes conform to the environmental regulations of the country of origin.

To the staff at the United Nations
Monitoring, Verification and Inspection Commission
(UNMOVIC)

Contents

Introduction

When I retired as director-general of the International Atomic Energy Agency (IAEA) in November 1997 and returned to Stockholm, I planned to write a book about the IAEA's inspection experience in Iraq and North Korea. But before I could start work on that project, Kofi Annan, the secretary general of the United Nations, asked me to become the executive chairman of the newly created UN Monitoring, Verification and Inspection Commission for Iraq (UNMOVIC).

Having studied at Columbia University's law school from 1954 to 1956, I was at home in New York and I loved the city. The fact that my younger son was now pursing his Ph.D. at my old university and that I was able to meet him and his wife for dinner every so often added warmth to my life. The ease and low cost with which one can telephone across the Atlantic allowed for daily conversations with my wife, Eva. To our elder son in Stockholm I kept writing letters, which eventually formed a diary that turned out to be of great help when I wrote this book. My family network provided love and stability during a period of excitement and pressure. Yirka and Ed Emerson, close and dear friends from my school days in New York, made sure that I got to see the important plays on and off Broadway. Our joint expeditions provided an essential counterbalance to my own life on and off the political stage over at the UN.

Some time in the spring of 2003 Per Gedin, an old friend from my student days in Uppsala and a very successful publisher, contacted me to say that I must write a book about my experiences in

Introduction

the Iraq affair. He brought me into contact with Albert Bonnier, who would become my Scandinavian publisher, and they got me to agree to write this book when I left the Commission. It was not difficult to persuade me to do so. I knew that I had lived through an important sequence of events in contemporary history. Diplomats and statesmen would describe their parts in these events from their various vantage points. I thought it was important that what transpired on the central UN stage should be described by someone who had actually been there.

I was lucky to be advised to contact the literary agent Jane Gelfman. She and Albert Bonnier encouraged me throughout the writing process. I have enjoyed and appreciated their sophisticated judgment, their friendship, and their professional competence. In Stockholm, Anders Mellbourn, director of the Institute of International Affairs, and in New York, Dan Frank, editorial director of Pantheon Books, have devoted much time and energy to helping me edit my drafts. I am very grateful to them for the skillful and gentle way they have gone about this difficult and hectic work.

Dimitri Perricos was always an energetic force. I knew that he would ensure that UNMOVIC inspections were professionally and competently carried out—and he did. He was kind enough to read through the entire book and helped me to correct errors when my memory led me astray. I am indebted to him for this and for all the valuable advice he has given me. I am also indebted to Ewen Buchanan and Geoffrey Allan for keeping me continuously informed via e-mail of what has been happening in Iraq since I left New York in the summer of 2003.

Stockholm
January 2004

Disarming Iraq

1

Disarming Iraq: Moments of Truth?

Invasion Instead of Inspection

On the afternoon of Sunday, March 16, 2003, I was in my office on the thirty-first floor of the United Nations Secretariat building in New York, the headquarters of the UN Monitoring, Verification and Inspection Commission for Iraq (UNMOVIC). Some of my close collaborators had joined me to put the final touches on a work program I was to submit to the Security Council.

When our commission was established by a Security Council resolution in December 1999, the Council had recognized that there might still be weapons of mass destruction (WMD) in Iraq, despite the fact that a great deal of disarmament had been accomplished through UN inspections after the end of the Gulf War in 1991. In November 2002, a new round of inspections had been initiated to resolve key remaining tasks in the disarming of Iraq.

Although the inspection organization was now operating at full strength and Iraq seemed determined to give it prompt access everywhere, the United States appeared as determined to replace our inspection force with an invasion army. After the terror attacks

3

on New York and Washington on September 11, 2001, a policy of containment—keeping Saddam Hussein in his box—and ensuring the disarmament of Iraq through UN inspections was deemed no longer acceptable.

The people around me were all solid professionals coming from different parts of the world. There was Dimitri Perricos, probably the world's most experienced inspector. A Greek and by profession a chemist, he had more than twenty years of experience with international nuclear inspections—in Iraq, North Korea, South Africa and many other places. He was the head of operations. Muttusamy Sanmuganathan, known to all as Sam, was from Sri Lanka. Both Dimitri and Sam had worked closely with me for many years in Vienna, when I was the director general of the International Atomic Energy Agency (IAEA). Ewen Buchanan, a Scot, was our manager of media relations and institutional memory. For years he had been a political expert and the spokesman of the previous inspection authority, the UN Special Commission (UNSCOM). There was Torkel Stiernlöf, who had been stationed in Baghdad and knew Arabic. He was about to return to his job at the foreign ministry in Stockholm after six intense months as my executive assistant. Lastly, there was Torkel's successor, Olof Skoog, an ambassador at the early age of 35 and on loan to me.

The military invasion of Iraq was all but announced and here we were at the UN sketching a peaceful way to try to ensure the country's disarmament! The military force, whose buildup had begun in the summer of 2002 and had been an essential reason why Iraq had accepted the inspectors back, had reached invasion strength and was now waiting to be deployed.

In the Security Council, all efforts to reach agreement on what might be demanded of Iraq in the next few weeks had collapsed. Proposals had been made by the British that Saddam Hussein should go before Iraqi television and declare his determination to disarm and to cooperate fully with the inspectors. The declaration would be accompanied by Iraq's fulfillment of a number of specific disarmament tasks within a very short time—perhaps ten days. (The approach had some similarity to the British efforts which ten months later would prompt Libya's leader, Colonel Muammar Qaddafi, to declare that Libya was stopping all efforts to acquire weapons of mass destruction and would open up for thorough inspection.) The U.S./UK would consider themselves authorized to take armed action against Iraq if they determined that Iraq was in non-fulfillment of the demands.

While the guidelines in the December 1999 UNMOVIC resolution were perfectly valid and called for a work program covering a first period of 120 days of inspections, the U.S., the UK and Spain had been taking their cues from Security Council Resolution 1441, adopted on November 8, 2002. In their reading, this resolution gave Iraq only a limited time and a last opportunity to cooperate to attain disarmament or else face "serious consequences." That limited time, in their view, had now expired. Others in the Security Council thought the process of inspections required more time. They were not ready, at this stage, to authorize "serious consequences"—armed action. Most member states of the Council were of the view that such a decision was for the Council collectively, not for individual members, as the U.S. and the UK insisted.

On this Sunday, U.S. president George W. Bush, British prime minister Tony Blair and Spanish prime minister Jose Maria Aznar Lopez had met for an hour on the Azores islands in the middle of the Atlantic and, for the record, made a last appeal to reluctant members of the Security Council to go along with the draft resolution on Iraq. Blair had stressed that they had gone an extra mile for peace, but Bush seemed already to be describing the blessings that would follow from armed action.

Most observers felt the war was now a certainty—and, indeed, it came. Although I thought the probability was very high, I was also, even at this very late date, aware that unexpected things can happen. I remembered how, in July 1991, after confrontations, the Iraqis had sent the IAEA a note admitting that they had tried several methods of enriching uranium. In October 1998, Kofi Annan, the secretary general of the United Nations, had secured an important concession from Iraq, prompting U.S. president Bill Clinton to call back bombers that had been sent to punish Iraq for its lack of cooperation. If, in the current situation, Saddam Hussein had made the kind of dramatic speech the British suggested, and offered quickly to solve a number of issues, there might well have been a suspension of the marching and flying orders and, instead, intensified inspections. Saddam did make a speech on his son's television channel, but it was not the dramatic gesture that the situation called for. In it, he noted that Iraq had *had* weapons of mass destruction in the past, but that it had none now.

As we were sitting around the table in my office, the telephone rang. It was Assistant Secretary of State John Wolf in Washington, calling to advise me that it was time to withdraw our inspectors from Iraq. No further notice would be issued and expeditious action was suggested.

Preparations for the Withdrawal of Inspectors

We had been preparing for this situation since the end of February, and in the previous few weeks had deliberately decreased the total number of our staff in Iraq. The chartered helicopters had already been removed by their owners. We had one airplane sitting in Baghdad and another was chartered to enable us to assist the UN by airlifting staff dealing with humanitarian assistance. Jeeps and buses for land transport would also be available, if this were to prove necessary.

It was now around 3 p.m. this Sunday in New York, and 11 p.m. in Baghdad. If Dr. Miroslav Gregoric, the head of our mission in Baghdad, were instructed immediately, the first planeload of staff would leave Baghdad the following morning. I was anxious to bring the people for whom I was responsibile to security as soon as possible. However, I was not the only one with responsibility. As secretary general, Kofi Annan had the highest managerial responsibility for all UN staff in Iraq. My colleague Mohamed ElBaradei, director general of the IAEA, was responsible for the nuclear inspectors in Baghdad. I phoned both. Mohamed did not want to hasten the process. He was anxious that the withdrawal should not look like a retreat.

Although the secretary general did not need permission from the Security Council to issue an order of withdrawal, he wanted to inform the Council before he gave the instruction. He decided that he would do so at a meeting the Council was scheduled to hold on Monday morning. This meant that the withdrawal could not take place until Tuesday morning. I was not happy about the delay, but I assumed Kofi Annan had reasons to be confident that this delay did not increase the risks.

Security Council, March 17: Resolution Authorizing War Withdrawn from Vote

Our inspectors in Iraq continued to work on Monday, March 17. They supervised the destruction of two Al Samoud 2 missiles, bringing the total number destroyed to seventy-two. They conducted a private interview with a biological scientist, bringing the total number of such private interviews to eleven. Inspection teams visited a dairy factory 140 kilometers north of Baghdad and two sites northwest of Baghdad. I worried about the risk of any hitches in the arrangements for their withdrawal on Tuesday morning. We had earlier received assurances from the Iraqi side, but I remembered that, in 1990, hostages had been taken.

The Security Council met at 10 a.m. To my dismay, Kofi Annan's announcement of the withdrawal of UN staff from Iraq did not come first. It was already 6 p.m. in Baghdad and every hour's delay in issuing instructions from New York would make the preparations for departure more difficult.

The tone in the Council was not combative or acrimonious. The struggle was over. The path of inspection had been blocked by the U.S., the UK and Spain, and a resolution implicitly blessing armed intervention had been blocked by the majority of states in the Security Council. The Azores meeting and all the working of telephones during the weekend had not brought any change in the positions of governments. The UK said that the draft resolution, which it had sponsored in the Council, *would not be put to a vote*. This was a tacit admission that it could not have passed. If the resolution had been submitted to a vote and rejected, the negative vote would have further undermined the doubtful claim by the sponsors that earlier resolutions by the Council authorized them to use armed force if and when they deemed that Iraq was in non-fulfillment.

Even though the UK and the U.S. pointed to the threat of a veto from France as the reason for this debacle—ignoring the possibility that China and Russia might have joined France—a majority of the Council had, in fact if not in form, refused to legitimize armed action. The UK persisted in stating that although the chances for a peaceful solution were now slim, Saddam could still take action to save the situation. The U.S. confirmed the advice that the UN should take expeditious action to withdraw staff.

France declared its opposition to any resolution that would authorize force and rejected the view that individual members could use armed force without Council authorization. France wanted UNMOVIC to present its work program for inspections and suggested the Council meet—perhaps at ministerial level, as Russia had urged—on Wednesday to approve the program. A time line should be set after which the Council would evaluate the results of the inspections. Mexico said there was at the time no justification for the use of force in Iraq. Angola said it had lived with war and insisted on the need to exhaust all peaceful means.

War Justified by Iraq's Failure to Disarm; Moment of Truth Expected

In a televised speech on the evening of Monday, March 17, President Bush issued an ultimatum to Saddam Hussein to leave Iraq with his family within forty-eight hours. Vice President Dick Cheney said that an offer by Iraq to disarm was no longer an option. Referring to Saddam Hussein, he said, "We believe he has, in fact, reconstituted nuclear weapons." His declaration was as firm as it was unfounded.

Secretary of State Colin Powell was more nuanced. At a press conference on March 17, he said the U.S. had become concerned about Iraq's sincerity shortly after the adoption of the new resolution in November 2002. The 12,000-page declaration Iraq had submitted a month later had, he stated, been an incomplete and untruthful rendering of their weapons programs. The U.S. had cooperated loyally with and assisted the inspectors. Despite some improvements, Iraq had not, however, provided the kind of cooperation demanded. The resolution which the U.S., the UK and Spain had now decided not to put to the vote would have given Iraq yet another last opportunity, but it had been blocked by France's threatened veto. So, although the UN would remain an important institution, the Security Council, in this case, had not met the test.

Perhaps it was convenient to blame the diplomatic failure on France, but it was evident that a majority of the members of the Council were against armed action at this juncture, though none of the states had excluded agreement on it at a subsequent stage. It is an interesting notion that when a small minority has been rebuffed by a strong majority, it is the majority that has failed the test.

There was no reference in Colin Powell's statement to the U.S. asserting a right to strike preemptively against Iraq. Instead, his legal justification given for the armed action was the same as that claimed by the UK: namely, that Iraq had not fulfilled its obligations under binding Security Council resolutions *to disarm* and that this entitled individual members of the Council to take action without the need for any collective decision by the Council.

With an expression used also by other U.S. spokesmen, Powell declared that the window on diplomacy was closing and that the "moment of truth" was arriving. Armed action, indeed, stands in contrast to diplomacy—but it does not necessarily stand for truth. There might be more to the saying "The first casualty in war is truth." Nor do I find it appropriate to make diplomacy the opposite of truth—to project it as lies or illusion. Diplomacy will often use language that understates the divergence of positions so as to minimize the gaps that have to be bridged and make reconciliation less difficult, but lying is not a part of diplomacy—at least not of good diplomacy.

The most important truth that U.S. spokesmen had in mind and expected to be revealed through the war was undoubtedly the existence of stocks of biological and chemical weapons and other prohibited items, and the people and programs related to them.

Withdrawal of UN Staff and Submission of Work Program to the Council

On Tuesday, March 18, Dimitri Perricos phoned at 7 a.m. and told me that our first plane from Baghdad had arrived in Cyprus and that the second was due a little later. All had gone well! They had even been able to take along sensitive equipment. The Iraqis had been most helpful throughout the operation. What a relief! Our inspectors would now stay in Larnaca for some days before being released to go back to their home countries. As they remained formally in our service until their contracts expired, they would still be available in the rather unlikely case that UNMOVIC would be asked to perform some verification function during the coming occupation. I was relieved that all our staff was out of danger, but I also felt empty, as after a school test for which you have braced yourself, and I was disappointed that we had not been given a reasonable amount of time to achieve the mission with which we had been entrusted. I had accepted the task of building and leading the new inspection organization three years before. It had become an expert and well-equipped force, and all agreed that it had done its job well as an effective and independent tool of the Security Council—for three and a half months. With the strong military pressure developed by the U.S. and UK, our Iraqi counterparts had toward the end become almost frantic in submitting material, seeking evidence and finding persons we could interview. I cannot claim we were confident that these efforts would lead to revelations and clarifications that would satisfy us and the world, but we were in a hopeful phase.

I felt the armed action taken was not in line with what the Security Council had decided five months earlier. The Council had not set a three-and-a-half-month deadline for inspections. Had there been any denials of access? Any cat-and-mouse play? No. Had the inspections been going well? Yes. True, they had not resolved any of the open disarmament issues, but in my view they had gone much too well to be abandoned and justify war. While the Iraqis had become frantic, though not very successful, about finding evidence of their own innocence, the U.S. had become frantic—but also not very successful—about finding convincing evidence of Iraqi guilt.

The Bush administration had long criticized the policy of containment (based most recently in the December 1999 resolution and consisting of inspection and monitoring, military pressure and sanctions), claiming it was insufficient to address the case of Iraq's weapons of mass destruction. It had now opened a quick campaign of armed *counter-proliferation,* which it claimed was justified under the Council's December 2002 resolution and which it expected to be the decisive way to ensure the eradication of weapons of mass destruction in Iraq.

What would have happened if the U.S. government had been willing to continue the traditional policy?

Without a military buildup by the U.S. in the summer of 2002, Iraq would probably not have accepted a resumption of inspections. However, if we assume this buildup and the return of inspectors, it is conceivable that a *moderate* continued buildup, continued inspection with no denials of access, and a guarantee of large-scale interviews with technical people in Iraq could have shown in time that there were no weapons of mass destruction. It would surely have been difficult to persuade both inspectors and the world, let alone the U.S., but if there had not been hopeful results by, say July 2003, when the 120-day period would have expired, it seems likely that a majority in the Security Council might have been ready to authorize armed action, which could have started with UN legitimacy after the summer heat—and revealed that there were no weapons.

For my part, I felt at the time that Iraq's inability or unwillingness to prove it had no weapons of mass destruction was a reason not to have confidence in the country and not to lift sanctions. However, since its level of cooperation was much better than it had rendered inspectors in earlier years, I did not think that inspections should be curtailed and declared a failure after only three and an half months—and used as a justification to go to war.

In the real world there was not a moderate buildup of military force but the relentless accumulation of a full-scale invasion army. Barring a conversion of Saddam and a "strategic decision" by him, this did not leave the U.S. much choice—if, indeed, it wanted one.

Was the War Predetermined?

Many people have suggested that the war was decided in Washington in the summer of 2002 and that UN inspections were allowed only as a way to fill the time until the military was ready. An *International Herald Tribune* article (September 4, 2003) citing *The Washington Times* refers to a "military report" to the U.S. Joint Chiefs of Staff showing that President Bush approved the overall war strategy for Iraq in August 2002. Time, political memoirs and declassification of documents will eventually uncover the truth.

My speculation—it is no more than that—is that the Bush administration decided in the summer of 2002 that, following the terror attacks on September 11, 2001, it should be ready preemptively to strike any identified enemy which it feared might pose a threat to the U.S. It saw Saddam Hussein as personifying evil, as successfully having thwarted the search for and elimination of weapons of mass destruction by UN inspection, as possibly shielding or cooperating with international terrorists and as one of the stalwarts against peace with Israel. It concluded, I think, that the president, having declared war on terrorism, needed to eliminate this perceived threat well before the next presidential election. The U.S. would have the military capability to do the job, as its engagement in Afghanistan was winding down and being partly taken over by NATO.

Where did this leave the UN and inspection? Dick Cheney is on record as saying in August 2002 that inspection was at best useless. His view was probably shared by the U.S. secretary of defense, Donald Rumsfeld, who was quoted as saying that the reality of inspections was that "things have been found [in Iraq] not by discovery, but through defectors" (*The Washington Post*, December 5, 2002). Nevertheless, a U.S. military buildup would take some time, and I presume it was concluded that there would be no great harm in engaging the UN in a last and probably futile attempt to disarm Iraq. If Iraq refused to readmit UN inspectors, a U.S. armed action could be seen not only as defending U.S. security but also as enforcing the demands of the world organization. If the inspectors were readmitted and again denied access to sites or subjected to other non-compliance, a U.S. armed action could, again, both serve U.S. security interests and uphold UN demands. And if Iraq were to readmit inspectors and deliver prohibited weapons, so much the better! Saddam would, regrettably, remain, but he would be a different Saddam.

In the following chapters I shall describe how events followed partly along a foreseen track, and how they derailed badly at the end. Iraq accepted renewed inspections. A U.S.-inspired resolution was unanimously adopted by the Security Council in November 2002, submitting Iraq to demands which, if not fully respected, could justify armed action. Some have suggested that the U.S. wanted the inspections to fail, noting the paucity of sites proposed for inspection by U.S. intelligence in November and December 2002 to support this view. I do not agree. The U.S. took a keen interest in the inspections at this time and urged us to expand them very fast and to conduct them "aggressively"—conceivably with a hope, or at least an expectation, that Iraq would deny us access, thereby violating the resolution and opening itself to "serious consequences."

From the U.S. viewpoint, the evolution in 2003 was problematic. While the inspectors identified and supervised the destruction of missiles that somewhat exceeded the permitted range, they did not find any of the WMD which were unaccounted for, nor did they get credible explanations for their absence. The Iraqis grumbled but behaved tolerably well. They did not even make any serious resistance to inspections of two presidential sites—in their eyes probably the most sacrosanct spots in Iraq.

The situation resulting might have been the worst possible from the U.S. viewpoint: Disarmament had not been achieved, nor had any good justification been created for armed action. Not surprisingly, the majority in the Security Council and strong public opinion in most countries, including the U.S., refused to go along with the use of armed force and demanded more time for inspections. There were political and diplomatic controversies between the U.S. and the majority of the UN member states, within NATO and among Europeans. Interestingly, this was not a clash between great powers as to *whether* Iraq should be disarmed, but about the method to achieve it. In the end, I think the amassment of an army of some 300,000 troops near Iraq and the approaching hot season made action inevitable. The armed force could not have been withdrawn without producing much more spectacular results than were taking place (such as the elimination of some seventy missiles), nor could it sit idly by in rising temperatures and just wait for some clear-cut and convincing reason to invade. It had to invade.

My conclusion was and remains that the armed action that was taken was expected but not irrevocably predetermined.

2

Inspection: Why, How, When?

Retirement from the IAEA; Time for Reflection
on International Inspections

After sixteen years of work in Vienna as director general of the International Atomic Energy Agency (IAEA), I retired in November 1997 and returned to Stockholm. Most of my time at the IAEA had been devoted to questions of the peaceful uses of nuclear energy, but I had also been much engaged in the operation of the agency's inspections and in its problems—the Iraqi violations, which had gone undetected; the implementation of the Security Council–mandated inspections after the Gulf War, which had been difficult; the supervision of the dismantling of South Africa's nuclear weapons program; and the agency's detection that North Korea had more plutonium than it had declared, which triggered a crisis.

Nineteen ninety-seven had been a very good year professionally: Several conventions had been adopted. I was happy to see the fabric of international rules extend and strengthen in the nuclear field. It was also of very great importance that after four years of work, the agency adopted an additional protocol to strengthen the safeguards agreements under the Nuclear Non-Proliferation Treaty (NPT). When accepted and ratified by states, this instrument would help increase the effectiveness of the verification regime, which was vital in light of the weaknesses that had come to light in the case of Iraq after the 1991 Gulf War.

A little earlier in 1997, my wife, Eva, had returned to Stockholm to work in the Swedish foreign ministry after years of international service in Geneva and Brussels. Our jobs had kept us separate for some ten years. It was nice to return to a life together. In retirement, I remained engaged in nuclear power and safety, the global environment, nuclear disarmament and non-proliferation. Eva was made an ambassador and given charge of Arctic and Antarctic issues in the ministry. We joked that after the collapse of the Soviet Union, this was the only bipolarity left in the world. She loved the job. On one point our interests directly intersected: the demilitarized status of the Antarctic and the right to inspections in the region.

International Confidence-Building through Inspection: The Antarctic Treaty of 1959 Marked the Beginning and the NPT of 1968 Was the Breakthrough

I now had time to think and write about the laws of war and disarmament. Why had sovereign states invented international inspection? What level of intrusiveness would states accept? I continued to closely follow the inspection processes in Iraq as well as in North Korea and was getting ready to write a book about the experiences I had gained at the IAEA in both cases.

Long before the Second World War there had been treaties prohibiting the use of specific weapons or means of warfare. Hague declarations of 1899 prohibited use of the so-called dum-dum bullet (which flattened against the human body and caused terrible wounds), use of "asphyxiating and deleterious gases," and—for a period of five years—"the launching of projectiles and explosives from balloons or by other similar new methods." After the First World War, during which extensive and horrible use was made of gas as a weapon, the Geneva Protocol of 1925 prohibited the use of both gas and "bacteriological methods of warfare." None of these agreements had any machinery for verifying compliance. It was thought that any violations would be visible. The risk of retaliation was seen as a deterrent against use and might well have been the reason why gas was not used during the Second World War.

The Antarctic Treaty, concluded in 1959, was an important effort to limit the all-embracing competition between the blocs. No military bases, maneuvers or testing of weapons would be allowed in the Antarctic. No nuclear explosions were permitted. Of special interest from my perspective was the treaty's stipulation that all areas of the Antarctic, including all installations, should be open at all times to inspection by "observers." The provision was a modest first step in using international inspection to create confidence that no activities occurred in violation of a demilitarization treaty.

The Non-Proliferation Treaty of 1968 and Inspections in Iraq

During the Cold War, nuclear weapons states were deterred from using these weapons against each other by the risk of mutually assured destruction (MAD). For other states, it was thought that the best guarantee against these weapons being used against them lay in their simply *not having them*. Since possession—but not use—could be kept secret, this precept required a system of inspections to assure the world that no state claiming to be non-nuclear would one day spring an unwelcome surprise. Such "safeguards" inspections were made obligatory for the non-nuclear-weapons states that joined the NPT, and the operation of the inspections system was entrusted to the IAEA. Standard safeguards agreements were concluded in accordance with a model approved by its member states. (Similar thinking led to the creation in 1993 of the Chemical Weapons Convention prohibiting the production, stockpiling and use of such weapons and establishing an inspection system.) Though the system represented a dramatic leap forward simply by being the first global on-site inspection system, and though it helped pave the way for inspections in other arms-control areas (e.g., between European states), the 1968 system eventually proved the difficulty of designing an inspections regime capable of satisfying all state parties while simultaneously fulfilling its mandate.

If you want a control system that gives a maximum of assurance, you can design it to be very fine-meshed and very intrusive, requiring that inspectors have the right to go almost anywhere, anytime, and demand any kind of documents. Such a system, however, has several potential drawbacks: It might prove extraordinarily expensive, it might force governments to open up their most diverse and sensitive sites to inspectors and it might give many false alarms. In the late 1960s, at a time when states guarded their sovereignty much more jealously than today, such an intrusive system was simply not feasible. The 1968 system, therefore, had few teeth. Its inspectors had no right to roam around a country looking for undeclared installations or activities. (Nor would this kind of activity have been meaningful without intelligence from member states, and at this time no channels had been established to provide such intelligence.) The inspected state also had the right to reject individual inspectors, and many made use of this right. The safeguards system as it was designed was too weak to ensure the discovery of clandestine installations in a closed society.

Another weakness was that the original system was designed primarily with open, advanced industrial countries in mind, and was aimed at creating confidence that no "significant" quantities of fissionable material (stated as twenty-five kilograms of uranium 235 or eight kilograms of plutonium) was diverted from declared nuclear installations to military purposes. (States like Germany and Japan and Sweden would have been technically capable of making nuclear weapons.) Over time, this system proved too weak to ensure the discovery of clandestine installations in a closed society. The Iraqi program that eventually came to light proved this, though it had only succeeded in producing about two and a half grams of plutonium and less than half a kilogram of uranium, at an average enrichment level of 4 percent. Bomb-grade enrichment would be 80 percent and above. The Iraqis had learned *how* to enrich uranium, but their industrial capacity was still very small.

Questioning the Reliability of Safeguards:
The Osirak Incident, 1981

In 1981, one country demonstrated clearly that the safeguards inspections performed by the IAEA in Iraq did not give it confidence. In a spectacular raid, Israeli planes destroyed the Iraqi research reactor Osirak, which had not yet started to operate. Israel was condemned by the IAEA, and in a resolution unanimously adopted on June 19, 1981, the Security Council described the action as "a serious threat to the entire safeguards system."

The United States, then with Ronald Reagan as president, joined in the vote condemning Israel. Ambassador Jean Kirkpatrick explained the U.S. vote by saying that "Israel failed to exhaust peaceful means for the resolution of this dispute." At the same time, Kirkpatrick's long speech showed a good deal of understanding for Israel's action: "It is surely not unreasonable to raise serious doubts about the efficacy of the Non-Proliferation Treaty safeguards system," she said, noting that safeguards inspectors are "not policemen; they can only inspect what has been declared."

Despite its questioning of the safeguards system's reliability, neither the U.S. nor any other government took the initiative to strengthen the system during the 1980s. There would at this time have been insuperable resistance to more intrusive inspections.

Although suspicions against Iraq existed, at the time no government or agency had any concrete evidence of Iraq's large, secret uranium-enrichment and weapons-construction facilities. They were neither known to the IAEA nor, it appears, to any national intelligence service. The agency continued to report annually that the safeguards inspections in Iraq had not detected any diversion of a significant quantity of fissionable material. This was true enough, but should be read with an awareness of the limitations under which the inspectors operated. Governments were no doubt aware of this, but the broader public might well have been lulled into misplaced confidence.

Could the Secretariat have done more? Yes, it could have performed inspections at Iraq's declared installations more often than it did. (Fewer inspections were done, in order to save resources.) It could have systematically scanned media for information and found a few suspicious items regarding Iraqi imports. Could states have been more alert? Yes, they might have had sharper export controls and better intelligence. However, during the Iran-Iraq War many states were more concerned about fundamentalist Iran and were probably not keen to ask questions and possibly rock the Iraqi boat. It is not likely that any of the measures the agency could have taken would have led to discoveries, but they might conceivably have led to useful controversies—alarms.

Designing the Security Council Inspection Regime for Iraq in March 1991: UNSCOM and the IAEA

With full international support and Security Council blessing, the short Gulf War succeeded in driving the Iraqi army out and liberating Kuwait. The war ended with a cease-fire, which was confirmed by Security Council Resolution 687, adopted on April 3, 1991. The resolution established an inspection regime under which Iraq was to declare all its holdings of weapons of mass destruction as well as facilities and programs for their manufacture. The declarations were to be verified by the newly created UN Special Commision (UNSCOM) in the spheres of biological and chemical weapons and long-range missiles, while the IAEA would be responsible for the nuclear sphere. Iraq was given a strong incentive to cooperate: No state would be allowed to import oil from Iraq until the Security Council, upon the reports of the inspectors, had concluded that all prohibited items and programs were eradicated.

When this resolution was adopted, I was not aware that there had been divided views in the first Bush administration as to whether the IAEA should be placed in charge of the nuclear inspections. With reason, it appears to have been argued by some that the agency was ready to start inspections almost immediately and that *not* giving it this task would undermine its authority and credibility.

Some foreign countries had also weighed in to support an agency role. Those in the U.S. administration opposing a role for the agency might have argued the desirability of a singular muscular inspection authority with very different practices from those of the IAEA safeguards system. Ambassador Kirkpatrick's judgment in 1981 might well have been remembered.

The inspection system designed for Security Council Resolution 687 (1991) was, indeed, different from the safeguards inspections. Above all, inspectors were to have unlimited access to sites and people, not just to declared sites. Assistance from national intelligence services to the new authority was contemplated. The new inspectors could be assisted by eyes in the sky, ears in the ether and, perhaps, spies on the ground. To prevent the budgetary committee of the General Assembly from poking its nose into the new system, its financing was removed from the regular UN budget. Additionally, the new commission was to be directly under the control of the Security Council, thereby guaranteeing a measure of independence from the secretary general.

Staff and equipment were to be contributed by member states on a voluntary basis. The recruitment of inspectors and other staff did not have to be on a broad geographical basis, as in the rest of the UN system. Staff would be provided free of charge by member states, an arrangement that would, in practice, facilitate close "liaison" between some staff and the national military or civil authorities in the countries from which they came. The arrangements made the operation of the system very dependent on those member states that were willing to contribute intelligence, staff and other resources. This gave UNSCOM many excellent staff members and some important intelligence but also a dependence, chiefly on the U.S. and a few other countries. In the longer run, this seriously reduced the commission's intended UN legitimacy, and it came to be seen as largely remote-controlled by a few states.

Under the safeguards system by which the IAEA had been operating, information received from member states in the course of inspections was considered to comprise industrial and commercial secrets, and was kept confidential. While it could in some circumstances be revealed to the Board of Governors, it could certainly not be passed to any national intelligence service in return for other information received. Further, no links between IAEA inspectors and the national authorities from which they might have come would have been tolerated. The inspectors were to be servants of the international organization. These patterns did not fit with the new design contemplated for inspections in Iraq. On the other hand, there was no institutional problem for the agency to operate inspections of different kinds: In most states there were NPT-type safeguards; in a few, like Israel, India and Pakistan, there were another type of non-comprehensive bilateral safeguards; there could now be yet another kind of inspections for Iraq under the Security Council rules. We thought it best nevertheless to set up a special IAEA action team for our work in Iraq.

Under the Security Council resolution, UNSCOM was to be responsible for all logistics, to provide "assistance and cooperation" to the director general of the IAEA. It was expected to have links to national intelligence agencies and—partly on the basis of the intelligence received—it was to designate sites for the IAEA to inspect beyond those declared to the agency by Iraq.

My Swedish colleague, Ambassador Rolf Ekeus, was appointed executive chairman of UNSCOM. He always had an American deputy with close links to Washington, the first being Robert Gallucci. In the IAEA, I appointed as the head of the action team an Italian, one of my former deputy directors general, Professor Maurizio Zifferero. He had a great knowledge of the nuclear fuel cycle and, in addition, long managerial experience. Dimitri Perricos, one of the ablest and most experienced members of our Safeguards Department, joined him. David Kay, an American who had no inspector training but had a talent for writing and a reputation for getting things done, was to take care of the administrative side.

A good deal of friction developed when we at the IAEA felt UNSCOM sought to treat the agency as a dog on a leash. The ambition might have been a reflection of the forces in Washington that had opposed any IAEA role in the inspections. When I found that UNSCOM was in full swing in New York recruiting members for an

IAEA inspection team, I felt that UNSCOM's "assist and support" mandate was being replaced by "insist and control." An even more serious matter was the difference in inspection style between the organizations: To UNSCOM, the IAEA inspectors seemed too much like proper civil servants; to the IAEA, some of the UNSCOM inspectors seemed to act Rambo-style.

The assembling, briefing and later debriefing of the team for each inspection mission at the U.S. military base in Bahrain, as well as the conduct of the teams in the field, contributed to making many inspections look like military operations. We were not alone in this impression. UN people who were in Baghdad for various humanitarian functions called UNSCOM staff "cowboys" and the latter reciprocated by nicknaming the UN staff "bunny-huggers." They probably included most IAEA staff in this category.

At no time, however, did any of the friction translate into reduced effectiveness. It simply lent an occasionally unpleasant aspect to what could have been an enjoyable and exciting cooperation.

IAEA Inspections in Iraq, 1991

The early results of the nuclear inspections were spectacular. Perricos, who headed the first IAEA inspection, on May 15–21, 1991, gave a detailed and colorful picture of it in an August 2001 presentation sponsored by the Institute for Science and International Security in Washington. He described how the inspectors had advance intelligence that an installation at Tarmiya might have been devoted to centrifuge enrichment of uranium, and how the inspectors concluded that this assumption, at any rate, was wrong. The Iraqis claimed that the site had been used for chemical processes like electroplating. The place was in ruins. The inspectors took hundreds of pictures. Returning to Vienna with the pictures, and helped by American experts who had participated in the making of the first atom bomb, they concluded that the site had, indeed, been used for the enrichment of uranium, but had employed the "dinosaur" method of electromagnetic isotope separation (EMIS), which had been employed nearly fifty years earlier, in America's World War II Manhattan Project. In the U.S., the separators had been named *calutrons* by their inventor, Ernest Lawrence, after his labs at the University of California at Berkeley. The Iraqis, it was later learned, had named their separators *baghdadtrons.*

At informal consultations in the Security Council on July 15, 1991, the Soviet ambassador, Yuli Vorontsov, asked me whether it was certain that the Iraqi enrichment program was not peaceful. I responded that it was not plausible that a developing country would devote a billion dollars to enriching uranium for power reactors when there was an ample supply of cheap enriched uranium in the world market and when, in any case, it had constructed no such reactors. The implication of my reply was that we suspected that Iraq aimed at a nuclear weapon. Similarly, in a report to the IAEA Board of Governors the same month, I noted that there could be no confidence that the three enrichment programs Iraq had by then admitted had peaceful purposes.

The revelation that Iraq had secretly enriched uranium without being detected shook the world. In the board of the IAEA there was agreement with my conclusion that a sharpening of the safeguards system was necessary. It also now became politically possible, which it had hardly been earlier.

The Role of David Kay

Before the reports were presented to the Security Council and to the IAEA board in July 1991, a dramatic second IAEA mission had taken place. When Professor Zifferero left the second IAEA inspection mission to attend a meeting of the Security Council, he appointed David Kay to take over the team as chief inspector. With crucial assistance from intelligence, Kay and his team succeeded at the end of June 1991 in outsmarting their Iraqi minders and reaching a truck park. There, they identified a number of trucks carrying calutrons. Courageously, the inspectors chased the trucks and photographed their loads until Iraqi staff began firing in the air. A high-level mission—including myself, the UNSCOM chairman Rolf Ekeus, and Yasushi Akashi, head of the UN Department for Disarmament—was sent to Baghdad by the Security Council to protest against the shooting. We showed the pictures to the Iraqis and pressed them to declare their enrichment program. Two weeks later, Iraq did declare that they had been trying to enrich uranium by several different methods. It was a breakthrough in the mapping of their nuclear program.

Nevertheless, it was not until the sixth IAEA mission that, through daring, skill and intelligence, a team, again with David Kay as chief inspector, succeeded on September 23 in finding a paper describing the planned Iraqi nuclear weapons program, and took it out of Iraq. This proved conclusively that Iraq was pursuing such a program. The second part of that inspection managed to find and seize a great number of relevant documents, but was detained by the Iraqis for several days at a standoff in a parking lot. David Kay and Bob Gallucci's smart decision to maintain continuous contact with world media throughout the standoff probably influenced the Iraqis to exercise restraint.

On the return of the team to Vienna, we held an all-staff meeting in the boardroom on October 4, and I gave David Kay the IAEA's distinguished service award "in recognition of his outstanding leadership, determination and courage during the sixth IAEA inspection in Iraq." A few days later, with Kay at my side, I reported on these events to the Security Council.

Smart and cocky (the U.S. Central Intelligence Agency is reported to have nicknamed him "Ramrod" when he later headed the U.S.-appointed Iraq Survey Group during the summer of 2003), David Kay must have felt a much greater kinship with the UNSCOM "cowboys" than with the IAEA that he served. As such, I was not greatly surprised when he published an article in *The Washington Post* in January 2003 in which he portrayed himself as an UNSCOM inspector—something he had never been. I was more surprised that in the same article he said that "looking for a smoking gun was always a fool's mission." After all, his fame from 1991 had been based on finding two excellent "smoking guns": the trucks loaded with nuclear equipment and the papers showing conclusively that Iraq tried to construct a nuclear weapon.

Regrettably, the appreciation which I and the agency showed Kay in 1991 was not reciprocated, and for more than ten years he took every opportunity to criticize the agency and myself. He has not hesitated to attribute to Mohamed ElBaradei and me statements that we never made.

On one matter, I came to recognize in 1991 that both David Kay and UNSCOM had a better instinct than I: namely, on the importance of searching for relevant documents. I had raised no obstacle to such searches, but my feeling was that we were in Iraq to look for weapons, and that documents were not weapons. However, the rich caches of documents which Kay seized that year showed that such a search could be highly rewarding—provided you had good intelligence on where to look. The documents did not lead to any weapons stores or, for that matter, to any weapons at all, but they were crucial and conclusive evidence about Iraq's nuclear weapons program.

I have no doubts that once the Iraqi side learned the lesson of Kay's 1991 success, further searches not based on specific intelligence, whether in ministries or elsewhere, would be meaningless. It cannot be difficult to find perfect hiding places for documents and diskettes.

On another matter, I felt and continue to feel that I had the wiser view. Inspectors, I believe, should avoid humiliating the inspected. I think a Rambo-style attitude on the part of inspectors antagonizes more than it intimidates. Inspection is not the pursuit of war by other means. Inspectors are not occupiers and should neither shoot nor shout their way in. Many inspectors have told me that Iraqi scientists and technicians provided more information in the wake of the 2003 Iraq war when they were talked to calmly than when they were bullied. This is not to suggest that in a brutal police state either method will stand much chance of eliciting information, when the revelation might mean torture and death to the witness.

To the Iraqi side, David Kay became like a red cape to a bull, and after he had left the agency, the Iraqi ambassador in New York sent a letter to the UN secretary general alleging that Kay had been an agent of the United States and "had been dismissed by the IAEA in a dramatic manner." The dismissal allegations were about as untrue as the allegations Iraq would make about me ten years later. Indeed, far from dismissing Kay, I had given him an award and recommended him for his new job. I sent a response letter to the secretary general, informing him that

> Mr. Kay was not dismissed by the agency. Mr. Kay left the agency on 15 January 1992 completely of his own accord to become Secretary General of the Uranium Institute . . . a post which Mr. Kay had applied for well before September 1991, when his name attracted world-wide media attention in the Baghdad parking lot incident. . . .

Most certainly, Kay had contacts with U.S. intelligence in connection with the inspections he led. This was part of the support built into the inspections program. I did not think at the time, though, that he was an American "agent." He had not come from the IAEA cadres of professional inspectors but had been an evaluator of relatively innocuous—though admittedly nuclear related—IAEA technical assistance projects. I might have been wrong, but I did not think that any American intelligence institution would spend an agent—or even a stringer—on such a post.

It is hard for me to assess how much influence Kay's never-ending criticisms against the IAEA, UNMOVIC and me personally have had over the years. I think it was limited in the U.S. departments of State and Energy, which had a good knowledge of the IAEA and of myself and had three times supported my reelection as director general. Until shortly before the heated debates in March 2003, no officials of United States had criticized the IAEA for its inspections under the Security Council mandate. However, David Kay worked in the intelligence and military environment of Washington, and I do not doubt that his views and tales strengthened the voices in those camps that were already skeptical about the role of inspection in general and of IAEA inspection in particular. Once a star inspector, Kay had come to the view that a military occupation of Iraq was the only way to eradicate the Iraqi weapons of mass destruction.

He did not know how successful the pursuit of inspections and sanctions supported by military pressure had been.

Inspections in Iraq, 1992–1998

In December 1998, all inspectors were withdrawn following an autumn of much Iraqi obstruction, and ahead of U.S./UK bombing.

The long period of inspections from 1992 to the end of 1998 had yielded much insight into the Iraqi weapons programs but no significant finds of hidden weapons. The techniques and tools of inspection developed much in this period, not least through the use of environmental sampling, through which even small particles found in installations or equipment or in the air could give conclusions about past presence of nuclear, chemical or biological material.

On the IAEA side, for which I was responsible, it was an uneventful period compared to 1991. We had our share of Iraqi intransigence, but suffered a little less animosity than they expressed toward UNSCOM. Early in the period, the IAEA secured the removal from Iraq of all fissionable material, which was flown to Russia. The agency further supervised the destruction of many large installations that had been used in the Iraqi weapons programs. Most of this was accomplished before the end of 1992. Our nuclear experts were able gradually to come to a full understanding of the Iraqi program and the infrastructure that had been built up, as well as how Iraq had obtained the technical knowledge for the centrifuge method of enrichment, which became its main endeavor.

In the report submitted to the Security Council on October 8, 1997, and for which I was responsible, the agency declared that a "technically coherent picture" of Iraq's past nuclear program had evolved, and that it saw no significant discrepancies between that picture and Iraq's latest declaration. However, the agency added, "some uncertainty is inevitable in any country-wide technical verification process which aims to prove the absence of readily concealable objects or activities." There was general agreement among governments at that time that there were no significant further "disarmament" matters to clear up in the nuclear dossier, only some "questions" to clarify.

For UNSCOM, by contrast, the period was a constant struggle. Like the IAEA, it supervised the destruction of much infrastructure that had been condemned for its links to Iraq's weapons programs. The commission also ensured the destruction of missiles and, in courageous operations, it took part in the destruction of large quantities of chemical agents. It claimed, indeed, that more weapons were destroyed under the supervision of its inspectors than had been destroyed during the Gulf War. I am not aware, however, that any significant amount of weapons or nuclear material was ever found hidden (i.e., found on sites that had not been declared). At the same time, with inadequate accounting on the Iraqi side, it could not be excluded at the end of 1998 that there still existed undeclared missiles, chemical weapons and biological weapons.

The Defection of Hussein Kamel, 1995

In August 1995, one of Saddam Hussein's sons-in-law, General Hussein Kamel, defected to Jordan, an event that had dramatic effects. Kamel was Iraq's minister of industry and former director of its Military Industrial Corporation (MIC), with responsibility for all of the country's weapons programs. During debriefings in Jordan, he claimed that all chemical and biological weapons had been destroyed on his orders in 1991. The statement was certainly significant, but without any corroborating evidence it could not be given credibility. More important was that the regime in Iraq chose to make available to UNSCOM and the IAEA a vast trove of documents related to prohibited weapons programs, documents it claimed that Kamel had hidden on his property, which was referred to by the media as the "chicken farm."

The Kamel affair has remained murky. It is possible that the regime feared that Kamel would reveal a lot of information about prohibited weapons programs, and so hurried to push the blame for hiding the information off on him. Irrespective of who was to blame, at least two significant revelations came out of the affair and were confirmed. One was that beyond simply having a program for the development of offensive biological weapons (a fact that UNSCOM had previously determined), Iraq had actually placed such agents in weapons ready for use—i.e., it had weaponized them. The other was that in August 1990 Kamel had ordered a crash program to make a nuclear weapon, using fissionable material from research reactor fuel that was under IAEA safeguards. That program had failed. Important as these revelations were for the knowledge and understanding of Iraq's programs and past actions, they did not result in the discovery and eradication of any more weapons.

In February 1996 Kamel was persuaded to return to Iraq, where the regime took its revenge by assassinating him.

Cheat and Retreat: Iraq's Cat-and-Mouse Games

A nuclear weapons program has its own industrial and physics logic, and the spectacular discoveries in the first half-year of inspections helped the IAEA to map Iraq's program and to eradicate most of it before the end of 1992. The mapping of the programs which fell under UNSCOM authority, especially the biological weapons programs, proved a more difficult task in the face of Iraqi efforts to conceal and procrastinate. It was natural that these strenuous efforts would lead UNSCOM and the world to believe that the regime was attempting to hide and retain prohibited weapons.

The resistance to transparency and inspection took many forms. One of the earliest was providing incomplete or false information, which led the Security Council to demand "full, final and complete declarations." When new declarations were rejected as inadequate and (as happened in the biological field) one "final" declaration after another was given, the situation became almost comic. Another form of resistance was directed against overhead surveillance, notably opposition to flights by American U-2 planes in UNSCOM service. There were also occasions when Iraqi helicopters endangered air safety by obstructing photographs taken by the U-2 planes. On yet other occasions there was resistance to remote-controlled monitoring cameras at missile factories.

Some resistance was directed at U.S. or UK nationals on the UNSCOM staff. In November 1997 this led to a crisis during which UNSCOM withdrew nearly all its staff from Iraq, leaving only a handful in Baghdad.

Denial of Access: The Sensitive-Sites, 1996

The most important resistance came in the form of denial of access for inspectors to various sites which, for one reason or another, the Iraqi side deemed sensitive—e.g., ministries and sites belonging to the Special Republican Guard or the security organizations. Objections were also sometimes raised to inspections during the Muslim day of rest.

In 1996 the Security Council asked UNSCOM's executive chairman, Rolf Ekeus, to visit Baghdad to secure access to all sites that the commission had designated for inspection. After talks between Ekeus and the Iraqi deputy prime minister, Tariq Aziz, a joint statement was issued on June 22. Iraq undertook to secure "immediate, unconditional and unrestricted access to all sites which the commission and the IAEA may wish to inspect," and the commission undertook "to operate with full regard for the legitimate *security concerns* of Iraq" (my emphasis).

Iraq's incentive to making the commitment lay in the agreement of the two sides to intensify their work in order to bring closer the day when the commission could report that Iraq had met its obligations, thus freeing the Security Council to lift economic sanctions. As emerges from Ekeus's report to the Security Council of June 24, 1996, the Iraqi commitment was made somewhat easier by Ekeus showing understanding for Iraq's sensitivities regarding inspection of sites they considered crucial to their sovereignty and national security. He informed the deputy prime minister that he believed

Iraqi concerns could be met by the chairman issuing "modalities [protocols] for the inspection of such sites," which he assumed would be few in number. Chief inspectors would be instructed to follow special procedures that would take into account Iraq's legitimate concerns regarding its security, while also fully safeguarding the rights of the commission.

The essence of the "modalities" issued for "sensitive sites" was that when inspectors came to such a site, entry would have to be delayed "a reasonable period of time" to allow the Iraqi side to make available a high-ranking official to "coordinate with the team in the inspection of the sensitive site." The entry would be made by not more than four inspectors, who would try to spend as short a time as possible at the site.

The solution was not welcomed by the U.S. and some other members of the Security Council, who felt that it introduced a limitation in the inspection rights that had been laid down by the Council. This was certainly how the Iraqis also saw the instruction. In reality, Ekeus had to some degree stepped on the Council's toes in order to avoid a crisis that might have led to the use of armed force. He wisely took the formal position that the modalities were only an internal instrument that he had issued in his capacity as executive. The problematic part was that any concession in the implementation of a Security Council resolution was a step taken on a slippery slope. Otherwise, it was hard to see that it was a disaster that inspectors had to wait an hour (or sometimes more) to enter a site. It is true that small things, like vials, diskettes and documents, could be removed and concealed while inspectors were waiting. However, stocks of prohibited weapons or equipment for the production of weapons could not be quickly removed.

The "Butler Modalities" and the Memorandum on Presidential Sites

On many occasions Ekeus's modalities worked well. However, in a number of instances there was trouble. An UNSCOM legend has it that in one bizarre case, when after many démarches the inspectors were admitted to a site declared sensitive and entered a building on the site, they found no less a person than Deputy Prime Minister Tariq Aziz, eagerly puffing on a cigar! It was sometimes hard, too, to understand why there had to be hours of haggling about the number of inspectors who were allowed to enter a building that would then prove to be empty. In none of the many inspections of sites belonging to the Special Republican Guard or security or intelligence organizations does anything significant and weapons-relevant appear to have been found.

Perhaps it was not unreasonable to think that the military units favored by Saddam Hussein would be the most likely to possess prohibited weapons. However, one might wonder in how many cases the selection of sensitive sites for inspection was based on intelligence and real suspicions that prohibited items would be found.

During this period, an UNSCOM campaign spearheaded by the American inspector Scott Ritter was underway and aimed at revealing the "concealment mechanism"—i.e., how Iraq organized the concealment of weapons, documents and data. The thought behind this campaign seems to have been that if you could not find the weapons but at least could show precisely how the Iraqi side organized its resistance to inspections, then its violation of the resolutions would be established. This line of action comprised much cooperation with intelligence and eavesdropping of Iraqi communications. Many of these inspections resembled minor military operations. An article in *The New Yorker* on November 9, 1998, titled "Scott Ritter's Private War" provided a vivid description.

In the summer of 1997, the Australian ambassador to the UN, Richard Butler, had succeeded Ekeus as UNSCOM chairman, but the commission's road continued to be rocky. Both UNSCOM and the world interpreted Iraq's conduct as evidence that it was hiding weapons. This reaction was understandable when inspectors' videotapes showed how files were moved and documents burned while the inspectors were forced to wait.

At the end of October 1997, the Iraqi government informed the Security Council of several decisions, one being that it would no longer deal with inspectors of U.S. nationality working for UNSCOM. Naturally a crisis ensued. The commission and the IAEA suspended all inspections.

Interestingly, both on this occasion and in a crisis about one year later, the Iraqi measures were directed against UNSCOM but not the IAEA. It was made clear to the IAEA in October 1997 that Iraq had no objections to working with inspectors of U.S. nationality in its teams: "All IAEA staff, inspectors and experts will be welcome as usual." The relations with the IAEA were, indeed, less confrontational. By this time the agency had made it clear that there remained few questions to solve in Iraq's nuclear dossier. Whether the distinction Iraq made was motivated by a wish to drive a wedge between the two organizations or by the fact that the IAEA had fewer American team members and did not take part in Scott Ritter's aggressive campaign, the IAEA nevertheless decided to act in unison with UNSCOM.

Following intense diplomatic activity (especially by Russia) and U.S. military pressure, the crisis was resolved. At a visit to Baghdad in December 1997, Richard Butler reopened the issue of inspections at sensitive sites. He secured some concessions from the Iraqi side concerning the modalities, e.g., about the number of inspectors who were to enter a sensitive site and about a shortening of the time they would have to wait before entering. However, on one point the Iraqis refused to retreat: namely, inspections of so-called "presidential sites." In February 1998 the matter got hot and Secretary General Kofi Annan dispatched a technical survey team to determine the precise size and perimeter of eight such sites that Iraq had declared off-limits. Following this mission and consultations with members of the Security Council, Kofi Annan went to Iraq and met with President Saddam Hussein and Deputy Prime Minister Tariq Aziz.

The deadlock was resolved and a memorandum of understanding was signed on February 23, 1998. Inspectors were to have access to the eight presidential sites, now precisely defined. However, in inspecting these sites, UNSCOM was to respect not only legitimate Iraqi concerns about sovereignty and security but also "dignity." A special procedure was laid down under which a group of senior diplomats was to accompany the inspectors, like chaperones. Inspections were given the more dignified name "entries."

End of Inspections; Desert Fox; UNSCOM and Espionage

After a period of eased relations in the spring of 1998, the climate hardened again. A group of international biological experts concluded in July that Iraq's declaration of its biological weapons program was not verifiable, and there was controversy about findings regarding the chemical agent VX. In early August the Revolutionary Command Council and the Ba'ath Party Command decided to stop cooperation with UNSCOM and the IAEA until the Security Council lifted the sanctions, reorganized UNSCOM and moved it to Geneva or Vienna. The decision was unanimously condemned by the Security Council in early September and again in early November.

Meanwhile, discussions in New York about a "comprehensive review" appear to have raised Iraqi hopes for an exit from the sanctions regime, prompting it to signal in mid-November that it was ready again to cooperate fully. Before embarking on any such review, the Security Council wanted to hear that the cooperation was, in fact, satisfactory—but this was an assurance UNSCOM was not prepared to make. In December 1998, Richard Butler submitted a controversial report to the Security Council concluding that Iraq had *not* in fact provided the full cooperation it had promised. In anticipation of U.S./UK bombings, he ordered the withdrawal of UNSCOM staff engaged in the inspection effort. They were evacuated in great haste from Baghdad, but other UN staff in Iraq stayed.

On December 17–20, the U.S. and the UK launched Operation Desert Fox, sending some one hundred cruise missiles to strike one hundred targets in Iraq. On November 19, Iraqi Vice President Taha Yassin Ramadan declared that UNSCOM's mission was over.

Despite the bombings, the Iraqi government perhaps was not displeased. The effect of the sanctions, which had crippled Iraq's economy during the first half of the 1990s and sent the population's standard of living plunging, had gradually been reduced through the UN Oil-for-Food Program. This allowed Iraq to sell increasing quantities of oil and to import increasing quantities of food and other products allowed by the UN sanctions committee. Iraq certainly wanted to get rid of the sanctions and be master of its own imports and economy. Each time the regime had made what it saw as concessions on the inspection front, it had been in response to the carrot being dangled in front of it: the possibility of an UNSCOM report that disarmament had been achieved, and a resultant lifting of sanctions by the Security Council.

Listening to U.S. statements, however, Saddam Hussein may well have come to doubt that cooperation with the inspectors would help, and to believe instead that the U.S. would allow sanctions to disappear only if he himself disappeared. If this was the case, why bother to cooperate with the inspectors? Indeed, why not play cat-and-mouse, teasing the UN and the U.S.? When the inspectors were kept out of the country after the Desert Fox operation, Tariq Aziz was said to have expressed satisfaction: It was enough to have sanctions. To have inspectors as well had been too much. How successful had the U.S./UK been? In bombing Iraq to force better cooperation with the inspectors, they had attained instead the end of those inspections. They would still have surveillance from above, but they would lose all information from the ground.

At this juncture the Iraqi regime probably began to feel some hope that the sanctions regime would erode on its own or even be lifted. It had been in place since 1990, but a large-scale illegal sale of oil enabled the regime to import what the elite and its supporters needed, plus some military items. In the outside world, public opinion was turning against the sanctions. They did not hurt the government, it was said, but only the Iraqi people—not least the children.

Some events in New York in the first part of January 1999 must also have gladdened the regime in Baghdad. Suddenly there was a lot of publicity indicating that UNSCOM had been infiltrated by intelligence agents from various countries, especially the U.S. and the UK. They had been members of the inspection teams and been able (or so it was reported) to give their home organizations information on military targets and the movements of the Iraqi leadership—both convenient for later bombings. According to media reports, there had been intelligence "piggybacking." Electronic eavesdropping equipment had been attached to UNSCOM activities, teams and remote-monitoring installations.

It was generally understood and accepted in the Security Council that UNSCOM should receive intelligence from national sources to assist it in mapping and eradicating the weapons of mass destruction programs. These reports, however, seemed to indicate that activities had taken place under the label but not the control of UNSCOM. Indeed, it was suggested that UNSCOM had not been given some of the information which was extracted, and which seemed to have focused on the security apparatus and the protection of Saddam Hussein. Richard Butler and his predecessor, Mr. Ekeus, both denied that they had ever authorized any activities that did not aim at benefitting UNSCOM's mandate, the eradication of weapons of mass destruction.

As I read all these news reports, which were published by indefatigable American investigative journalists, I had little doubt that the larger part, at any rate, was true. I could see that the generally accepted starting point had been that intelligence should "share" the information they had with the inspectors to help them in their mandate. Gradually, "sharing" came to mean that the intelligence partners "shared" all the UNSCOM information they wanted, while information they obtained through piggybacking might not have been "shared" with UNSCOM.

The publicity about the intelligence affairs critically damaged UNSCOM, which was seen by many as an instrument in large measure controlled by the U.S., rather than as a tool of the Security Council. Scott Ritter's descriptions in interviews (and later, books) of American domination of UNSCOM and of his own extensive cooperation with American and Israeli intelligence had an impact, even though they were in part refuted by Richard Butler and Rolf Ekeus. Articles were written which suggested that UNSCOM was dead. The Iraqi regime, which had long accused UNSCOM of espionage, felt vindicated.

There was no agreement between the five permanent members of the Security Council on where to go. Many considered UNSCOM so discredited that it should be discontinued. Some felt the aggressive conduct of UNSCOM—which even the U.S. had tried to temper on various occasions—had been counterproductive, and that a kind of UNSCOM-lite should be created, giving missile inspections to the UN disarmament department and chemical inspections to the organization that had been set up at the Hague specifically for such work. Others pointed to the difficulty of creating something new and starting from scratch.

The French suggested that in all likelihood everything possible had been done to discover weapons from the past, and that the UN should transition to the monitoring phase and to preventing a future revival of Iraq's weapons program. The French also urged that a lifting of the sanctions should be considered. The Russians submitted an informal working paper that contained many ideas that were close to the French position. The U.S. wanted neither to lift sanctions nor do away with UNSCOM, but seemed open to the idea of declaring the nuclear sector ready for transition from disarmament to monitoring. Faced with all this disarray, the Council decided at the end of January 1999 to set up three panels, all to be led by the Brazilian ambassador, Celso Amorim, who was president of the Council at the time.

With remarkable speed, Ambassador Amorim and his panels produced three reports, the first of which concerned disarmament. The panel concluded that "the bulk of Iraq's proscribed weapons programmes has been eliminated" and suggested that the presence of inspectors was the most effective way to provide assurance that Iraq did not retain, acquire or rebuild prohibited weapons. The panel warned against believing that any system could bring 100-percent certainty and suggested a concentration on the remaining priority tasks. The system could range from routine monitoring to very intrusive inspection. The panel cautioned that any information should be assessed "strictly on the basis of its credibility and relevance to the mandate" and that the relationship to intelligence providers should be one-way only, even if it was recognized that some dialogue was necessary. The report demanded effectiveness, but warned against unnecessary confrontation. The legal framework for UNSCOM could remain, just in "renovated" form.

The Iraqi government almost immediately rejected these ideas and said there could be no return of inspectors unless sanctions were lifted. Long negotiations followed among Council members. Meanwhile, Richard Butler and many of UNSCOM's staff left. The many experts whom governments had provided as inspectors did not have to be released; they had come for specific missions only, and then gone home.

It was not until December 1999 that the Council was able to adopt the new Resolution 1284, which on major points followed the panel's recommendations.

UNMOVIC became the "renovated" UNSCOM. While the system from 1991 had envisaged a complete lifting of sanctions only in return for a complete eradication of all prohibited weapons programs, the new resolution also opened the possibility for a suspension of sanctions in return for Iraqi "cooperation in all respects," leading to progress in the resolution of key remaining disarmament tasks.

In my quiet corner in Stockholm I had been quite happy with the report of the Amorim panel, and I felt the same way about the new resolution. It seemed to me that, through the report and the resolution, many of the lines that we had taken in the IAEA in the past nine years had been upheld:

- Inspectors were to be broadly recruited and become international civil servants with loyalty to the UN only. The end of a dominant recruitment of gratis staff from some big states was implied.
- UNMOVIC was to have a clear United Nations identity and should, accordingly, not be remote-controlled by any state. As such, it could develop and retain international legitimacy.
- There was no suggestion of any mechanism for swapping inspection information for intelligence.

- Inspection should be effective and could be highly intrusive, but should avoid being unnecessarily confrontational.
- UNMOVIC would have all the rights and prerogatives of UNSCOM.

In January 2000, Secretary General Kofi Annan set about looking for someone he could nominate as executive chairman of UNMOVIC.

I was curious to see who it would be.

3

Out of the Ice-Box
and Into the Frying Pan

A Tourist Trip to the Antarctic, January 2000

In the simple hotel we stayed at in Chalten, Patagonia, you could receive telephone calls but you could not call out. On January 19, 2000, the hotel received a message asking me to call the secretary of the Swedish foreign minister or the Swedish embassy in Buenos Aires—but I could not return the call. There was no way the staff could determine the charge. I offered ten dollars as a round sum for a brief call to Buenos Aires. No. Twenty dollars? No. I gave up and we walked down to the public telephone station and sent a fax telling Stockholm when I would be available for an incoming call the next day.

We had left winter in Stockholm for summer in the Antarctic and a trip to Patagonia on the way. My wife, Eva Kettis, had the responsibility for Arctic and Antarctic issues in the Swedish foreign ministry. She wanted to see with her own eyes what they were talking about at the conference tables. I had heard much about the beauty of the Antarctic and was happy to join her.

The fax worked, and the next morning, the call came telling me that the UN in New York would be interested in having me as executive chairman of the new inspection organization for Iraq, the United Nations Monitoring, Verification and Inspection Commission (UNMOVIC). The Swedish foreign minister hoped I would make myself available. I said I was skeptical. Was there no one else who could do it? Would I be ready to take a call from the undersecretary in the French Foreign Ministry, who was eager to explain? OK, I could do that at the end of the day, after our hike. . . .

We had a beautiful long hike in the impressive Fitzroy environment. Sunny. Beautiful forest and fine path to Laguna de los Tres. The year before I had had a big operation on my spine and felt it was wonderful that I could now walk for seven and a half hours without any pain.

Back in Chalten after the hike I took the incoming call from the French undersecretary at Quai d'Orsay in Paris, Gerard Errera. He had been the French disarmament ambassador in Geneva as well as an excellent governor on the Board of Governors of the International Atomic Energy Agency. I knew him well.

He explained how difficult it was proving in the Security Council to agree on a new chairman. He thought I was perhaps the person everyone could agree on. It would be for a year or a year and a half. I remained skeptical. Surely there were lots of others? I was enjoying my retirement and hiking with my wife. I mentioned some other names. Could they return to me if they found no one else? Well, yes.

I discussed the situation with Eva. I thought we had lived separately for too many years, when I worked at the IAEA in Vienna and she worked in Geneva and, later, Brussels. She was now thoroughly engaged in her job and pleased to have me returned home as a retiree. I kept the household going and she kept the polar regions going—insofar as Sweden had any influence.

To my surprise, Eva did not reject the idea out of hand. She knew that when I retired from the IAEA in 1997 I'd felt that Iraq was unfinished business. She also knew that I had felt that a less aggressive style of inspection than that which had often been practiced by UNSCOM might bring better results. If I wanted to try, she would understand. We left it there and hoped the questions would go away. Had not one of the most famous of all Frenchmen, de Gaulle, said that the cemeteries are full of indispensable men? (His generation had not discovered that the cemeteries are also full of indispensable women.)

On Saturday, January 22, our bus took us to a sweet town called El Calafate (the blueberry). Having been let down by the airline, which was to take us to Ushuaia, the world's most southerly town, our group was queuing at a tourist office to learn what was to happen next. A young lady called my name and I thought Eva and I would be among the lucky to get plane seats. No, the young lady informed me that someone by the name of Kofi Annan wanted me to phone him. The young lady had no idea that Kofi Annan was the secretary general of the United Nations, but other people standing in line did and looked curiously as Eva and I stepped out in search, for a second time, of a local telephone station.

Kofi Annan was still looking for an UNMOVIC chairman. I knew about several names that had been turned down. Rolf Ekeus, who had been the chairman of UNSCOM from 1991 to 1997, had allowed his name to go forward. I had been surprised that Rolf wanted to have a second go, but in any case he was turned down by some of the permanent members of the Security Council. I was sure that the U.S. had wanted Rolf. Had the Iraqis persuaded Russia and France to exercise their veto, or did these states feel that UNSCOM under Rolf (and even more under Butler) had come under U.S. domination? I did not know. It was a fact that the IAEA had stood for a less humiliating style of inspection, but I doubted that my name could be pleasing to the Iraqis. They were infuriated that, despite the general agreement that seven years of IAEA inspection had left no significant nuclear issues open, we had not recommended the closing of the nuclear dossier.

I felt a bit of challenge building up inside. The dominant feeling, however, was one of unease. I had settled down and ended my career. I planned to hike and to write a book about IAEA efforts in Iraq and North Korea. I got through to Kofi Annan, who explained that they still had no other name than mine, that the job was not easy and that he wanted to know if, nevertheless, I would be ready to take it. I said I remained skeptical but did not rule it out if they really could not get someone else.

We were not among the lucky ones who got seats on the plane, but after long bus rides we reached Ushuaia and the chartered Russian exploration ship, *Akademik Joffe,* that was to take us and a few hundred other tourists to the Antarctic. We were lucky with the weather and enjoyed the fantastic scenery, the birds, the millions of penguins, the seals and the whales.

Accepting the Chairmanship?

On January 26, Rolf Knutsson, in Kofi Annan's office, reached me through the INTELMAR radiophone system and explained that the secretary general was about to leave for Moscow and needed to know if I would be available as chairman of UNMOVIC. He said there was no other name and they were sure my nomination would have unanimous support in the Council.

All right, I told him.

Why had I agreed to come out of retirement? I felt strongly that although UNSCOM had displayed great skills in analysis and, shall I say, "prowess" in the field, in the long run its "inspectors at war" attitude and its identification with Western intelligence had been counterproductive and discrediting. It had succeeded in provoking and antagonizing the Iraqis without bringing further clarity. I had heard many times from inspectors that they thought the IAEA had often got more information through a more restrained, professional UN style. It would be tempting to try this approach with UNMOVIC.

Another reason for accepting was that it is simply difficult to say no when the secretary general of the UN tells you that you are the only name they can agree on and you know the task very well. A third reason was that I felt healthy and strong and I like to do things. Moreover, I thought it would be only for a year or a year and a half.

After having consulted the Security Council, the secretary general appointed me and it was decided I should enter into service on March 1, 2000.

The exploration ship was an excellent place to think without being disturbed by phone, since it was difficult to get through. On my return to Stockholm, the U.S. secretary of state, Madeleine Albright, reached me personally by phone, congratulated me and promised full U.S. support. I also had a warm message of support from Prime Minister Blair of the UK.

Interestingly enough, an article had appeared in a Swedish newspaper declaring that I was about the worst possible choice for the UNMOVIC chairmanship. The article's author, Per Ahlmark, had been deputy prime minister of Sweden for two years some twenty-five years earlier and still styled himself "former deputy prime minister." People supposed there was some old quarrel between him and me. No, we had been good friends in those days and I had hardly seen him since. This was the first of many mean and insulting articles Ahlmark published all over the world, including in *The Wall Street Journal*. When he cited statements he claimed I had made to David Kay, and when he wrote that Kay ought to have been given the Nobel peace prize for his inspections in Iraq, I assumed that Kay had generously provided him with material and ideas. The press in Stockholm asked me for my comment on Ahlmark's article and I said it was more important for me to have the Security Council's confidence.

Arriving in New York

I arrived at the UN on February 28 for an unofficial visit and was taken to the thirty-first floor of the Secretariat building, where I shook hands and said hello to all our staff. I was horrified to discover how little space each staff member had. In the afternoon I had half an hour's informal talk with Secretary General Annan, whom I had met many times before when I was at the IAEA. As always, I found him warm and wise, and he was well-versed in the whole Iraqi affair. His office is modest in size and has a nice view of the East River, with a huge Pepsi-Cola sign sitting as a colorful decoration on the other side.

The next day, March 1, I paid another brief visit to the secretary general, but this time officially. I also paid a visit to the president of the Security Council, who this month was the ambassador of Bangladesh, Iftekhar Ahmed Chowdhury. I promised him that I would keep in touch with all the members of the Council, not only the great powers, the P-5.

Now I was in charge of UNMOVIC and moved into the chairman's office. My executive assistant, Torkel Stiernlöf, was in the room next to mine, and Olivia Platon, my personal assistant, was at a large desk outside my room. She kept me and everybody else and all documents in order with a firm hand but a cheerful smile and laughter. Charles Duelfer, an American who had been deputy executive chairman, had left. I had phoned him from Stockholm and said that I knew he had handled the situation very well since Butler's departure but felt that the commission needed a clean break and recommended that he should resign. He did so, and I drafted an appreciative letter of thanks to him for the secretary general. We met for lunch a few days after my arrival. I had asked Duelfer to resign from the UN inspection commission, and I was pleased that he was appointed to head the U.S.-organized Iraq Survey Group when David Kay resigned from it in January 2004, not having found any of the weapons of mass destruction he had told the public were there.

Naturally, I had an all-staff meeting on the first day. Many specialists who had been seconded by governments to UNSCOM free of charge had left already, and the remaining professional staff and support staff was perhaps around fifty persons.

There was a press conference. I said Iraq tended to look at inspection as a penalty which it wanted to minimize. It should rather see inspection as an opportunity to maximize. The world would not believe what Iraq said, but it would believe the commission. Cooperation with us gave them an opportunity. I said further that intelligence was useful but had to be examined critically. There was a good deal of disinformation. We would welcome intelligence, but it was to be largely a one-way traffic. In reply to a question, I said no organization could completely protect itself against infiltration, but that if I found anyone working for an outside agency I would fire him or her.

Organizing UNMOVIC

One part of UNMOVIC which I did not have to organize was the College of Commissioners. Resolution 1284 (1999) had requested that the secretary general appoint suitably qualified experts to meet regularly, review the work of the organization and give professional advice and guidance to the chairman and on the reports he submitted to the Security Council. Many thought this was meant to be a check on the new chairman. I always felt it was a fine group on which to test ideas. Some of the members, like those from the U.S., the UK, Russia and China, came from their central government. Others, like those from France and Germany, were unaffiliated experts. Some were experts in a particular field, like biology or missiles, but all were well versed in the history of inspections in Iraq. It was an excellent group. We persuaded it not to use interpretation and not to keep any formal records, and thereby managed to make the discussions lively and helpful. These discussions sometimes helped our staff to understand the questions their reports would prompt from governments as opposed to colleagues. I made great use of the group and felt more confident when I knew I had its support. Sam, or Mr. Muttusamy Sanmuganathan, was the secretary of the College and he made sure that they were kept well informed about any important developments or documents.

Resolution 1284 stipulated that the executive chairman should submit an organizational plan for UNMOVIC to the Security Council within forty-five days of entering into service. This meant April 15. While I was still in Stockholm, several governments had sent missions to me with advice and blueprints for the new inspection authority. The U.S. representatives, Assistant Secretaries Robert

Einhorn and David Welch, had refrained from giving any detailed advice and simply said that the plan should be my own, "without undue pressure from member nations." The undersecretary for disarmament in the UN, Jayantha Dhanapala, had also kindly come over to Stockholm and brought a whole helpful dossier that he and his people had prepared for the start-up of UNMOVIC.

The Iraqis gave no sign of accepting inspections anytime soon, so I and my colleagues could concentrate on drafting the organizational plan, on staffing and training, and on starting the work to identify which disarmament issues remained.

Organization and administration may sound dull, and I cannot say that these are my favorite areas of work. However, I know that if you are to achieve results you must have competent people, some order and decent human relations. In a national government, the political opposition may watch and attack ministries and departments for their work. International organizations have few natural enemies, but they do have more than a hundred member-state bosses looking over their shoulders.

The government representatives who had seen me in Stockholm had given me much good advice regarding UNMOVIC's organizational structure. I had felt encouraged by the advice from the U.S. side that UNMOVIC should be technical and not politicized. I realized, of course, that when other states had suggested there should be some checks on the chairman, it was because they felt that the UNSCOM secretariat and chairman had been overly dominated by U.S. influences.

I was determined to give UNMOVIC the independent UN profile that Brazilian Ambassador Celso Amorim's report, which had paved the way for the resolution, suggested. We would listen to all, but we would carry out only the instructions of the Security Council. There was an important feature facilitating this course: a small portion—0.8 percent—of the revenues from the sale of Iraqi oil under the Oil-for-Food Program would go to us for our expenses. The income would depend upon oil prices and how much oil Iraq would pump, but it might come to $100 million for a year, which we thought would be enough even when we were fully in operation.

We would need assistance from governments in many ways—e.g., intelligence, satellite imagery, some advanced equipment and expert advice—but we would not require cost-free staff or ordinary equipment, such as planes, helicopters and communications. We set about drafting the formal organizational plan and making practical arrangements.

- We did not accept the advice that the chairman should have one assistant from each of the five permanent members of the Security Council. What would have happened if the five "assistants" were not in agreement? Nikita Khrushchev had once demanded that the UN secretariat should be divided into a troika: one third from the East, one third from the West and one third from non-aligned states. This would have built vetoes into the secretariat. Yet this time a kind of pentarchy had been suggested! If adopted it could have brought politicization and paralysis.
- We eliminated the post of deputy executive chairman, which had always been a direct channel to authorities in Washington.
- We announced to *all* missions—except that of Iraq—that we would hire staff competent in the fields of biological and chemical weapons and missiles and would appreciate if they stimulated applications. However, we would also accept applications which came from outside government channels.
- All staff would be on UN contracts and be remunerated by us. We would train all staff and have a "roster" of specialists who could be called up and contracted for service in inspection teams in Baghdad or at headquarters in New York.
- Although it had been suggested to us that we start with a clean slate and retain no professional staff from UNSCOM, we decided to go for a policy of renewal and continuity. Former UNSCOM staff who were highly competent and who would contribute experience and institutional memory could stay, if they wished.

- We would at all times have a substantial number of staff resident in Baghdad, with an ability to organize several parallel inspections every day.
- We would not make use of the so-called gateway facility at the U.S. military base in Bahrain, where UNSCOM teams had gathered and been briefed/debriefed before and after inspection missions.
- We would appeal to member states for intelligence, especially for information that could lead inspectors to sites suspected of having weapons of mass destruction. However, this was to be in the main a one-way traffic. In principle, findings would either remain confidential or go to the Security Council.
- Only a special officer and the chairman would be entitled to receive intelligence. When use was to be made of intelligence in an inspection, the head of operations and the chief of the team would have to be brought in, as agreed with the provider of the intelligence.
- We would make much use of satellite imagery, both commercially purchased and given to us by governments.
- We would not make use of or allow any electronic eavesdropping.

Staffing

The "renewal and continuity" policy served us very well. It gave us Rachel Davies, an Englishwoman who had served UNSCOM, as the head and excellent manager of the information division, handling the whole database and all our work under the Oil-for-Food Program. A bright and cheerful soul with a phenomenal memory, Rachel relieved me of most problems on those fronts. John Scott was in principle in retirement from the UN Legal Department and UNSCOM, but stayed with us as a consultant and to provide institutional memory. We knew each other from our days at Cambridge University in the 1950s. We had both participated in the seminars of

Professor Hersch Lauterpacht, who later became a judge at the Hague. Alice Hecht, a Belgian and a longtime UN hand, came also from UNSCOM. She knew all the administrative ropes—and persons—in the bureaucratic forest, and how to move them when it was needed. She was assisted by Nina Pinzon from Colombia, who exemplified the kind of hard-working administrative miracle workers without whom huge organizations would collapse, with no one getting a salary or a pension or payment for a travel claim.

With the organizational plan endorsed without any changes by the Security Council, we began recruitment on a larger scale. We brought candidates for interviews to New York and sent teams of two or three of our senior staff to interview groups of candidates in Vienna, Paris, Bangkok, Dacca, Sydney and Buenos Aires. While UNSCOM had been obliged to take many staff from countries that were ready to second them free of charge, we were able to recruit freely and obtained a more geographically balanced composition. With the exception of Jordan, no Arab state nominated candidates. I took this to mean that they thought it would irritate Iraq to see Arab brethren among the inspectors, and that they heeded this presumed Iraqi objection.

Training

Nikita Smidovich, a Russian, was put in charge of the training program. He had been one of UNSCOM's most experienced and successful inspectors. UNSCOM had never had time to train inspectors—staff supplied by governments had been taken directly from their home bases to briefings at the "gateway" in Bahrain and then to one-the-job training. The resolution that established UNMOVIC, on the other hand, explicitly required training. We decided that all our staff was to have a one-month basic training course covering the Security Council's objectives, past inspections in Iraq, techniques and equipment used in inspection, and what had become known and remained unknown in the different weapons disciplines. We also included mock inspections. A few lectures were devoted to Iraq's geography, political history, culture and religions. Detractors of UNMOVIC tended to refer to such subjects as sissy "sensitivity" courses. We ran many basic training courses and shorter advanced courses and took care to place them in different countries. I myself lectured at all the major courses. In one of them I tried to describe with some adjectives the way I thought inspectors should conduct themselves:

Driving and dynamic—but not angry and aggressive
Firm—but correct
Ingenious—but not deceptive
Somewhat flexible—but not to be pushed around
Calm—but somewhat impatient
Keeping some distance—but not arrogant or pompous
Friendly—but not cozy
Respectful of those you deal with—and also demanding of respect yourself

I also reminded them that a light tone or a joke may sometimes break a nervous atmosphere.

I realized that the Iraqis read all my lectures and did not like all they saw when, after a lecture at a training course in Ottawa in June 2001, the Iraqi newspaper *Al-Thawra* wrote: "We say to Hans Blix: the American and Zionist language he is speaking is very clear and Iraq will not accept him and will never accept his spies."

Preparation for Future Inspections

I sometimes wonder how we would have managed if Iraq had invited us to start inspections in the summer of 2000. We did not yet have any new trained staff and only a limited grasp of the dossiers. Even without inspections, we had our hands full. We organized groups to analyze which issues were unanswered in the different weapons disciplines. What *could* remain? This required a lot of search into the enormous archives of UNSCOM and required a reorganization of the database to make relevant data retrievable and ready for new inflows. Other staff analyzed sites that had been visited in the past and updated them with new satellite information. Which sites should we give priority? Some staff examined where needed equipment could be purchased without delay. They went to the huge UN store in Brindisi in the south of Italy to see what could be delivered quickly, from jeeps to handheld radio telephones.

Some staff worked out routines for the taking of biological and chemical samples—no insignificant matter in evidence collection. Others worked out safety regulations for the handling of hazardous material. The lawyers drafted regulations regarding matters of confidentiality. A whole handbook was worked out systematizing all the rights and obligations that had been given by the Security Council to the inspection authorities in nearly ten years of resolutions. There was much to do and the mood was mostly cheerful. While UNSCOM's relations with the rest of the UN Secretariat and the secretary general's thirty-eighth floor had been so-so, especially during Butler's time, ours were excellent. We had good help and advice from experienced senior officials like Kofi Annan's chef de cabinet, Iqbal Riza; the head of the Disarmament Department, Jayantha Dhanapala; and the deputy head of the Political Department, Danilo Turk. We did not need to be introduced to the people at the IAEA. Close contact and cooperation with Mohamed ElBaradei and Jacques Baute, the seasoned head of the agency's action team for Iraq, was a given.

From 2000 to September 11, 2001:
The Iraq Bazaar

The 1999 adoption of Resolution 1284 did not mean that the Security Council was fully agreed on what policy to follow vis-à-vis Iraq. There had been four abstentions: China, France, Malaysia and Russia. There was an eagerness to get the inspectors back and, at the same time, a certain "sanctions fatigue." Yet, no plausible alternative methods had been recognized as likely to bring pressure on Iraq to cooperate with the inspectors. The latest UK/U.S. bombings had only had the effect of getting the inspectors out.

The resolution was clearly meant to be a complement to but not a replacement of Resolution 687 (1991). Under the 1999 resolution, sanctions could be suspended rather than lifted, and this in return for cooperation evidenced by "progress" on "key"—rather than *all*—remaining disarmament issues. Nevertheless, the Iraqi government declared itself opposed to the new resolution and said it was a trap. It argued that the U.S. would see to it that if suspended, sanctions would never be lifted. Moreover, even after suspension Iraq would be, according to the resolution, subject to "effective financial and other operational measures." What were these measures, and which were the "key" remaining issues? Iraq maintained that there were, in fact, no weapons of mass destruction and thus no disarmament issues.

In 2000, Iraq sat down in the global political bazaar with an attitude of "wait and see and chat." The inspectors were gone. The sanctions were condemned by a broad world opinion and in any case they had become less painful, and were eroding. Isolation was reduced. More foreign airplanes were landing. Businesspeople came to Baghdad. The revenues from the Oil-for-Food Program provided many billions of dollars and huge purchase orders were so placed as to produce maximum political benefit—or punishment. Sometimes the Iraqi side denounced the idea of resumed inspections. In July 2000, the foreign minister, Mr. Mohammed Saeed al-Sahaf (who later gained worldwide fame as Iraq's information minister), describing the impending defeat of coalition invaders even as U.S. tanks rolled into Baghdad, said that UNMOVIC "would return American, British and Israeli spies to Iraq." On other occasions the Iraqi side allowed the impression to arise that there could be some normalization "packages" comprising such elements as an end to the no-fly zones maintained by the U.S./UK. Inspectors might be allowed back, but sanctions should be lifted as soon as they did. There should be a timetable for their stay, and no visits to presidential sites.

The French and the Russians seemed to think that some concessions were necessary if the resolution was at all to be implemented and inspectors were to return. They suggested an early agreement on the "financial and administrative measures" that would come into play at a suspension of sanctions, so Iraq would know what carrot it would be given. Similarly, they wished UNMOVIC to specify which, in its view, were "key" remaining issues—without awaiting, as the resolution envisaged, the opportunity to first carry out a period of inspections and assessment. They were, further, keen to see the secretary general engage in a "dialogue" with the Iraqis to get the ball rolling. A new memorandum of understanding covering a package of issues could be an instrument for the necessary adjustments.

At meetings I had on August 22, 2000, with Secretary of State Madeleine Albright and National Security Adviser Sandy Berger, I was told that in the U.S. view there should be no "re-writing" of the resolution.

In October 2000 and, as we shall see below, in January 2001, the UK did not seem closed to the idea of some arrangements which would hold out hope for a suspension of sanctions within six months.

In 2001, two Iraq-related items claimed attention before the terror attacks on September 11, 2001, filled the scene. One was the reform of the sanctions system; the other was the dialogue between the secretary general and the Iraqi government.

In a report released January 10, 2001, the outgoing U.S. secretary of defense, William S. Cohen, warned that Iraq had rebuilt at least its weapons infrastructure and might have begun covertly producing some chemical or biological agents. A spokesman at the British Foreign Office said they shared the U.S. suspicions (which were not new) regarding factories rebuilt after the allied bombings in 1998, but that they *had no hard proof or hard evidence* to substantiate the charges. It was added that since the UN inspectors had left Iraq in December 1998, "the international community had no way of verifying such suspicions." At about the same time, the junior Foreign Office minister Peter Hain told Reuters, "The key is getting weapons inspectors back in and getting sanctions suspended, and that could happen within 180 days of letting the inspectors back in."

On April 3 and 4, 2001, I visited President Bush's new national security advisor, Condoleezza Rice, and the new secretary of state, Colin Powell. Both of them stuck to the position that Iraq had to accept Resolution 1284. Neither of them gave any indication of a hardening U.S. position. Colin Powell said there was a review of policy aimed at putting focus on the issue of weapons of mass destruction and to stop the erosion of the sanctions. Both assured me of U.S. support for UNMOVIC, and Colin Powell said he would look into the question of providing intelligence.

In March 2001, the Joan B. Kroc Institute for International Peace Studies had published a study on "Smart Sanctions" in Iraq. It coincided with a more general search for so-called "smart sanctions" designed to influence policy-makers but not hurt the general public. In Iraq, many said, the result of UN sanctions had been the inverse. It appears that the institute's study became the blueprint for U.S. efforts to reform the sanctions system, which on November 29, 2001, led to the adoption by the Security Council of Resolution 1382. While the U.S. had to abandon ideas of tightening Iraq's borders against smuggling, the resolution removed the onus on the U.S. and UK having to vote in the UN Sanctions Committee against a variety of Iraqi imports that appeared desirable from a humanitarian viewpoint. Everything that was not prohibited for import in a huge, exhaustive list now became permitted, and the heavy job of examining contracts was placed on UNMOVIC and the IAEA. Rachel Davies and her information division handled it with great skill and a small increase in staff. The reform was significant, but as I saw it, the sanctions system had for several years been a mechanism for preventing the export to Iraq of items that could be of military use rather than a means of pressing Iraq to accept inspections.

I had found some statistics from which I drew that conclusion:

- In 1990, when the sanctions were first introduced, the value of Iraq's imports had been $7.6 billion.
- In each of the years 1991, 1992, 1993, 1994, 1995 and 1996,

when the sanctions were fully effective, the value of the imports had decreased to $1.0 billion.

• In 1997, when Iraq was allowed to sell oil and import under the Oil-for-Food Program, the value of imports had been $4.2 billion.

• In 1999, the import value was at $8.52 billion, and in 2000 at $13.7 billion.

Oil prices had gone up, of course, and statistics can be misleading, but the numbers suggested to me that while the sanctions had broken the economic and industrial backbone of the country during the first part of the 1990s and brought misery, they worked chiefly as a control of, not a break on, legal imports in 2000, when there was no longer a limit on how much oil Iraq could export.

The Terrorist Attacks on New York and Washington, September 11, 2001

The terrorist attacks on September 11, 2001, hit the United States like an earthquake. While the action was perpetrated by an amorphous group of terrorists, it brought the world's only superpower to a war footing, and while the terrorists had used no heavier weapons than boxcutters to hijack the airplanes and control their passengers, the action immediately raised the question of what would happen if terrorists or "rogue states" were to possess weapons of mass destruction. One conclusion was that if the United States had reason to suspect any such threat, it must strike first—preemptively. In the absence of any threatening terrorist movement apart from Al Qaeda, many eyes fastened on an old intransigent evil entity— Saddam's Iraq. It had been concluded by all that his nuclear program was finished, but defectors and satellite imagery spoke about reconstruction of various facilities and new teams of scientists. Although no links were known to have existed between Iraq's rather secular Ba'ath regime and Al Qaeda, nevertheless Saddam, it was asserted, had had contacts with terrorists. Mind-sets were transformed around the world and have remained so, but nowhere more than in the United States and in the Bush administration. Even as late as January 15, 2004, U.S. Vice President Cheney, referring to the threat of a terrorist attack in the United States, is reported to have said that the battle, like the Cold War, could last generations and that a new kind of mobilization was needed, requiring more overseas bases so the United States could wage war quickly around the globe.

On January 10, 2002, I went to Washington. Attitudes had certainly changed. Colin Powell made a distinction between the bilateral path to Iraq and the multilateral. The UN stood for the latter. He doubted that the present Iraqi regime would ever comply with the Security Council resolutions. However, he commended UNMOVIC for its role and work. The undersecretary for disarmament, John Bolton, said that UNMOVIC would need support from and unity among the P-5, especially in the initial phase after Iraq allowed the return of inspectors. The Iraqis might try to extract concessions, and he did not rule out another cat-and-mouse game. Undersecretary Douglas Feith in the Department of Defense asked if there was not a risk that some inspectors could learn on the job the best ways of concealing material and documents from inspectors. I wondered if he meant one should only have Americans, Brits and a few other nationalities, and it occurred to me that Iraq had learned its uranium-enrichment techniques from German engineers.

Condoleezza Rice said she did not think it would be beyond Saddam to use or transfer weapons of mass destruction. Right now the U.S. priority was to deal with Al Qaeda but, hopefully, the international community would also focus on Saddam. The war in Afghanistan had had a useful demonstrative effect, she said, which the president had understood early on. Like Colin Powell, she concluded that the administration did not believe Saddam would deliver what was expected of him—though it would, of course, be happy if he did.

On January 28, 2002, President Bush delivered his State of the Union address in which he named Iraq, Iran and North Korea as the "axis of evil."

The Secretary General's Dialogue

The dialogue between the secretary general and the Iraqi government had grown out of the Ba'ath leadership's belief in early 2000 that they had the upper hand and could get some kind of package deal that would, among other things, end the sanctions. Although the idea of a package in the shape of a memorandum of understanding was supported by the French and the Russians, the Iraqis consistently overestimated their hand. The U.S. and UK never accepted the idea, feeling that any proposed package was likely to be a dilution of the compromise they had settled for in Resolution 1284. The French took the view that this might be necessary to make Iraq readmit inspectors.

No doubt Kofi Annan felt pressure from developing countries, including most Arab countries, to move the matter out of the dead end. However, he could not enter into a dialogue "without preconditions," as the Iraqi side suggested. He obviously had to start from the premise of the binding resolutions of the Security Council. From his side, the dialogue was mainly about getting Iraq to accept inspection, which the resolutions demanded. From the Iraqi side it was mainly about using the inspection issue as leverage to make gains on other issues, such as sanctions. Wisely, he limited himself for the most part to listening to Iraq's long lectures about its grievances.

One session took place February 26–27, 2001, with Iraqi Foreign Minister al-Sahaf. At this stage, the Iraqi side did not want to hear about Resolution 1284 and UNMOVIC. Kofi Annan conferred with me before the meeting, but I did not take part. After the session, al-Sahaf was asked by the press about UNMOVIC and said simply it was "a non-entity." And Blix? He is a "detail" in the non-entity. Journalists turned to me for a comment, and I said I thought the Iraqis had given me a promotion, as they had earlier only called me a spy.

A year later, on March 7, 2002, there was a second session of the dialogue. This time the Iraqi delegation was headed by the new foreign minister, Dr. Naji Sabri, who was said to have been elevated to his post thanks to Saddam's younger and ever more influential son,

Qusay. Dr. Sabri was more affable (and even sometimes cheerful) than his loud and barely civil predecessor, though hardly less propagandistic. The Iraqis were expected to do less lecturing this time and even show some flexibility, perhaps even on inspections. They raised no objection to my joining Kofi Annan for the talks. The secretary general of the League of Arab States, Amr Moussa, who also attended the meeting, had visited President Saddam Hussein in January and talked to him about inspections. Saddam had explained that the inspections were insulting.

During the talks, Kofi Annan gave me the opportunity to explain how we had organized UNMOVIC and how we looked upon our task. I stressed that credible inspections should be in the interest of both Iraq and the UN. Lax inspections had no credibility. What struck me was how aggrieved the Iraqi side appeared—or at least wanted to appear. I did not have an impression of a lack of sincerity, rather of people living in another world of thinking.

Public Discussion in the U.S. and UK, Spring 2002

At this juncture the discussion of the possibility of armed action against Iraq had started in the U.S. In testimony in the U.S. Congress on March 1, Robert Einhorn, former assistant secretary of state for non-proliferation, said it was doubtful if anyone in the world would believe a statement by Saddam Hussein in a letter of February 7 to the Turkish Prime Minister: "As pertains to the weapons of mass destruction, Iraq, which no longer has any of these weapons and has no intention of producing them, is in the forefront of those who are keen that our region be free of weapons of mass destruction."

Einhorn further said that "a consensus seems to be developing in Washington in favor of 'regime change' in Iraq, if necessary through the use of military force." He noted that President Bush had called for the return of inspectors, but there was speculation that the purpose of this was to provide justification for military action if Baghdad, as expected, refused to admit the inspectors.

There was also a lively debate in the UK. In an interview with

NBC on April 5, Prime Minister Tony Blair said about Saddam Hussein: "We know he has stockpiles of *major amounts of chemical and biological weapons.* We know that he's tried to acquire nuclear capability" (my emphasis). This was only two and a half months after the Foreign Office had said there was no hard evidence. The mind-set was changing. The Iraqi foreign minister, Naji Sabri, challenged the British to send a team of British experts to Iraq to locate the items they claimed existed. After a weekend visit to President Bush in Texas, the British prime minister said in Parliament on April 10: "The time for military action has not yet arisen . . ." and further that Saddam could avoid the wrath of the United States and Britain by allowing United Nations weapons inspectors to return to his country unfettered. It is tempting to think that President Bush had agreed with him that the inspection path must be tried.

On April 16, 2002, Walter Pincus in *The Washington Post* reported Secretary of Defense Rumsfeld as saying about inspectors that "for the most part anything they found was a result of having been cued to something as a result of a defector giving them a heads-up." Pincus reported further that the deputy secretary of defense, Paul Wolfowitz, in January had requested a CIA investigation into my performance as head of the IAEA between 1981 and 1997. I could sense in this the hand of my former employee, David Kay. When asked about the inquiry, the Defense Department played it down and said I had their full confidence. In another article on April 15, Walter Pincus reported that the CIA had concluded that as chief of the IAEA I had conducted inspections "fully within the parameters he could operate." Some officials had said that Mr. Wolfowitz "hit the ceiling" because the report on me failed to provide sufficient ammunition to undermine me and the UN inspection program. Even more interesting was Pincus's report that Wolfowitz and his civilian colleagues in the U.S. Department of Defense feared that new inspections could "torpedo" their plans for military action to remove Hussein from power. He quoted an official as saying that "the hawks' nightmare is that inspectors will be admitted, will not be terribly vigorous and not find anything. Economic sanctions would be eased, and the U.S. would be unable to act."

May Round of the Dialogue

The next round in the dialogue between the UN and Iraq took place in New York May 1–3, 2002. Minister Naji Sabri had ended the meeting in March by putting nineteen questions to the UN, and I now gave factual answers to those which concerned inspection. I prefaced my remarks, however, by saying that the Iraqi side had given the impression in March that the greatest problem in the relations between Iraq and the UN was how Iraq could again acquire confidence in the Security Council. I said this was to underestimate the problem. There was the other side: that Iraq needed to cooperate with UNMOVIC and the IAEA in such a way that the Security Council and the world gained a high level of confidence that the weapons of mass destruction had been eradicated in Iraq.

At this meeting the Iraqi side had two new prominent members in their delegation: General Dr. Amir Al Sa'adi, who from then on became my opposite number, and Dr. Jaffar Dhia Jaffar, both high-class intellectuals, both described as presidential advisers. Jaffar was a brilliant nuclear scientist whom Saddam had thrown into jail and then released and kept alive in exchange for his services. Mohamed ElBaradei, myself and our experts met with Al Sa'adi and Jaffar and their colleagues in a "technical subcommittee." Jaffar had arrived late to New York, having been delayed in Amman because his visa for the U.S. took time and his luggage had been lost on the way. It was said that on the journey he had been approached by an intelligence agent who told him that his luggage had been detained to be searched, and also asked whether he was ready to defect. Whatever the truth, he was angry and criticized Mohamed ElBaradei fiercely for not having given Iraq a "clean bill of health" in the nuclear field in 1998. While I understood him—there were no disarmament issues left in 1997–1998, only minor questions—I do not think he understood that closing the nuclear dossier would not have helped to lift sanctions so long as other dossiers had many open issues.

Not surprisingly, the Iraqi side tried to extract concessions in return for an acceptance of resumed inspections. The "package" was still alive, although its time had long since passed—if it had ever been there. Now they wanted some sort of assurance that if they accepted inspections the threat of aggression would be lifted. Thus the presence of inspectors would also be a form of protection. They knew that Kofi Annan had no powers in this regard and that it was unlikely the Security Council would give in.

More practically important was that, before any inspections resumed, they wanted us to tell them which disarmament issues we deemed still to be open after eight years of inspection and clarification. We refused this approach, and insisted on following the procedure laid down by the Security Council. Iraq had had no inspections for nearly four years. Only after a period of inspections on the ground could we proceed to define the disarmament issues which were open—old or new—and those among them that were "key" issues. The Iraqi side was, in effect, trying to achieve a limitation on the scope of the inquiry before agreeing to it. We sought to get into a discussion about the practical arrangements for resumed inspections. Questions of right to access, the flights of helicopters and so on had caused many controversies in the past. As our rights were laid down in many resolutions and other instruments, there was nothing about which to negotiate. Rather, we wanted to tick off a great many items to ensure that we saw eye to eye and did not land ourselves in controversy from day-one of the resumed inspections.

July Round of the Dialogue

Although the continued public discussion in the U.S. about possible armed action against Iraq must have worried the Iraqi side, we do not know how much of this was communicated to Saddam Hussein. In June, before the next round of the dialogue, there was no indication of a more flexible position. Quite the contrary.

Clearly, several things I had said had stung them. One related to my insistence that we needed more *evidence* (e.g., documentation) from the Iraqi side showing what had happened to different stocks of weapons. We had been told that there were no more documents.

I doubted this was true. Precisely at this juncture the Iraqis declared that they had discovered carloads of stolen Kuwaiti state archives in Baghdad and were ready to give them back to Kuwait. I could not resist remarking in an informal Security Council consultation that perhaps they could also find more weapons documents. My remark resulted in an angry letter of June 10 from the Iraqi foreign minister to the secretary general in which I was accused of "blocking prospects for success." Moreover, the minister wrote, "the remaining disarmament issues are merely a matter of academic and of historical interest and have little to do with present realities."

In another letter to Kofi Annan on June 17, in advance of the July session of the dialogue, Naji Sabri continued to urge "a comprehensive solution" in which, above all, the "unlawful sanctions" would be lifted. The word "inspection" was evidently too stark to use. Rather, he wanted, within the structure of the comprehensive solution, to develop "a formula for transparency to answer any concerns of the United Nations concerning the ascertainment of the truth of the United States allegations."

In Vienna, as a gesture of goodwill, we did examine a few disarmament issues during the "technical subcommittee talks." Our counterparts appreciated the thoroughness with which we went about our analyses, but did not reciprocate by discussing even one of the many practical arrangements that we pointed to—for instance, regarding flights into Iraq, helicopter operations, lodging, or regional offices in Basra and Mosul. I had argued, and they had not disagreed, that a resumption of inspections should have a good and "flying start," but they were still balking and focused exclusively on their effort to limit the scope of inspections. I had also suggested that a "new general declaration," shedding light on or solving some of the issues that in the past had been seen as unresolved, might provide new momentum, if backed up by credible evidence. This, I think, was the first time the idea of a new declaration was advanced. Little did I know that it would result five months later in a dossier of some 12,000 pages—regrettably without bringing us much forward.

Views expressed in the media had hinted that there was a political global warming on the Iraq issue and that the talks in Vienna could tip the scales toward war or peace. Hundreds of journalists were waiting downstairs with their cameras and microphones. When we concluded the Vienna talks on July 5, 2002, however, no progress had been made. Kofi Annan could not very well set a date for a new session and contribute to a false impression that the dialogue was going somewhere, and as I had seen no readiness on the Iraqi part to discuss practical arrangements for inspections, I was also not willing to agree to and set a date for a further separate meeting of the "technical subcommittee." Instead, a statement was written expressing the bare minimum: The secretary general would remain in contact with the Security Council and the Iraqi delegation would report to their authorities. It had been agreed to maintain contacts, "including continuing discussions on technical matters."

On his return to Baghdad, Foreign Minister Naji Sabri said it was very clear that I had bowed to U.S. pressures. By refusing to hold meaningful discussions about what had been achieved through inspections since May 1991, I had blocked talks on the return of inspectors to Iraq. Ten days later, however, he sought to put a more positive spin on Vienna. Briefing ambassadors in Baghdad, he added to the rich lore of the old city by saying that in Vienna, "a breakthrough was achieved": the secretary general was to convey Iraq's questions to the Security Council. There was even some hope on the inspection front, although "the head of UNMOVIC hesitated to accept Iraq's proposal due to U.S. pressures as it seems . . ." He expected that contacts on the political and technical levels would continue. A few days later, on July 24, he was quoted in the London-issued Arabic newspaper *Al Hayat* as saying that the inspectors' return should be connected to the other elements in the Security Council resolutions and must be done on the basis that "the search was completed in the past decade."

The Iraqi stance was puzzling. Talk of armed action was growing louder in the U.S. Even while we were in Vienna, *The New York Times* published an article about a Pentagon invasion plan for Iraq. While no reference had been made to it, everyone had read it, and it was like a slap in the face that ought to have softened the Iraqi position. Yet the Iraqi side persisted in accepting resumed inspections only as part of a "comprehensive solution." Was Saddam Hussein not well informed or was the Iraqi conduct simply a piece of hard bargaining in the bazaar? Their obvious need was for a guarantee that in return for resumed inspections there would be no armed attack. If they did not feel confident that UNMOVIC would be much different from UNSCOM, they might also have wanted some guarantee that UNMOVIC would not provide the U.S. intelligence that would be of use for possible future attacks. In an interview in Belgium on July 24, Naji Sabri touched upon both these elements. However, he must have known that the U.S. would never have given a guarantee not to attack and that even if I was determined not to allow UNMOVIC to be misused, I could not give a 100-percent guarantee.

In two successive letters from Sabri to the secretary general at the beginning of August 2002, the Iraqis tried to get me to Baghdad for continued "technical talks." Even though they dangled the possibility of dealing with the "practical arrangements," the proposals remained based on the premise that before any inspections resumed we should agree which disarmament issues were open. As the Security Council had retained for itself the final decision of which were "key" remaining disarmament issues—rather than making decisions on the scope of issues a matter of agreement between Iraq and UNMOVIC—the procedure proposed could not be accepted. In various Iraqi communications, the negative response was said to have been inspired by me and caused by American pressure on me. They were completely wrong. I felt they had stonewalled in Vienna and just persisted in a procedure that was unacceptable. They needed to cool their heels a bit and get more anxious for inspections before we met for another round of talks. In one Iraqi letter it was said that Iraq had information that I went every second week to Washington to consult with the State Department. Actually, I had not been there since June 18, and, as it turned out, my next visit would not be until October 4.

The tone seemed to become harder on inspections. In an interview in Baghdad on August 27, 2002, Iraq's vice president, Taha Yassin Ramadan, attributed the negative response from New York to the "new spy"—me—being directed by the U.S. "We have affirmed," he said, "not just now, but for years, that Iraq is free of weapons of mass destruction and that the inspection committees, which are actually espionage committees, have accomplished all their missions in Iraq. There is nothing left concerning the subject of disarmament."

This would become a lost opportunity for Iraq. Had they accepted inspection pure and simple and gone through all the practical arrangements, they would have gotten a somewhat more lenient inspection regime than the one the Council decided on a few months later. From my point of view, this outcome was not a bad thing.

4

Inspections, Yes, But How?

Mid-August to Mid-September 2002:
Preemptive Invasion or Peaceful Inspection?

From the middle of August to the middle of September, a brew of many ingredients, currents and countercurrents was simmering. Where did I myself stand? On August 18 a BBC interviewer noted strong indications that the U.S. would take military action against Iraq regardless of the debate over inspections. What was my view of the situation and the invitation I had received to come to Baghdad? Would there be any inspections?

I said that if the Iraqis concluded that an invasion was inevitable they might also conclude that prior inspections were pointless. It was my impression, however, that the concern that they might have weapons of mass destruction was an important element, and that giving unfettered access to inspectors could play an important role. What did I expect to find in Iraq? "I'm not assuming at all that the Iraqis have retained weapons of mass destruction," I said. "At the same time, it would evidently be naïve of me to conclude that they don't. . . . So on-site inspection is important." Did I have any idea what the Iraqis might have? "Well, we listen to . . . various intelligence organizations, but they are not putting any evidence on the

69

table, and it would be our job to go to the various places they might have talked about and see on site whether there was something or not."

In September 2002 an important document, *The National Security Strategy of the United States of America,* was released. It supported the concept of preemptive action. Evidently influenced by the terrorist attack on the U.S. it stated:

> We must be prepared to stop rogue states and their terrorist clients before they are able to threaten or use weapons of mass destruction against the United States and our allies and friends . . .

and further:

> . . . the United States can no longer solely rely on a reactive posture as we have in the past. . . . We cannot let our enemies strike first. . . .
>
> To support preemptive options, we will:
>
> • build better, more integrated intelligence capabilities to provide timely, accurate information on threats, wherever they may emerge;
> • coordinate closely with our allies to form a common assessment of the most dangerous threats; and
> • continue to transform our military forces to ensure our ability to conduct rapid and precise operations to achieve decisive results.

In speeches on August 26 and 29, U.S. Vice President Cheney was clearly advocating preemptive invasion rather than peaceful inspection. In the first of the speeches, he said:

> A return of inspectors would provide no assurance whatsoever of his [Saddam's] compliance with U.N. resolutions.

On the contrary, there is a great danger that it would provide
false comfort that Saddam was somehow "back in his box."

The vice president evidently saw defectors as a better source of
intelligence. He said that the information obtained from Saddam
Hussein's defected son-in-law and the documents obtained from his
chicken farm "should serve as a reminder to all that we often learned
more as the result of defections than we learned from the inspection
regime itself."

He did not mention that in his debriefing in Amman in 1995,
General Hussein Kamel had said that he had ordered the destruction of all weapons of mass destruction in 1991. He also ignored the
fact that hardly any weapons had been found at non-declared installations. Instead, Mr. Cheney said, "Simply stated, there is no doubt
that Saddam now has weapons of mass destruction. . . ."

It was evident that the terrorist attacks on the United States had
influenced his thinking. He advanced two arguments that would
often reappear in the public discussion: "time is not on our side"
and "the risks of inaction are far greater than the risk of action."

On preemptive action, he said, "If the United States could have
preempted 9/11, we would have, no question. Should we be able to
prevent another, much more devastating attack, we will, no question."

As for the reactions in the Arab "street" after such action, he said
in a sentence that has been often quoted (and was itself a quote of a
statement with which one may assume he agreed), "the streets in
Basra and Baghdad are 'sure to erupt in joy in the same way the
throngs in Kabul greeted the Americans.' "

On a trip to Europe in the first week of September I went to
Brussels, then joined German foreign minister Joschka Fischer on
his election campaign bus, and lastly saw Prime Minister Tony Blair
in London. All seemed at this time to favor inspection rather than
invasion. In my long talk with Mr. Fischer I got the impression that
the German government, like most others, was convinced that Iraq
retained weapons of mass destruction but also feared that a U.S.
invasion of Iraq might destabilize the whole region.

The British Foreign Office talked about giving Saddam Hussein a deadline for accepting inspections. The implication of a deadline would appear to have been that military action would be taken if the UN's demands were not heeded. I note, in this context, that in his preface to a report of September 2002, Prime Minister Blair advocated inspection first. He wrote that

> the inspectors must be allowed back in and to do their job properly; and that if he [Saddam] refuses, or if he makes it impossible for them to do their job as he has done in the past, the international community will have to act.

Not only European voices but also many in America, like that of Brent Scowcroft, national security adviser to the first President Bush, urged caution. Within hours of the vice president's speech, the U.S. State Department's spokesman, Richard Boucher, said that "We're doing our utmost . . . to get U.N. inspectors back to Iraq."

It was almost as if the U.S. administration was making a virtue of speaking with different voices. Former Secretary of State Henry Kissinger was reported to have said that the war talk in Washington enhanced the possibility of Saddam agreeing to comprehensive inspections and that the goal of full disclosure through inspections "is not achievable without the threat of war." It was an interesting observation: deterrence by discussion. In California on August 27, Secretary of Defense Donald Rumsfeld said that "the president's not made a decision with respect to Iraq. . . . There is a discussion, a debate, a dialogue taking place in our country and the world, as it properly should."

However, with Mr. Rumsfeld suggesting that the administration was in no rush to decide whether or not to take military action, one might think that the president had in fact decided against invasion at this early time.

Had Mr. Blair talked the president into a period of UN action while the military—not yet ready for invasion—increased the pressure? Maybe some in the U.S. administration hoped that Iraq would reject the resumption of inspections or, if they accepted, would obstruct inspections and thereby give a justification for military action. A big question is whether already at this stage a time limit had been set within which inspections—in the U.S. view—would have to succeed or else invasion would be undertaken. Before the hot season began in Iraq in April?

Action on the UN Scene in New York

On Thursday, September 12, the secretary general of the UN and the U.S. president both addressed the General Assembly of the United Nations. Kofi Annan came first and turned to the burning points of the day. On multilateralism he said, "Choosing to follow or reject the multilateral path must not be a simple matter of political convenience. It has consequences far beyond the immediate context."

There was also a warning that preemptive military action—perhaps in the name of counter-proliferation?—might not acquire legitimacy but without the support of the UN:

Any State, if attacked, retains the inherent right of self-defense under Article 51 of the Charter. But beyond that, when States decide to use force to deal with broader threats to international peace and security, there is no substitute for the unique legitimacy provided by the United Nations.

On Iraq he had this to say: "Efforts to obtain Iraq's compliance with the Council's resolutions must continue." The acceptance of weapons inspections was vital. "If Iraq's defiance continues, the Security Council must face its responsibilities."

President Bush reminded the General Assembly how Saddam Hussein had defied the organization year after year. He continued to develop weapons of mass destruction and was a threat to UN authority. If the Iraqi regime wished peace it would immediately forswear, disclose and remove or destroy all weapons of mass destruction. The president pledged that the U.S. would work with the UN Security Council and that if Iraq again was defiant, the world must move deliberately and decisively. It was a forceful speech, which was received positively. There was only one word missing, we noticed: inspection.

After President Bush's speech, most people concluded that the U.S. had decided to go the multilateral path. Others were not so sure. A new resolution on inspections was talked about and some warned that the U.S. would load it with so many difficult demands that the Iraqis could not but say no. This could be used as a justification for military action.

On Sunday, September 15, Kofi Annan asked me to come down and see him at the UN. He told me that he expected the Iraqis to declare that they accepted the return of inspectors and wanted early discussions in Baghdad or Vienna about practical arrangements. Great, I said, and added that I wanted the talks to be in Vienna. We should not rush to Baghdad and raise expectations in the world that the Iraqis had given their wholehearted acceptance of inspections, only to come out saying that the conditions offered were not adequate. We might look as if *we* were blocking inspections! We should go to Baghdad and offer Iraq the benefit of inspection only when they accepted the practical arrangements we needed: full and free access, landing rights and a host of other things. I told Annan that I knew the U.S. wanted to get rid of the "sensitive sites modalities" that Ekeus had adopted, as well as the memorandum of understanding on entry into presidential sites. Both were, in the U.S. view, restrictions on the access that the inspectors should have. I would take the view that the "modalities" were not binding, but I could not touch the memorandum since the Council had endorsed it.

Kofi Annan received Naji Sabri's official letter about the decision "to allow the return of the United Nations weapons inspectors to Iraq without conditions" on Monday afternoon, September 16. This, it said, was an indispensable "first step towards an assurance that Iraq no longer possesses weapons of mass destruction" and, equally important, toward a "comprehensive solution" of the question of sanctions and other issues. The Iraqi government was ready to discuss "the practical arrangements necessary for the immediate resumption of inspections." The letter referred to appeals by the secretary generals of the United Nations and the League of Arab States and others, but not to the U.S. military pressure and the discussion about war. I sensed and I felt relieved that Kofi Annan must have influenced them to explicitly mention the practical arrangements.

On Tuesday morning, September 16, I phoned the Iraqi ambassador to the UN, Mr. Mohammed Aldouri, to suggest immediate talks, taking advantage of the presence in New York of some persons in charge of our inspections on the Iraqi side, notably General Hussam Amin, the head of the National Monitoring Directorate, the official Iraqi organization dealing with the inspections. In my office that same afternoon we had a good talk. I gave them the list of the practical arrangements we had wanted to discuss in Vienna and, as they had not come to the meeting prepared for talks, we agreed on another meeting in Vienna in the week beginning September 30. This gave them—and us—some time for preparations. General Amin had addressed me as "Your Excellency" that afternoon—quite a career leap after first being named a "detail in a non-entity" by Foreign Minister al-Sahaf in 2001 and then a "spy" a month ago by Vice President Ramadan.

On Thursday, September 19, I briefed the Security Council informally on our preparations to date. When could we start in Baghdad? In about two months, I said, and this turned out, in fact, to be a good prediction. The whole situation was like a plane sitting on the tarmac, its pilot going through the checklist to be sure that he's ready to take off. Thankfully, we had a little longer time, and of course, we had prepared for this moment. We could proceed immediately with the chartering of a transport plane and helicopters, the purchase of equipment, and so on. Having waited for two and a half years and spent many efforts on training, we now had all the people we needed. However, they were not waiting in our corridors. They had to arrange for leaving their normal jobs, and that would take a little time.

The Crude Roots of Resolution 1441 (2002)

The UK and U.S. did not at the time regret that our discussions with Iraq about practical arrangements were not scheduled immediately. They were preparing a new Security Council resolution on inspections, and it would be necessary in due course to take into account in any practical arrangements. I was aware of this, and intended to make any arrangements subject to new Security Council decisions.

The discussion of a new resolution on inspection continued in the corridors. The Iraqis made it known that they were against it and hinted that they might rescind their invitation for renewed inspections if the conditions were changed. What they particularly feared, I would guess, was a clause authorizing armed force in case of non-compliance, or some time limit within which the Security Council had to be satisfied that there were no unresolved disarmament issues left. Some states felt no new resolution was needed and that we could operate on the basis of existing ones. I was, personally, in favor of a new text, and I made no secret about it. It seemed reasonable to me that since we were starting afresh and in an atmosphere that was much more demanding of Iraq than that which had prevailed when Resolution 1284 had been adopted a year before, we should be given language we could use against any renewed cat-and-mouse play.

During the week of September 23–27, we learned more about the contents contemplated for the resolution, and toward the end of the week I was given a draft that made my few hairs stand up. It read more like a U.S. Defense Department document than like one drafted by the UN. Just as the U.S. initiative on "smart sanctions" in 2001 had drawn on the study of a private institution, this draft seemed to have drawn on a study by the Carnegie Endowment for International Peace, which had held a workshop on inspections in Iraq in April 2002 and had presented a paper on a "new approach" in August. Normally, I have great respect for this institution, but this time I could not agree with their proposals.

The well-meaning ambition of the study seems to have been to avoid war by finding a compromise between those who advocated an armed invasion and occupation of Iraq and those who wanted to see a resumption of the existing UN inspection system. The result was an approach called "coercive inspections." Among the participants in the workshop were some military experts and former UNSCOM inspectors. I had been startled at two points made in the executive summary of the April meeting:

- "UNMOVIC is a weak inspection body that needs to be strengthened or replaced."
- "A multilateral *cover* would provide legitimacy and generate international support. In this regard, Security Council resolutions are important and P-5 unity is crucial" (my emphasis).

I was puzzled. Rolf Ekeus, a former executive chairman of UNSCOM, had been a prominent member of the study group, but he had also been a candidate to become the chairman of UNMOVIC. He was cited as saying that "a weaker inspection system was a glaring hole in Resolution 1284, which should be thrown out of the window." Had he been willing to become chairman of a commission that he thought was not strong enough, and with whose inspection system he could find such fault? Had Resolution 1284 done away with any of the rights that UNSCOM had had? And had he been willing to help run "a multilateral cover" providing legitimacy? Had not the Amorim report and some provisions in Resolution 1284 seen it as necessary to strengthen the international legitimacy of the inspection authority by stressing broad international recruitment of staff rather than drawing them from states ready to provide them gratis? Had not the reason for replacing rather than extending UNSCOM been that it had lost its international legitimacy precisely by becoming too much of a "multilateral cover"? Ekeus had also contributed a special chapter to the study in which he urged intelligence "support" for the inspectors. He had reported that with the help of supporting governments UNSCOM had applied "some in-country listening arrangements in support of inspections" and that there was a temptation for supporting governments to use the system for "extracurricular" purposes. Indeed, many U.S. media reports between January 5 and 15, 1999, reported extensively on these activities, and even an interview with Ekeus himself in the Swedish media on July 29, 2002, had shown how this electronic eavesdropping had gotten out of hand, how UNSCOM had become a "multilateral cover."

In an early draft of what some six weeks later became Resolution 1441, I identified the following features to which I held serious reservations:

> • "any permanent member of the Security Council may recommend to UNMOVIC and the IAEA sites to be inspected, persons to be interviewed . . . and data to be collected *and receive a report on the results*" (my emphasis);
> • "any permanent member of the Security Council may request to be represented on any inspection team with the same rights and protections accorded other members of the team";
> • UNMOVIC and the IAEA "shall be provided *regional bases and operating bases throughout Iraq*" (my emphasis);
> • UNMOVIC and the IAEA shall have the right to establish "no-fly/no-drive zones, exclusion zones and/or ground and air transit corridors, (which shall be enforced by UN security forces *or by member states*)" (my emphasis).

What would happen, I asked myself, when representatives of the P-5 on the inspection teams did not agree during missions? It was the same problem as with the pentarchy proposed (though not by the U.S.) in the UNMOVIC secretariat. Evidently the P-5 would be entitled to "recommend" sites to be inspected, the mode of inspection, and so on, and to receive a subsequent report. There seemed to be an idea, further, that UN security "forces" could be supplemented by forces from member states—including, apparently, even members other than P-5. This was certainly not the mission I had been willing to head, and I could not imagine that the P-5 would buy it.

With this draft in my baggage I took the plane to Vienna to discuss practical arrangements with the Iraqis.

Practical Arrangements

The talks in Vienna lasted two days, Monday, September 31, and Tuesday, October 1. Again the plaza outside the Vienna International Center was filled by TV and radio. It was amazing to find such public attention being paid to issues like the unimpeded inspection of so called "sensitive sites," about where our planes should land in Baghdad, etc. The media began to sense that inspection was the alternative to war.

Before the formal meeting began on Monday morning, Mohamed ElBaradei and I gave the Iraqi delegation—General Amir Al Sa'adi, General Hussam Amin and Ambassador Saeed Hassan—a short paper in which we put them on notice that we suggested Iraq should refrain from requesting the application of "modalities" and the memorandum of understanding on presidential sites. The talks were difficult but never disagreeable. The main line we had established was that procedures which had been used by UNSCOM and which had worked well in the past should continue.

I had had a concern that the Iraqis, advancing various security reasons, would insist that our plane would be required to land about 100 kilometers away from Baghdad, as UNSCOM's had had to do. However, a solution was found by which our flights in and out of Iraq would use Baghdad's big international airport and our helicopters would use the Rashid Airport. It worked out quite well, too. We had little difficulty about a host of other issues. It was harder to do away with Ekeus's and Butler's "modalities" for inspections of sensitive sites, but, helped by the background of strong political and military pressure, we did. Thus, there remained no sanctuaries and only presidential sites were subject to a special agreement. We could only register our proposal to put these sites on the same footing as others. We also did not receive a green light on some other points, such as surveillance flights, interviews without "minders" and a guarantee of safety when flying in no-fly zones.

Some points made by the Iraqi side had amazed me. In this high-tension situation they had suggested that minders who would escort inspectors outside regular working hours should be paid for overtime by UNMOVIC. This, they said, would make the minders more "enthusiastic." I demurred that it was the Iraqi side's job to keep them enthusiastic.

Back in New York, we briefed the Security Council on Thursday, October 3. The members were pleased with the outcome and asked for a written document on all the conclusions we'd reached. We prepared one, and as we had not made such a neat list in Vienna we sent it to the Iraqi side for confirmation. On a few points the replies we later received were not quite satisfactory, in particular regarding air operations in no-fly zones, interviews, surveillance flights and regional offices.

The Iraqi side now felt that it had helped to clarify all the practical arrangements and that the inspections should start immediately—and above all, should start within the legal framework of existing resolutions and not under some new regime. We were not yet ready to dispatch people and equipment. We were also conscious of the ongoing negotiations about a new resolution. It would be awkward to start inspections under one regime and find, after only a short time, that it had to be modified because of a new resolution. Even worse would have been if, in the midst of our inspections, the Iraqi side rejected a new regime.

The Development of the Draft Resolution; A Discussion in Washington

After Mohamed ElBaradei and I had briefed the Security Council in the morning of October 3, the P-5 ambassadors came to my office in the afternoon to talk about the resolution. I affirmed that I thought a new resolution could mark a new chapter and could be helpful to prevent any resumed cat-and-mouse play. The next day we were invited to the State Department in Washington. Quite an array of U.S. luminaries attended the primary meeting there: Colin Powell, Condoleezza Rice and Paul Wolfowitz, plus people in uniform like General Peter Pace, vice chairman of the Joint Chiefs of Staff, and people from the National Security Council and the office of the vice president. I came with Dimitri Perricos and my executive assistant, Jarmo Sareva, an experienced and unflappable Finnish diplomat who had succeeded Olof Skoog. The IAEA group consisted of Mohamed and the head of his action team, the nuclear expert Jacques Baute; a legal adviser, Laura Rockwood; and the head of his New York office, Gustavo Zlauvinen.

Colin Powell asked me to present my views on how the inspection regime could be strengthened. I welcomed the efforts being made and was pleased to offer some comments and suggestions:

- The rights of the inspectors under the existing regime could not be said to be weak and should be confirmed. For instance, inspectors could go into the headquarters of the security forces and ministries, yet—since 1994 at any rate—information but not much hardware had been found. Despite defectors and satellites, whatever secrets they had were well guarded.
- We welcomed new provisions that would help us to prevent a repetition of Iraq's cat-and-mouse play and lead to the acquisition of credible information.
- Legally we could start inspections without any new resolution, but it would be more practical to wait until we knew whether a new text would require additional practical arrangements. It might also settle some matters we had not been able to thrash out in Vienna.
- A consensus in the Security Council was vital. To operate inspections with half the Council for and the other half against would be bad.
- A clause signaling forceful action in case of non-

81

compliance would be valuable. Iraq did not move without forceful, sustained pressure, and it simply shrugged off economic sanctions.

- I questioned why the Iraqi side had asked for at least a fifteen-minute delay before inspectors could enter "sensitive sites"—a request we'd rejected. Would that be enough to hide weapons? Was it a matter of dignity?

- We would be glad to have the presidential sites put on par with others.

- We did not like the idea of attaching security escorts to inspections. If there was an incident involving armed Iraqi units and armed escorts it could act as a trip wire and force the hands of governments. This would be a kind of semi-occupation without real power. It was better to have forces in the region but outside Iraq.

- I favored—and had myself advanced—the idea of requiring a new declaration. The system was based upon the concept "they declare, we verify," not just "they open doors, we search." If they had something still hidden, maybe they could find another "chicken farm" full of documents—but did they have any weapons of mass destruction? Al Sa'adi had denied it and said they would be weapons of self-destruction.

- We needed free access to persons and the right to private interviews, but receiving defectors in our Baghdad offices would be problematic; how would we get them out?

- Like other states, P-5 members of the Security Council were able even now to give inspectors any "recommendations" they wanted regarding sites to inspect or persons to interview, but the inspectors should only report back to the Council, not to individual members. Intelligence should be mainly a one-way traffic.

- Having P-5 "representatives" on UN inspection teams was unwise and marked a reversal of the approach of Resolution 1284, which had sought to strengthen the UN identity of the inspection teams. P-5 representatives would presumably report home about military sites they visited. UNSCOM had been too close to supporting governments and, in the end, had lost its UN identity and legitimacy.

• The Security Council was free to determine whatever model it wished for inspection. In June 1950 it had recommended that member states make military forces available for a united command under the U.S. to fight the Korean War (Resolution 84). It was free to give the inspection job to the P-5, but the inspector should not then be considered a UN operation.

Mohamed ElBaradei also stressed that unity in the Security Council was vital to making Iraq cooperate, and, further, that preserving legitimacy required a UN identity. The following discussion was brisk, with Ms. Rice and Mr. Wolfowitz taking fairly tough lines. The latter asked me if I did not believe that Iraq had weapons of mass destruction. I replied that I had read the recent paper which the British government had published—the one that claimed Iraq could deploy weapons of mass destruction in forty-five minutes. I thought it was a good paper but was struck that all the way through it stated that "intelligence suggests" or "intelligence tells." This was not evidence.

After the meeting, Colin Powell, Condoleezza Rice, Mohmed ElBaradei and I talked alone for a while. Powell intimated that the U.S. might provide more intelligence if they felt sure that information would not be compromised. A greater presence at the center in UNMOVIC would help. I said we would be transparent about how we handled all intelligence we received from the U.S. but we could not allow ourselves to be an extended arm of the CIA. I wondered if he understood that if I were to add an American to my office to look after intelligence everybody would immediately say, "now the U.S. is taking over UNMOVIC." Perhaps he wondered if I understood how important such a presence might be to the Pentagon.

It was, as always, a civilized, professional talk. Afterward Powell went with us down to street level where we made a few comments to the assembled journalists. I said good-bye and stepped into a big

Volvo that the Swedish ambassador, Jan Eliasson, had sent to take me to his residence for a drink. As I left, I thought Powell was probably having kind thoughts about me that day. Not only did I leave in a Volvo, which I knew was a favorite car of his, I had also delivered some heavy arguments against various lines in the draft resolution that must have troubled the State Department. Most of them came out later, probably through the efforts of various Security Council members, but I may have contributed.

Colin Powell in New York, October 17; Igor Ivanov in Moscow, October 22

Nearly two weeks after the big meeting in Washington, Colin Powell was in New York and asked me to see him at the Waldorf Astoria Hotel. The signals I had been picking up from the press and various individuals at the time were mixed. Some said that the U.S. was only feigning interest in the UN and that its war plans were already made. Others said that the draft resolution was moving forward. I did not see that increasing military pressure and readiness for armed action necessarily excluded a desire for a peaceful solution. If that was what the U.S. wanted, strong inspections would be needed. The draft resolution we had discussed in Washington had been extreme, and it was doubtful whether it could even have had a majority support in the Security Council. From what I heard of the further negotiations, the U.S. had dropped the absurd and unworkable clauses about UN inspections being directed by five permanent members of the Security Council. It was also ready, I had heard, to live with a blurred clause about the consequences of non-compliance, enabling them to take unilateral action if they deemed this necessary.

I walked over to the hotel from the UN and met Colin Powell alone for half an hour. He said that the U.S. was serious about wanting a solution without armed force and impressed on me how important it now was to beef up our inspection plans and machinery. The U.S. would help us in any way it could. I explained to him how far we had come in our preparations but was cautious about promising any fast increases beyond what we had planned.

A few days after this talk I was in Moscow for a conference on non-proliferation and was invited to see Foreign Minister Igor Ivanov. He might not yet have received the latest drafts that were discussed on the resolution, but I found him reacting even more strongly than I had done to the early version of the draft. I agreed with many of his comments but pointed also to some features and provisions I thought could be helpful—as I had done with the Americans in Washington.

Visiting the White House, Wednesday, October 30, 2002

On Monday morning, October 28, Mohamed ElBaradei and I briefed the Security Council on practical aspects of the then-current draft of the new resolution. I said that the demand for a new declaration and the provision which would put access to presidential sites on the same basis as other sites were welcome. I had some doubts and reservations about a few other provisions. Why provide that we should select the best available experts as inspectors? Did we not already?, I asked. I thought to myself that this harmless, even redundant-looking provision must have been the result of suggestions from some who were convinced that UNSCOM's system of drawing experts gratis from the big Western states was superior to the UN system of recruitment on a broad geographical basis. I was not going to fight about the provision, but it angered me. Did we have a UN system of inspection, or was the UN providing cover for a Western operation?

On Monday evening Colin Powell called me to talk about the resolution, and said it would be good if I saw the president. By Tuesday it was all organized: Mohamed ElBaradei and myself would meet Mr. Bush in Washington on Wednesday. President Bush's White House keeps early hours, so at 8:30 that morning a van picked us up at the hotel and took us all the way up to the West Wing. This time I did not have to go through the various elaborate security procedures that are normally necessary when entering the area.

While the other members of our team were left to wait and join us later, Mohamed and I were taken first to Vice President Cheney, who throughout our meeting did most of the talking and gave the impression of a solid, self-confident—even overconfident—chief executive. In talking about the world at large he always took the security interests of the United States as his starting point, he said. He stated the position that inspections, if they do not give results, cannot go on forever, and said the U.S. was "ready to discredit inspections in favor of disarmament." A pretty straight way, I thought, of saying that if we did not soon find the weapons of mass destruction that the U.S. was convinced Iraq possessed (though they did not know where), the U.S. would be ready to say that the inspectors were useless and embark on disarmament by other means. I commented that we were aware there are limitations on what inspections can do and that without detailed intelligence it is hard to find objects hidden underground, or mobile objects. Nevertheless, you can check industries, military installations, get in anywhere, monitor the country. It was obvious this meeting was not meant as a real exchange of views. Perhaps it was just to put us on notice.

From here, we walked over to meet the president, who greeted us in a friendly manner, telling us that he was honored to receive us. His manners contrasted starkly with the vice president's measured way of talking and moving. He makes a boyish impression, moves with agility, and frequently changes his posture in his chair. He explained to us that the U.S. genuinely wanted peace. With some self-deprecation, he said that, contrary to what was being alleged, he was no wild, gung-ho Texan bent on dragging the U.S. into war. He would let the Security Council talk about a resolution—but not for long. He mentioned the League of Nations. He said that the U.S. had confidence in me and Mr. ElBaradei and would throw its full support behind us. I responded that we appreciated the U.S. support and considered it essential for success.

It was not a substantial conversation and was presumably not meant to be one. Rather, I thought it was meant to be a demonstration—especially with Mr. Cheney, Ms. Rice and Mr. Wolfowitz appearing to agree with Mr. Powell—that the U.S., at least for the time being, was on the multilateral track, sincerely trying to advance in step with the UN. It was an affirmation that, despite all the negative things that Mr. Cheney and others in the administration had said about the UN and about inspection, the U.S. was with us for now. After our visit, White House Press Secretary Ari Fleischer said that the president wanted to stress that the United States wanted to work with the inspectors to make sure they were able to carry out the disarmament of Saddam Hussein. An official was also quoted in the Associated Press that day as saying that, "taking a cue from Blix, the administration is easing its demand that Iraqi scientists who worked on weapons programs be interviewed outside the country. The revision would approve such interviews but not insist on them." There was, in reality, no change in the U.S. attitude on this matter. Colin Powell stated at some point that the provision was an authorization, not an instruction. However, on hardly any other point was there such drawn-out difference between the U.S. and us.

From the president, we walked over to Condoleezza Rice's office and were abandoned by Mr. Powell and Mr. Cheney. To start with, it was just Ms. Rice, her deputy, Mohamed and I. Here there *was* an exchange of views. She said that she understood we must maintain our UN legitimacy and that this was in the U.S. interest as well. She even seemed to understand our view that intelligence must in principle be a one-way traffic. She told us that the U.S. had lots of ideas how we ought to go about our job and how we could be "helped." One of them set us worrying: The U.S., she said, had now decided to give the grave task of disarming Iraq to the UN; accordingly, there was a need for "a philosophical agreement on how to do this," perhaps through letters of agreement on certain practical arrangements. I did not reply to this suggestion. I thought that while there could be "arrangements," even written ones, between us and supporting governments (e.g., about lending us equipment or providing services, like those of the U-2 planes), a "philosophical agreement" was a different matter. Our "philosophical" basis lay in the resolutions of the Security Council and would not be supplemented by any bilateral agreements. There were, indeed, attempts made later by the U.S. side to come to common understandings of how we should best pursue our job, but as will be seen below, we deflected many of them and never made agreements on the subject.

After a fairly substantial discussion between the four of us we were joined by Mr. Wolfowitz and by our colleagues who had traveled with us from New York, filling the national security adviser's small office. The question of taking scientists out of Iraq and interviewing them abroad came up again. Mr. Wolfowitz said it would be like issuing a subpoena: we would just tell the Iraqis that they would have to put up with our taking people out. I said I suspected that people would tell us they were not willing to leave their country, knowing that relatives would remain behind, exposed to revenge. Was he suggesting that we should subpoena people like Tariq Aziz to come to us abroad?

Where did the U.S. stand on the inspection path to disarmament? Perhaps this was the wrong question. There had been and there remained different positions. Some perhaps hoped that there would be no agreement on a resolution. The president had said they would not wait for long for the UN, and had mentioned the League of Nations. Others perhaps expected that the Iraqis would soon refuse to comply with some obligations under a new resolution—an outcome that would be even more likely if the resolution contained draconian provisions. Nevertheless, wherever different U.S. factions were standing, we knew what our job was and for the time being the U.S. was supporting inspections.

Two days after my visit to Washington, on November 1, the Iraqi ambassador at the UN, Mr. Aldouri, visited me. I told him I thought we had been invited to Washington to hear that the U.S. had chosen the UN path and was throwing its weight behind the inspection process. President Bush had said that he would much prefer a peaceful solution but was firm on the absolute need to disarm Iraq. I said that U.S. patience might be limited and that it was desirable to get to a positive start. We then talked about the declaration, and the ambassador said he was much concerned that this was "the real hidden trigger." What if there was nothing to report? I said the declaration had to be plausible and credible. Iraq would need to look at its stocks and stores. Joking with him and alluding to the document-studded chicken farm of the defector Mr. Kamel, I said maybe they could find a camel ranch. He left with a bitter laugh.

November 2002: Resolution Adopted; U.S. Ideas for Inspection

On November 8, the Security Council adopted Resolution 1441 by unanimous vote, the Syrian delegation having received last-minute authorization to vote in favor. The text declared in no uncertain terms that although Iraq was in breach of earlier resolutions it was being given one last opportunity. Iraq was requested to provide immediate, unconditional and active cooperation to the inspectors. Any further "material breach" would lead the Council "to consider the situation and the need for compliance"—diplomatic language for possible armed action. There were, however, some major differences of interpretation, especially between France and the United States. The French consent was given on the understanding that a "material breach" could only be registered and acted upon on the basis of a report from the inspectors. I am sure that several other members of the Council were of the same view. They did not wish to issue a blank check. However, it was the French who carried the ball. The U.S. did not read such constraint into the text.

At this stage, the differences in interpretation faded into the background in the general delight that the Council had come together and had come out strong. Although the text had paled somewhat in comparison with the first U.S./UK draft, which had sent shock waves, it was still a draconian resolution that would not have been accepted by any state that was not under direct threat of armed attack. For good measure, it declared that all the practical arrangements that I and Mohamed ElBaradei had listed in our joint letter to the Iraqi side would be binding on Iraq. No need to discuss them with the Iraqis again! This was the first—and probably the last—time in my life that a letter I had written was elevated to world law.

Would Iraq accept the resolution within the week given to it? Perhaps there were some on the U.S. side who hoped not. However, on November 13 Iraq did send a long letter that was both angry and lamenting but declared that it would "deal with" the resolution.

Ever since Iraq declared that it would accept inspections we had been in high gear with our preparations. One question that could have been very problematic had been settled swiftly: the base from which we would go to Iraq. UNSCOM had used Bahrain as a gateway to assemble their teams and fly into Baghdad. We still had the old offices there, but there had been drawn-out discussions with Bahrain about a renewal of the UNSCOM agreement. I did not think the difficulties Bahrain had raised were a way of saying no, but time was getting short and I decided to try another option. I turned to Cyprus, which had a lot of experience in handling UN missions. In very little time their Foreign Office and their New York representative, Ambassador Sotos Zackheos, had helped us arrange to use Larnaca as the base for an office and for a transport plane. As most of our people going to Baghdad would come from the West, this was a practical choice. An added advantage, we found in due course, was that the flight path from Larnaca to Baghdad avoided the complication of going through the U.S./UK no-fly zones.

Member states had been helpful to us from our start in early 2000 but largely left it to us, with the advice of our College of Commissioners, to plan the future inspections. We counted on keeping some two hundred people in Baghdad, in addition to a number of biological, chemical, missile and multidisciplinary teams of about ten inspectors each. If we needed a larger team for some mission we could combine several ordinary teams. We had planned for a number of helicopters with a total of about forty people serving them. Computers, communication equipment (including secure lines) and whatnot were all on order. We knew a great many sites we wanted to inspect and a great many questions we wanted to ask.

Once the U.S. had decided to support the inspections, we expected they would lend a helping hand, but soon came to worry about too generous an embrace. In various ways we learnt how the U.S. now—a little late in the day—thought we should go about the job. The U.S. press was already being told by people in the administration that we were going to follow the recipes given. On November 10, Steven Weisman reported in *The New York Times* that the inspectors planned to "force an early test of Saddam Hussein's intentions by demanding a comprehensive list of weapons sites and checking whether it matches a list of more than 100 priority sites compiled by Western experts." Really?

Mr. Weisman also reported that "many administration officials say they would far prefer a cold rebuff by Mr. Hussein, rather than have him cooperate. . . . Speed is important, military experts say, because the cooler winter months, ending in February or March, are the optimal time for an attack against Iraq." Demanding quick access to highly sensitive sites was seen as posing some problem, however: "The [U.S.] experts say the inspectors cannot move so quickly that it looks like a deliberate provocation to Iraq." The advisers who came up to New York from Washington did not tell us all this, but they had much advice, some of it helpful.

One of their suggestions was a "top down" approach: We should launch inspections at high-level authorities, like ministries, and have experts check the computers there to learn what was going on and where things were to be found. Someone commented that it was not necessary to teach us how to suck eggs. For my part, I drew the conclusion that the U.S. did not itself know where things were. Further, I would have presumed that the Iraqis had learnt in 1991 that ministries are not a safe place for papers or archives when inspectors are around. I also had a slight suspicion—supported by the article cited above—that one idea behind the advice was to try, if there were no documents of interest, to at least provoke the Iraqis, perhaps even achieving a denial of access. We did not exclude the top as a target but we had other priorities, and while we were glad to have sites recommended, we made inspection choices ourselves and, for evident reasons, we were not telling anybody which they were.

Another suggestion was that we overwhelm the Iraqi side with so many inspections that they would not be able to cope with controlling us well. For this purpose we ought to double the number of our inspectors in a short time. This was not really practicable. For a military giant that could mobilize several hundred thousand people to the Gulf in a matter of months, we must have looked ridiculous. However, our plans, which we had to follow if we were not to land in chaos, were not dimensioned for such an increase. Equipment, lodging, transport—all would have to change. We also wanted all our people to be trained by our own experts. I repeated that we had to learn to walk before we could run, and in any case we would not have succeeded in overwhelming the minders—Iraq had an ample supply of this species. During one of my visits to Baghdad I complained that on some inspection the ratio of minders to inspectors had been 10:1 and Dr. Al Sa'adi agreed that a normal ratio would be 1:1. This left a good reserve supply.

We fully accepted and assured that all intelligence the U.S. passed to us would be handled securely. The Americans' preferred method of assurance was to have someone with U.S. security clearances positioned high up within our operations, but we could not accept that. Our independence was part of the legitimacy that the Security Council had requested. Our intelligence man was Jim Corcoran, a Canadian and a professional known to many services. We had confidence in him, and he would tell the U.S. how we ensured the security of intelligence. To date, I have not seen evidence that any intelligence we received was compromised.

We also resisted demands for "sharing" our information with anybody's intelligence organization and running joint operations. We knew that such activities had given some good yields in the early 1990s but they had also gradually resulted in intelligence piggybacking on UNSCOM, thus contributing to its demise. We were ready, of course, to give enough information to intelligence services to enable them to determine what we needed, and we were also prepared to give some feedback on results achieved as a result of information obtained. For instance, what, if anything, did we find at a site that had been indicated to us? The question of where to draw the line had no easy answer. What we knew was that it had been very wrongly drawn in UNSCOM. Considering how misleading much of the intelligence given us eventually proved to be, perhaps it was a blessing that we did not get more. What we came to discover was that no sites given to us by intelligence were ever found to harbor weapons of mass destruction.

No question was more discussed, privately and publicly, than that of taking Iraqis thought to have relevant knowledge abroad to record their testimony, a matter I have touched on above. While interviews generally were an important tool, I never thought the idea of taking people out of Iraq was realistic. At one stage I thought we were being positioned to provide UN cover in effecting defections that U.S. intelligence thought desirable and do-able. I said publically that we were neither an abduction nor a defection agency. When I pointed out the risk of an "accident" when the Iraqi side found us trying to bring such a person to our plane, a U.S. expert commented that "most of these guys [have] devoted themselves to production of weapons of mass destruction, anyway." This comment did not increase my readiness to go down the path proposed. I talked to other governments and intelligence services about the concept and found nowhere any understanding for it. The U.S. was ready to promise asylum not only to the informant but to a reasonably sized family of ten or so coming with him, provided that the name of the informant was on a U.S. list. But if the Iraqi government really did not want the person to leave, would it not tell him that while his children and brothers and sisters could come with him, he did have an aunt in Kirkuk or an uncle in Basra, did he not? . . . Perhaps the real purpose was to achieve a provocation, hoping that Iraq would balk and a violation of the Resolution 1441 could be noted.

Paris–Larnaca–Baghdad–London–New York, November 15–23, 2002

On November 15, I left New York for Paris in the company of a CNN crew and Torkel Stiernlöf, who had come back as my executive assistant. We had brief meetings in Paris with Foreign Minister Villepin and his advisers, including the very able former French representative at the UN, Mr. Jean-David Levitte, who was moving to Washington. I had also the opportunity to meet the Mexican foreign minister, Jorge Castaneda, whose father—also a foreign minister and a fine international lawyer—had been an old friend of mine. From there we went to Baghdad via our new stopover in Larnaca.

We arrived in Baghdad on Sunday, November 17, to a chaotic media situation at the airport—a not uncommon situation in those months. They had prepared a stand where we were supposed to talk but we were surrounded long before we could reach it. I told the press that we had come for the sole reason that the world wanted to be assured that there were no weapons of mass destruction in Iraq. If such assurance had been attained in 1991, Iraq would have been saved a decade of sanctions. I hoped it would happen now, and promised that we would provide correct and "effective" inspection. Only this would give credibility to our results.

We were comfortably lodged on the top floor of the Al Rasheed Hotel. Dr. Al Sa'adi opened our talks on Monday, November 18, by saying a little cheekily that they had hoped we would come a month earlier, when Iraq had first accepted inspections. I responded that we would have liked to come many months earlier. After these light jabs we got down to discussing how we should organize our cooperation under the resolutions which guided them and us. We discussed how the timelines of December 1999's Resolution 1284 had to be reconciled with those of the new Resolution 1441. The main subject on their mind, however, was the declaration required of Iraq under paragraph three of the new resolution.

On my part there were several practical things I wanted to settle. We wanted the Iraqis' assistance in establishing an office in Mosul, in the north of the country; we wanted more space for our offices at the Canal Hotel; we needed to iron out a number of points regarding identity cards for our staff. I also wanted to come to an understanding ensuring that there would be no media circuses during inspections, as it had become quite clear that Iraq intended to have its media keep watch on the inspectors' movements. We would not meddle with what they allowed the media to do on their territory, but on the sites we inspected we would not tolerate any media presence. To enable the Iraqi side to start making preparations, I also put them on notice that we would request lists naming all persons who had been engaged in past weapons programs.

On Tuesday, November 19, we first had a talk with the foreign minister, Naji Sabri, then had more meetings with the Iraqi side before we briefed the diplomatic corps about our start-up and met all the UN agencies headquartered at the Canal Hotel and elsewhere in Baghdad. I wanted to demonstrate to them that we were part of and cooperated with the entire UN organization. Their aims were humanitarian, and so were ours—eliminating weapons of mass destruction was also a humanitarian mission. We were together. At a press conference at UN headquarters—organized by our own people this time, to give some degree of order—I announced that the first inspection team would arrive around November 25 and that the first inspection was expected to take place on November 27. When asked about the declaration and the difficulties Iraq might have in reporting about so many types of items over such long periods, I said that "producing mustard gas is not like producing marmalade. You keep track of how much you make and what happens to it."

On the way back to New York we stopped over in London, where I was invited to see Prime Minister Blair. He was kind but did not seem to expect that Iraq would in the end declare very much. It would fall to the inspectors to search, he feared, and there was a risk that the Iraqis would fall back into their old cat-and-mouse game.

The first inspection took place on November 27. This was twenty-five days before we would have needed to launch inspections under the terms of the resolution. Within a week we had carried out some twenty inspections, including the Al Sajud Palace, a presidential site beside the Tigris River. When Dimitri Perricos came with his inspection team to the presidential site, they were not immediately let in. Perricos first showed impatience—which comes easily to this hard-driving veteran Greek inspector, who was the IAEA's point man in Iraq in 1991 and later in North Korea. After waiting ten minutes, Perricos withdrew to his jeep, telephone in hand. The doors of the building were quickly opened and the inspectors were let in to examine what turned out to be a luxurious presidential guesthouse. Inspectors routinely photograph what they see to be able to check the next time whether any changes have occurred. They look for equipment of various kinds and often take samples of soil, liquids or dust to analyze. In this guesthouse there were no archives, document files or stores of chemical or biological weapons and no sensitive equipment to tag, but there was lots of marmalade in the refrigerators.

There was no doubt that the innumerable presidential residences and buildings could be used to house illegal labs or as storage facilities, especially if they were off limits to inspectors. The inspection of such sites had, indeed, been a sensitive matter during the UNSCOM period, touching, in the Iraqi view, on sovereignty and, perhaps even more important, on the dignity of the head of state, i.e., the president. However, it had been settled by the new resolution that these sites had no special privileges. There were no sanctuaries and no privileged sites anymore.

After our inspection at the presidential site, Vice President Ramadan declared that we had sought to provoke them to commit a breach of the resolution—an action, he said, that was "loaded with landmines." He also complained about our refusal to have journalists present at sites during inspections. But Perricos said that we were getting results. For example, about a dozen Iraqi artillery shells containing the chemical agent mustard gas had been secured at a previously known desert installation.

The inspections were gearing up. More people and equipment arriving meant more inspections at more sites. It went remarkably well, but was still just a beginning. The helicopters for transport and surveillance were not yet there, and the labs that would allow us to analyze samples taken at sites for traces of chemical or biological agents were not yet in place. While some in the Bush administration said the effort was undermanned, we were counting on having about one hundred inspectors in Baghdad by Christmas.

For all our activity, the most intense and concerted effort in Baghdad at this time was actually on the Iraqi side, as they worked to put together the declaration that was due to the Security Council by December 8.

5

The December Declaration

A central provision of Resolution 1441 required Iraq to submit a "currently accurate, full, and complete declaration" of all aspects of its prohibited weapons and delivery programs as well as "all other chemical, biological, and nuclear programmes, including any which it claims are for purposes not related to weapon production or material."

The resolution's detailed description of what was to be declared under "all aspects" was as long as the time given to do it was short: thirty days. The punishment for not fully meeting the requirement was severe: "False statements or omissions . . . shall constitute further material breach," which could lead to "serious consequences"—a euphemism for armed action.

The Purpose of the New Declaration

The idea of self-declaration is as basic to arms control as it is to income tax systems. The weapons inspector or tax man should not need to go and find what you have. Rather, you know what information is required and you have it, so it is for you to collect all the relevant data and submit it for scrutiny. You declare and the inspector verifies. However, tax men often do more than just check the counting in your declaration. They look around in various ways to see if there were any items which should have been declared but were not. The same is true for arms inspectors. For instance, they may make inquiries of exporting countries, they may study satellite images for signs of new or expanded arms facilities, they may visit sites indicated not only by the inspected state but also by defectors or intelligence. Yet, the declaration is basic. And so it was in the case of Iraq.

After the Gulf War in 1991, the idea had been that Iraq should make comprehensive declarations, the inspectors should verify them, and all items and activities that were prohibited should be eliminated under the inspectors' supervision. Thereafter the Security Council would free Iraq from the economic sanctions and only long-term monitoring would remain to ensure that there was no renewal of programs for prohibited weapons. This plan had not turned out as neatly as the resolution had foreseen. There had, to be sure, been significant results in the analysis of declarations, in the mapping of programs, and in the destruction of weapons and facilities. However, during the inspectors' search of sites and interrogations, there had also been eight years of cat-and-mouse play. Declarations submitted had been erroneous and incomplete, and new ones had been demanded. As a result, one "full, final and complete" declaration had been followed by another—with little confidence that any one of them was full, final or complete. Rather, it was all described as "cheat and retreat."

Was there any point then to demand, in the autumn of 2002, yet another omnibus declaration before the restart of inspections? In my view, yes. During Kofi Annan's dialogue with the Iraqis in Vienna in the summer of 2002, I had suggested to the Iraqis that such a declaration could be used in a "fresh start." My idea was that if Iraq were to accept renewed inspections—at that time a big if— they should do it to achieve success, and this would require that they distance themselves from the declarations and methods of the past. Any prohibited stocks of weapons or other prohibited items or activities should be listed in a new declaration. I was sure that if they felt the need to save face they could always pretend that some general or other official had hidden the stuff.

The U.S. may have had other ideas when the requirement of a new declaration was included in the resolution. The U.S. was firmly convinced that Iraq had weapons and other items that should have been declared. If the Iraqis declared them, fine. However, the Bush administration probably doubted that Iraq would declare any illegal weapons and was anxious that Iraq was violating the orders of the Security Council. A declaration requiring extensive information and giving Iraq little time to prepare it might serve as a tripwire leading to visible violations that justified "serious consequences." Such calculation, if indeed it was there, did not have much success, although the U.S. tried, especially shortly before the war, to claim that a few items found (but not hidden) should have been declared. Much later, David Kay, the chief U.S. inspector in occupied Iraq, sought to pin Iraq to a violation of the resolution for having failed to declare some equipment that had dual use. My own optimistic speculation that the declaration could serve the Iraqis as an instrument for fresh revelations and a fresh start also did not become reality. No significant disarmament issues were solved by the new declaration. What was generated was a lot of work, big piles of paper, a wild circus and some resentment.

How Could Iraq Respond Appropriately to the Demand for a New Declaration?

During the informal discussions in the Security Council before the adoption of the October resolution, I had mentioned that a country with a sizeable petrochemical industry might have difficulty in providing within thirty days a full description of all its peaceful chemical programs. I thought putting such a requirement in the text betrayed a lack of seriousness. I met some understanding. The text was not altered, but the U.S. ambassador said that some delay in that part of the declaration could be tolerated.

After the adoption of the resolution, Mohamed ElBaradei and I traveled to Baghdad in November 2002 to set the stage for the first inspections. Our Iraqi counterparts asked us how they could possibly provide all the information required for the declaration in such a short time. This was not an easy question to answer. If, in fact, many prohibited items did remain and the Iraqis were aware of them, it would be relatively easy to declare them. Of course, the world would then say that its view that Iraq had been lying in the past had been confirmed. There would also continue to be doubts that everything had now been declared, but it would also fuel some fresh hope of getting to the bottom of the barrel, and armed action would become more difficult.

On the other hand, if, as the Iraqis claimed, there remained little or nothing to declare—if all biological and chemical weapons that had been deemed unaccounted for had in fact been destroyed in the summer of 1991 without the presence of any inspectors—the Iraqis would have a big job finding and presenting credible supporting evidence. While understanding the difficulty the Iraqis might be facing, Mohamed and I would not, of course, give any advice that they might use as an excuse for in any way limiting their response. We replied that we were not authorized to explain anything on behalf of the Security Council. Nevertheless, we said we assumed that, for the Council, Iraq's declaring weapons of mass destruction would be the most important. Iraq should look into its stores and stocks. If they declared zero they would need to present more documentation. As regards programs, which were far removed from weapons, perhaps they could list them with indications of sites and note that more information could be made available on request.

How Can the Security Council Avoid Being a Proliferator?

In Resolution 1441 the Security Council required that Iraq should provide its declaration to "UNMOVIC, the IAEA and the Council." Nothing extraordinary, you may think. No, except that the declaration was expected to contain "cookbooks"—information from which it could be learned how to make weapons of mass destruction. Earlier declarations by Iraq had not been given to the Council but only to the inspectors. On this occasion the president of the Council would receive the declaration and distribute copies to all fifteen members of the Council. Hence, they might all learn, for instance, how to make VX, the most modern and lethal chemical weapon, and about the Iraqi method of developing a nuclear bomb. Moreover, a document that went to fifteen member states might soon be on the Internet. The Council, which had assumed the task of preventing the proliferation of weapons of mass destruction, might face the horrible prospect of acting as an international proliferator itself!

Although we had for some time tried to alert various members of the Council to the problem, it came up only at an informal meeting of the Council on Friday, December 6—two days before the arrival of the documents. There was much talk about various conventions obliging states—including, of course, those in the Security Council—not to contribute to proliferation.

I was asked if UNMOVIC and IAEA, examining the declaration texts, could on behalf of the Council excise any risky parts. Yes, I said, if we were asked by the Council to do it. After some discussion an informal understanding emerged in the Council: UNMOVIC and IAEA should examine the texts submitted and perform the censoring. When the job was finished—it would inevitably take some little time—the expurgated version would be circulated to all members of the Council.

All hell broke loose when news of this arrangement reached Washington. Would UN inspectors decide what Washington could read!!?? Ideas swirled about how and why the full text with its risky recipes could be transmitted immediately on arrival in New York to the P-5—the permanent members of the Council—who, it could be assumed, already know the "recipes" while the E-10—the elected members of the Council—would have to wait for the expurgated version that was fit for "innocents." On Saturday morning I declined to go along with a suggestion to simply disregard the Friday agreement and hand the whole text to the P-5 on Sunday. I said I was the servant of the whole Council. I had been given guidance at the Council meeting and would follow it. However, I would do whatever the president of the Council, acting on behalf of the Council, asked me to do.

A weekend of global phone traffic followed. Colin Powell and other foreign ministers were hard at work and all non-permanent member states were persuaded to acquiesce in not getting the full text of the Iraqi declaration. The president of the Council, ambassador and former Colombian minister of justice Alfonso Valdivieso, was in the hot seat and so, I am sure, was his country's president in Bogotá. Eventually Ambassador Valdivieso told me that a new understanding had emerged that the P-5 should provide advice to UNMOVIC and the IAEA on what, in their views, needed to be excised from the declaration. To do this, the P-5 must have the text immediately upon its arrival. The E-10 would only later get the version that was excised with the help of the P-5. One member of the Council, Syria, had refused to give its consent to this new arrangement, but was ignored. Later, Syria declined to comment upon a text which some of the members had seen in full and others had viewed in a censored version. The resentment of the procedure, which treated members of the Council as unequal, was fully shared by all the elected members, long sore about being treated as second-class states. The Russian ambassador, Sergey Lavrov, summed up the situation accurately when he said that the procedure had been bad but the result was good.

Getting the Iraqi Declaration to the Security Council Members

The distribution of the Iraqi declaration was a bit of a circus. The document was due in Vienna and New York on Sunday, December 8, and the Iraqis had told us that if they themselves were to bring it to New York they would lose a number of the valuable thirty days at their disposal for putting the text together. As we, unlike the

Iraqis, could go from Baghdad by air and had staff doing so on December 8, we offered to receive the declaration in Baghdad on Saturday, December 7, and bring it to New York ourselves on Sunday. One of our staff members, Surya Sinha, who not only had proven to be a good lawyer but had also consistently shown excellent judgment in operations, carried the bags containing the documents from Baghdad to New York. He was accompanied and helped by an experienced UN security man, Eric Brownwell. Both were young and strong—necessary qualifications since the declaration contained in their hand-carried bags ran to some 12,000 pages. This precious luggage was transported from Baghdad to Cyprus by our own plane on Sunday morning, and then without any complications through Athens and Frankfurt to New York, where the two men were met by UN security and brought directly to the UN.

Dimitri Perricos and I were alerted to be at our offices in the UN building to receive the bags. When we entered the UN compound at 8:25 in the evening, the lobby was full of cameras and media. In the absence of any bags to photograph, they contented themselves with us. We had only small talk to offer and were happy when Surya and Eric appeared a few minutes after us, tired but bearing the desired but rather plain-looking bags, which were duly recorded by dozens of cameras. The next act, which the media did not record because they did not have access inside the Secretariat, was the arrival in our UN office of two other young men who, like rested horses, were to take the bag addressed to the Security Council to its next station. Mr. Bye, a nice and able secretary of the UK mission, was there because the UK was responsible for coordination among the P-5 that month, and would receive the unexpurgated text of the declaration on behalf of those states. The other gentleman was Mr. Duffy, an equally nice and able secretary from the U.S. mission. He was to arrange that the declaration be taken by helicopter to Washington, where copies of all 12,000 pages would be speedily made for all the P-5 states.

The master of the unique ceremony, Security Council President Alfonso Valdivieso of Colombia, was still missing. We waited with the bags sitting like big gold nuggets on the floor in the center of my office. Eventually the Permanent Representative of Colombia and his advisers arrived—exhausted, I sensed, after thirty-six hours near the telephone and innumerable not altogether agreeable conversations. In the presence of UNMOVIC staff I symbolically put his hand on the bag addressed to the Council and he directed me to transfer the bag to the representative of the P-5, Mr. Bye, who together with his U.S. colleague disappeared with it, to the satisfaction of the great powers and the distant fury of the ten elected members of the Council.

I never inquired about the logistical capacity of Washington to make five or more copies of 12,000 pages. Considering how easily documents in general leak in that city, I suspect the capacity is mature. The UN capacity, by contrast, was limited, and we knew it. Fortunately we had staff experienced in solving such problems. It was UNMOVIC's task to judge in a very limited time what should be excised. To get down to this task as quickly as possible, we needed a few copies of the text so we could distribute different parts to a number of staff, who would immediately get down to reading and analysis and, in some cases, translation from Arabic. Igor Mithrokhin, a former Russian army officer and an old UNSCOM hand, was not only a very able analyst and former inspector in the chemical sector but also a highly practical man. Before the end of Monday the commercial copying capacity that he had engaged and supervised in New York had spawned the copies we needed, and our staff was engaged in the necessary task.

Analysis of the Declaration; My Briefing to the Council on December 19, 2002

It turned out that the main body of the declaration was about 3,000 pages and that 5,000 pages were supporting documents in Arabic. In due course we received advice from the P-5 capitals as to what they advised us to excise. All the P-5 stressed that these were recommendations only, and that they would accept our judgment. This was perhaps not so surprising. After all, the need to "advise" us had been invented as a subterfuge to allow the P-5—mainly Washington—immediate and full access to the text. Nevertheless, it was a relief to find that we would not lose any precious time in reconciling different views on what should be excluded. As we studied the advice offered, we further noted that views were not very divergent.

We were able to freeze the "sanitized" text on Monday evening, December 16, after one week's work. The next day, copies of this text were produced for each of the fifteen members of the Council. Distribution was deemed unnecessary for much supporting text in Arabic, but even so the text copied for each recipient amounted to about 3,500 pages. It was available for all members in our offices on Tuesday evening, December 17. The ten non-permanent members had only one day to study it before I was to comment on it at an informal meeting of the Council on December 19. Few if any of the members could bring it to their capitals in one day.

Not surprisingly, given the time constraints imposed on them, the Iraqis had not been able to arrange everything in the best order. Some texts had been included in two places, one even in five different places. Conceivably the great volume was presented to counter any accusation that they were not complying with the demand, but I also had the feeling that there could have been an element of spite: Ask for an unreasonable amount of information and we will throw volumes of papers at you! These volumes consisted in large measure of reprints of declarations that had been sent to UNSCOM in the years before the inspectors left at the end of 1998. What new information there was—some of it useful—related mostly to development of missiles and peaceful developments in the field of biology during the period of 1998–2002. The declaration had certainly not been used as the hoped-for occasion for a fresh start, coming up with long-hidden truths. It looked rather like a repetition of old, unverified data. Was it renewed stonewalling? While providing a few new documents and some which had previously been denied to UNSCOM, the Iraqi side claimed they had nothing more. We doubted this was true, but could not prove it.

In my briefing of the Council on December 19, I noted that the biological section was essentially a reorganized version of a declaration provided to UNSCOM in September 1997. The chemical area of the text was an updated version of a declaration submitted in 1996. The missile part also had largely the same content as a declaration of 1996, with updates added. I reported to the Council that our preliminary examination of the declaration had not provided material or evidence that solved any of the unresolved disarmament issues. At the same time I noted that while individual governments had stated that they had convincing evidence contradicting the Iraqi declaration, UNMOVIC was neither in a position to confirm Iraq's statements, nor in possession of evidence to disprove them. I said further that the opening of doors in Iraq—which was going rather well— was not enough. Statements needed to be supported by documentation or other evidence. Only so did they become verifiable. I ended my briefing by saying that the growing arsenal of inspection tools available to UNMOVIC could not guarantee that all possibly concealed items and activities would be found, but with the extensive authority given to UNMOVIC and the backing of a united Security Council, the tools would make any attempted concealment more difficult.

The U.S. ambassador, John Negroponte, commented that Iraq had spurned the opportunity given to it, that the declaration was an insult to the Security Council and that the absence of data constituted omissions. He noted, in particular, that there was no information about mobile facilities or the procurement of uranium, and that it denied that unmanned aerial vehicles (UAVs) had any link to the dispersal of biological agents. He concluded that Iraq was in further material breach of its obligations. (During the postwar occupation we learned that the mobile facilities to which Ambassador Negroponte probably was referring appear more likely to have been for the production of hydrogen than for biological weapons. The reference to uranium procurement appears to have rested on a contract found to have been a forgery, and the UAVs were found to have been intended for surveillance rather than for the dispersal of biological agents.) The French ambassador noted that there was little new information in the declaration and that the inspections were still at a preliminary stage. The Russian ambassador commented that the U.S. had not presented any evidence in support of its claims, and the Mexican ambassador said he saw no evidence that Iraq had weapons of mass destruction—nor, indeed, did he see evidence to the contrary.

The Growing Buildup of UN Inspectors—and of U.S. Armed Forces

The analysis of the declaration continued after the meeting in the Council on December 19. The buildup of UNMOVIC capacity continued with more trained inspectors, equipment and helicopters. By the end of the year we expected to have about one hundred inspectors in Iraq—more than originally planned but far fewer than the U.S. had urged. We wanted an orderly buildup, not chaos.

The members of the Security Council—including France and Russia—had been disappointed that Iraq had provided no significant new evidence. Kofi Annan called me on December 21 after a meeting in Washington about the Middle East. Colin Powell had told him that he had been pleased with the manner that UNMOVIC and the IAEA had processed the declaration. Blix was as reliable as a Volvo, he had said. Being aware that one of Powell's favorite hobbies is working on Volvo engines, I took this as praise.

Meanwhile, the U.S. military buildup continued at an order of magnitude far beyond that of the inspection buildup. By the end of January the U.S. forces were expected to number around 100,000. The Americans did not see any Iraqi "cracking" or confession in the face of the growing military threat, nor was there any clear-cut casus belli. This must have troubled them. I find the following note in my diary from New Year's eve:

It has been an intense year. The inspection path must be and must be seen as an alternative, not a prelude to armed action. I do not think that the U.S. has made up its mind to go to war even though they are taking all the steps in that direction. It serves to scare the Iraqis. And should the Iraqis not provide maximum cooperation, the U.S. might determine that the inspection path is hopeless. There is presumably a momentum built into the great buildup of troops. Can Bush refrain from letting the coiled spring jump without losing face? He will need some manifest action by the Iraqis to hold the spring down.

January Developments

December 2002 had been a month of considerable buildup of our inspection capability, and we'd had a fair amount of Iraqi cooperation, including prompt access to all sites UNMOVIC wished to inspect. January 2003 became a month of lowered expectations and increasing tension.

We had the impression in UNMOVIC that the positive attitude shown by Iraq on process might be combined with a less than forthcoming attitude on questions of substance. Some of our inspection-related requests were seized as occasions to bargain for something in return. For instance, our request to use American U-2 planes for surveillance was first met by a proposal that we should help Iraq to get more modern radar for some Iraqi airports. There was certainly no general and spontaneous action to demonstrate to the world that Iraq was seizing this new opportunity to cooperate with the inspectors and clear up the past. For the most part our inspectors were received correctly, but with an attitude of suspicion. Complaints were voiced publicly on very trivial matters. We were not back in a cat-and-mouse game, but we did not seem to be moving toward the resolution of the weapons questions, which I felt was needed to avert war.

On the U.S. side the military buildup continued and there was a growing expectation that armed force would be used. However, although the U.S. had concluded that Iraq's declaration had been deficient and that it was not complying with Resolution 1441, it seemed intent on waiting for the update which Mohamed ElBaradei and I were to present to the Security Council on January 27, sixty days after the first inspection.

The Security Council Meeting of January 9, 2003

During the lead-up to the 27th, the Security Council had asked ElBaradei and me for an informal "pre-update" briefing, which took place on January 9. By now all the members of the Security Council had had time to analyze the declaration, and both Mohamed ElBaradei and I were there to provide comments based on a more solid analysis than had been possible in December.

In my prepared remarks I noted that there had been no denial of access and that no "smoking gun"—the colloquial term used for unequivocally prohibited items or activities—had been found. I voiced my disappointment by stating as our overall impression that the declaration was "rich in volume but poor in new information about weapons issues and practically devoid of new evidence on such issues." I was wondering, though I did not articulate the question, whether we were back to the wrestling matches of the past, back to squeezing out explanations.

UNMOVIC did not assert, I said, that there were proscribed items or activities in Iraq, but the absence of any finds at inspected sites was no guarantee that such items and activities could not exist elsewhere. If they did exist, they must be declared and eliminated under our supervision. This was a line that I would repeat many times. It was in contrast to the flat assertions of the U.S. and the UK that proscribed items and activities *did* exist and could be used almost immediately. There was still time for it. If this did not happen there was no way the inspectors could close a file by simply invoking a precept that Iraq could not prove the negative.

At this juncture I was sometimes asked by the media what my gut feelings were about Iraqi weapons. I consistently refused to answer such questions, saying simply that my job as executive chairman of the inspection organization was not to express gut feelings but to present findings based on inspection or analysis. Looking at the material before us as a lawyer, I could not exclude the possibility that the Iraqis had destroyed both weapons and documents and that little or nothing was left. My gut feelings, which I kept to myself, suggested to me that Iraq still engaged in prohibited activities and retained prohibited items, and that it had the documents to prove it.

The Absence of Evidence

Although I did not explicitly cite U.S. Secretary of Defense Donald Rumsfeld, I was in substance concurring with a statement he had made that "the absence of evidence is not the evidence of absence." I did so with pleasure because I thought the line was both smart and true, and because it was not often I agreed with Rumsfeld. He demanded positive evidence to be convinced of the absence of prohibited weapons in Iraq. OK, we all did, and few were impressed by Iraq's argument, taken from criminal law, that it should be presumed innocent unless proven guilty. Who would attach a presumption of innocence to the regime of Saddam Hussein?

The inspection regime was not a criminal trial. It was a process through which the world sought to gain confidence that Iraq *had* rid itself of all weapons of mass destruction. Someone acquitted in a court for lack of evidence would be set free, but would not automatically regain the confidence of society. To be reintegrated into the international community, Iraq needed to convince the world that it had no prohibited weapons. It needed to do so by presenting evidence to the inspectors. If it failed to do so, the inspectors would not jump to the conclusion that weapons remained; however, they would also not be able to rule out that possibility, and the result would be that the world would have no confidence about the absence of weapons. Another matter was that many people seemed to have no difficulty in attaching a presumption of guilt, flowing from the past behavior of the regime. Here I would not follow them. I would not make any presumptions.

In my conversations with the Iraqis and in my speeches I

explained that evidence could be of the most varied kind—e.g., budgets, letters of credit, production and destruction records, credible interviews with knowledgeable persons—but bare assertions and declarations by the government did not constitute evidence. Although the Iraqi side did find a few new documents and presented some which they had refused to give UNSCOM in the past, new documentary evidence that would help solve unresolved issues was, on the whole, not forthcoming. Names of persons who could have been interviewed and whose testimony might have been helpful were provided only during the last period of our inspections—too late to be helpful.

The U.S. and UK were ready with their conclusions. The failure to present relevant documents meant that there were "omissions." For these, as for false statements, the resolution stipulated draconian consequences. Perhaps sensing that their cases were not very solid, they did not yet push very vigorously for the conclusion that Iraq was in further "material breach." I could not help wondering to myself what would happen if Iraq did not, in fact, have more documentary evidence! Absurd thought, but could denying that you possess documents which you do not in fact have constitute an "omission"?

The Time Lines of the Resolutions

In my presentation on January 9, I had said I understood the Council's wish for more frequent reporting, and I mentioned innocently that in accordance with Resolution 1284 (1999), which had established UNMOVIC and given it guidelines for the work, our next quarterly report was not due until March 1, 2003. The inspection regime had not started on November 8, 2002. when Resolution 1441 was adopted, nor did it end with the update on January 27, 2003. In conformity with the older resolution, UNMOVIC was obliged to come to the Council in March with a draft work program listing key remaining disarmament tasks.

It became clear from U.S. Ambassador Negroponte's comments

on my remarks that the U.S. did not want to hear about anything so remote in time. He said that the Council was now dealing with Iraq's "last opportunity," offered under Resolution 1441. We should not allow ourselves to "slide into" the leisurely schedules of Resolution 1284. He was aware of the Washington clocks, which had been set by the latest resolution and were ticking fast.

In UNMOVIC we were acting under the various clocks set by all Security Council resolutions and were obliged to try to reconcile them. The two resolutions—one from December 1999 and the other from November 2002—sat side by side but represented different outlooks and different ways of influencing Iraq. At the end of 1999 the Security Council had been divided on the Iraqi issue and had also tired of it after nine years without any hope of a satisfactory solution. The economic sanctions, which were supposed to induce the demanded disarmament, seemed threatened by an increasingly critical opinion among governments and the public. So the Council decided to seek a new exit to the deadlock and held fresh carrots in front of the Iraqi government. Iraq would not have to clear up all the disarmament questions of the past. The solution of key remaining disarmament issues and a period of genuine cooperation would lead to a suspension of the sanctions. Inspection and monitoring would continue even thereafter, until the Council decided otherwise. If the inspectors reported failure of cooperation, the provisions provided for automatic reactivation of the sanctions. The philosophy was that of containment: There would be effective and continuous inspection and monitoring and, hopefully, a readiness to react in case of attempted breakouts by Iraq.

The new resolution, in contrast, had been adopted about a year after the September 11 terrorist attacks on the United States. The tiredness of 1999 was gone, and the angry mood of the United States had done away with any margins of tolerance. Any deviation from the stiff demands of the resolution was to be reported immediately; it might constitute a "material breach" and lead to armed action. Containment and carrots were out; sticks were everywhere.

We thought that the U.S. military buildup would help to make the Iraqis cooperative. However, it was for the Council to conclude whether to apply the stick or move along with inspections, hoping that shortly the combination of military pressure and inspection would result in a verified elimination of all weapons of mass destruction.

In a diary note made in the evening after the discussions in the Council on January 9, I made the following reflection:

> There may be difficulties ahead for the U.S. If we have a denial of access or if we stumble upon some stock of VX or anthrax then the material breach will be easy [to establish]. However, if nothing dramatic occurs it will be hard for the U.S. to garner support for armed action. I doubt the U.S., if it tried, would even get a majority for a resolution authorizing armed force. And if it did not have such a resolution, going it alone would have much less support in American opinion and might not allow the U.S. to deploy from Turkey or Saudi Arabia.

Meeting with Condoleezza Rice in New York, January 14, 2003

On January 14, Condoleezza Rice, the national security adviser to the U.S. president, came to New York, and I was asked if I could join her for a talk. Normally representatives of governments will call on UN officials in the Secretariat, just as ambassadors in capital cities visit the foreign ministry. I received many foreign ministers and even a prime minister in my drab and modestly sized office on the thirty-first floor of the UN Secretariat building. Although it had a nice view of the beautiful Chrysler Building, it was so small that an Iraqi minister had once said "it was not big enough to shout in."

On this occasion it had been suggested that the presence of Condoleezza Rice in the UN building might spark speculation and that to avoid it I might come to Ambassador Negroponte's office across the street. I did. The ambassador has a nice, moderately sized office—much bigger than mine—with a view of the UN. For face-to-face talks there are two sofas placed opposite each other and a couple of chairs. Tea is often served. From my experience in previous talks with Rice, I knew that she relied on her rational arguments and not on the authority of her position. I always liked that. She is an intellectual and we always had very direct discussions. They were never disagreeable, even on points on which we disagreed.

Rice did not react visibly, as John Negroponte had done in the Council, to my description of the possible timetable for the Iraq issue under the resolution from 1999. Perhaps she did not feel a need to show her hand, or perhaps she did not feel the U.S. timetable was firmly locked. I was inclined to the latter explanation because it did not seem to me that she excluded the possibility that the Iraqi regime would crack under the increasing military pressure and reveal whatever weapons stocks it had. This was a possibility I myself was hoping for. At this stage my gut feeling was still that Iraq retained weapons of mass destruction. The early opportunity to declare them, regrettably, had been missed in 12,000 pages. Perhaps more military pressure would do the trick? I had nothing against inspection backed by pressure, but how far could the game of chicken go?

I told Rice the latest from the inspection front. Earlier we had felt that U.S. intelligence agencies had not been very forthcoming in providing us information about sites to inspect. I had said in interviews that some of these agencies had seemed like librarians who sat on their books and did not want to lend them. We had no such complaint now, I told her. We needed site-related intelligence and we now got some. We were about to act on two such cases.

I further told her we had found that Iraq had imported missile engines illegally, but by themselves the engines did not constitute weapons of mass destruction. There had been testing of missiles able to reach farther than the permitted 150 kilometers. Although we did not have evidence showing it, we suspected there might also be a readiness in Iraq for a jump start of production of prohibited weapons. We did not yet have arrangements in place with the Iraqis for the safe use of the American U-2 planes. The list the Iraqis had given us of people who had been engaged in prohibited weapons programs had contained fewer names than those we had in our archive, and we would ask for supplements. We performed useful on-site interviews, but the conditions for private interviews in Baghdad were still unacceptable and we had not yet concluded how to take people for interviews in Cyprus without endangering them and their families. On the last point Rice, like others on the U.S. side, showed little understanding for our qualms and stressed that this might be the only way to get honest statements. I stated my reservations: Even if a scientist came out with a family of twelve he could still have an uncle somewhere in Iraq whose life could be threatened. Moreover, television footage of Iraqis pressed by the UN to leave their own country for interrogation might damage our reputation.

I was puzzled by the spin the media sometimes put on our conversations in New York, suggesting that Rice had told the international official in no uncertain terms what he should do: e.g., take Iraqi scientists out of Iraq for interviews. While I often learned from her and Colin Powell what they thought would be desirable action, I never sensed a peremptory tone in my discussions with either of them. These talks were invariably held in an atmosphere of mutual respect and courtesy.

Iraqi Conduct

Our inspectors made two important discoveries shortly after my meeting with Condoleezza Rice. On a visit to a large ammunition store that had been declared by Iraq and been inspected several times before, our inspectors found a crate of warheads designed for chemical weapons. There were no chemical agents in them, but they should have been declared. The big question was, were they the tip of the iceberg, or debris from the vast chemical weapons program of the past? The Iraqis almost immediately appointed a commission of officials to look for any further weapons that might have been "overlooked." More were found, both by them and by us. Did the new commission signify a genuine effort or was it merely a show? We did not know.

The second find was a stash of documents on research regarding the enrichment of uranium by laser technique and regarding laser guidance for some old types of missiles. It was found in the home of a nuclear scientist. Our team had some difficulty in getting access and there were demonstrations in the street against the intrusion into a private home. It could have been even nastier if our team had not included an excellent woman inspector, Kay Mereish. Only women were at home at the time, and we would not have liked to commit the offense of sending male inspectors in to search. Was this storing of documents at a home part of a general pattern of concealment, as had been suggested to us by intelligence? Or was it, as the Iraqi side claimed, simply a scientist taking home papers that he should properly have kept in his office? The Iraqis appointed another commission with extensive powers to look for and seize relevant documents all over Iraq. Again, was this serious or a gesture?

There was no nuclear information unknown to the IAEA in the documents. Both Dr. ElBaradei and I felt that the appointment of the two Iraqi commissions could be a positive step. If Iraq had hidden weapons or documents and now felt that it was getting too dangerous to keep them, there would be less loss of face if the Iraqis themselves made the finds and turned over the materials. We wanted revelation, not humiliation. In retrospect, the two commissions never came up with any finds except an early one of four additional empty chemical warheads.

The Iraqis were surprisingly prickly in their judgment of the inspectors' conduct. On one occasion, during the first week of inspections, after an inspection of a "presidential" site, the Iraqis voiced displeasure, calling the inspectors spies. On another occasion, the head of the National Monitoring Directorate (NMD), General Hussam Amin, complained in writing that an inspector "while walking in a provocative and improperly flamboyant manner" had said that "it seems you have nothing chemical or biological, but there is a smell in the air." Nevertheless, General Amin ended his letter to the head of our Baghdad office with the assurance that "nonetheless, we shall continue to cooperate with you and this conduct [the flamboyant walking, etc.] shall not affect the level of our cooperation."

There were frequent Iraqi complaints that questions put by inspectors were improper and could only be understood as provocations or attempted espionage. One inspector had asked for the telephone number of an air base, its organizational structure, etc. On one occasion an inspector's request for information as to who were the investors in the Nineveh Free Trade Zone was turned down. We were concerned that this might be a precursor of a more general position that the Iraqi side would determine which questions were permissible. That would have been unacceptable. It was for us to determine what questions were relevant.

On our side, we could well understand that given the background of past close relations between many UNSCOM inspectors and some national intelligence services (notably the U.S.), and given the possibility of early military action by the U.S., the Iraqis did not appreciate questions that went beyond what was strictly relevant to the issue of weapons of mass destruction, especially if they related to conventional defense. We also recognized that every question put by a hundred or more inspectors might not be relevant. We told the Iraqis this, and assured them that there was no spying. We did not transmit any information to any government, nor did we find any inspector doing so—if we had, we would have fired him or her. Naturally we took steps to guide the inspectors as to what questions would be relevant. Although in public Iraq repeatedly cried espionage, even at the level of Vice President Taha Yassin Ramadan, the complaints did not become a big issue. My impression was that the unease about inspection had to come out somewhere and that the Iraqi side was constantly adding new files to a dossier of cases which they could one day use should they decide to stop the inspections.

There were some cases of demonstrations against the inspectors, though hardly threatening ones. They occurred at our Baghdad office, at a hospital site and during the inspection of the private home that yielded nuclear documents. The most absurd complaint, and one that was lodged with fanfare and escalated to a high level, concerned some inspectors' sightseeing visit to a mosque in Baghdad. The inspectors had been well received by the sheik and been guided around in all innocence. However, shortly thereafter an imam called on all Muslim clergymen in the world to denounce the "inspection" of the mosque, and the head of the NMD claimed that questions had been asked about underground shelters and the mosque's relations with the government, etc. I doubted that our counterparts' complaints were in good faith and suspected that the noise level was due to their wish to exploit a matter that touched religion.

In my updating of the Security Council on January 27, I said that "demonstrations and outbursts of this kind are unlikely to occur in Iraq without initiative or encouragement from the authorities. They do not facilitate an already difficult job, in which we try to be effective, professional and, at the same time, correct. Where our Iraqi counterparts have some complaint they can take it up in a calmer and less unpleasant manner."

By the end of January two significant matters were left without satisfactory conclusion: our operation with U.S. assistance of U-2 planes and our interviews in Baghdad.

Flying the U-2 Planes and Other Surveillance Aircraft

Mohamed ElBaradei and I had raised the subject of using the U-2 and other surveillance planes during our talks with the Iraqis in Vienna at the end of September 2002. We did not get very far at that time, despite the fact that UNSCOM, our predecessor, had used such planes and there had been routine procedures for it. UNMOVIC was now buying commercial satellite images of many sites. These pictures had high resolution and gave excellent fresh information, which could be compared with the information we had of the sites in our vast database. However, the planes traveled at a lower level than the satellites and they had some capabilities which the satellites lacked, so we wanted them. An American U-2, a French Mirage, a Russian AN-30 and a French or German drone would also provide a visible political demonstration of the support we had from the great powers.

The right to launch such flights was unequivocally inscribed in the November resolution. Having assured ourselves that the U.S. was willing to perform U-2 flights for us and that the French and the Russians would also offer their special planes, we informed the Iraqis about the procedures we wanted to follow. They did not reject our plans, as this would have been a contravention of the resolution, nor did they advance clear-cut conditions, presumably in the awareness that their acceptance of the resolution had to be "unconditional." Rather, they demurred that the continuation of daily attacks by the U.S./UK in the no-fly zones raised difficulties. The Iraqi air defense units, they said, had to act in self-defense against this daily aggression, which was not sanctioned by the Security Council. To protect our planes we would need to ensure that allied bombings in the no-fly zones were suspended when our surveillance aircraft were in the air. Further, again in order not to endanger our surveillance planes, Iraq would need our help to get modern civilian radar at Basra and Mosul.

To the U.S., an Iraqi downing of a U-2 in UNMOVIC service would no doubt be regarded as a clear sign of defiance. On the other hand, the Iraqis would understand that shooting down an American U-2 plane, despite the triumph it would represent in the face of the humiliating no-fly zones, in all likelihood would trigger war. They would surely want to avoid that. They were probably playing poker with us to get something out of our request, although their cards were weak. But what about the risk of "accidents" by trigger-happy Iraqi air defense crews?

Although my impression was that the U.S. would have sent U-2 planes on our behalf even without an Iraqi assurance of safe flights, we wanted to minimize the risk of attacks, and so the discussion dragged on. It was clear that Iraq's stance on this issue originated above the level of my opposite number. It was linked to Iraq's resistance to the no-fly zones. The regime wanted to use the U-2 issue as leverage in the no-fly-zone question. This was futile. The matter of the surveillance planes had been settled by the resolution. I found, however, that resistance seemed to weaken somewhat when we talked about our intention to use French and Russian surveillance planes as well as American ones. It was as if the humiliation was diminished when the presence of U.S. planes would be diluted by planes from less hostile countries.

The issue of the surveillance planes was not resolved until February. There would be no suspension of the no-fly zones, nor any radars for Basra and Mosul. We would follow the same procedures as UNSCOM. Before we had to suspend our inspections in Iraq, there was time for a number of American high-altitude U-2 flights but for only one French Mirage flight, at a lower altitude. The Russian AN plane, which was to fly at the lowest altitude and could perform surveillance also at night, came so late to the scene that there was no time to get it into operation. The Russians had at first asked for payment to provide the service of their plane and we had refused, as the other planes were free of charge. Not that we had financial difficulties—Iraqi oil money footed the bills—but we always tried to keep expenses down. After some discussion and high-level political intervention in Moscow, Ambassador Lavrov told me that the Russian government had promised to operate the plane for us free of charge. At this point we ran into the problem of where to station the plane. The Kuwaitis did not want it. I guess they had enough with a huge American military buildup on their territory. By the time the problem was solved by Syria expressing readiness to host the Russian plane, the matter had dragged on so long that it was too late.

The Problem of Interviews in Baghdad

UNMOVIC also had to deal with resistance from the Iraqi authorities to another right which the November resolution had given us: that of conducting interviews. When Mohamed ElBaradei and I had first broached the subject during the talks in Vienna at the end of

September 2002, before the resolution had been adopted, our Iraqi counterparts had said that they had no problems with our interviewing individual Iraqi scientists or other staff. They added innocently that it was, of course, up to the individuals to decide if they were willing to be interviewed. There had been instances in the past, they said, when the interviewees had felt intimidated by the UNSCOM interrogators and had sometimes been misunderstood. For this reason the interviewees might want to have representatives of their own authorities present, who could correct any misunderstandings. In their view this was no more unusual than someone requesting the presence of consular officials of their country when giving testimony in a foreign state.

We pointed out that there had sometimes been a whole crowd of official Iraqi "minders" present during UNSCOM-led interviews and that the witnesses clearly had been intimidated by these people rather than by the inspectors. According to UNSCOM, the minders had often interrupted the witnesses and told them that their memory was wrong or that they had misunderstood.

Our inconclusive discussions the previous year in Vienna on this point had been settled by the UN resolution, which clearly stipulated that we should have the right to private access to any persons, i.e., interviews without the presence of any Iraqi minders. This did not quite solve the matter. As we began calling people for interviews in Baghdad, we met refusals to come to our offices and an insistence on having some Iraqi witness or, at least, permission for the interviewee to tape the interview. Having considered these requests, we concluded that most likely they were the result of instructions from the authorities, and so must be rejected. But how could we get the persons to come and speak, if they refused? Could we simply order the National Monitoring Directorate to bring us the persons we wanted and make sure they were ready to talk without any witness or tape recorder? This, in effect, was the advice from American officials. If it did not happen, Iraq would have committed a violation of the resolution. Of course, a totalitarian state would have no difficulty delivering people to us. But could the UN allow itself to draw on the uncontrolled power of the totalitarian state? Without saying that we wanted to do that, we made it clear to the Iraqis that we would see it as something very serious if we could not exercise the right given to us by the Security Council. Moreover, we said, if there was nothing to hide then the interviews should work in their favor, even more so if the absence of Iraqi officials and tape recorders increased the interviews' credibility.

Before the end of January the Iraqi side had promised to "encourage" persons to accept our requests for interviews, and after a period during which we sent interviewees home if they demanded to have a "friend" present or a tape recorder running, we succeeded in carrying out one-to-one interviews in a small number of cases. Some of these talks were informative, but we never had illusions that the persons spoke freely.

The question of taking scientists or other persons who might have information of interest to us and interviewing them outside Iraq was controversial from the moment it appeared in the first draft of what became the November resolution, and it remained so until the inspections were suspended. Although the resolution talked about the matter as a right and not a duty for UNMOVIC, the U.S. was increasingly insistent on the right being used. Other member states were as skeptical as we were. Was the U.S. insistence really motivated by a conviction that this would be a way of getting relevant information? Or was the purpose to assist in the defection of certain people, or to provoke a rejection by the Iraqi regime? Interviews of Iraqi scientists conducted later, during the occupation, suggest that some would not have wanted to leave their country, while others would not have dared to go. It was one of the few cases in which I felt strong U.S. pressure.

A Mid-January Balance Sheet and a Talk with Kofi Annan

Mohamed ElBaradei and I were invited to Baghdad for stocktaking and to solve outstanding practical problems before the updating of the Security Council scheduled for January 27. Our visit was set for

January 19 and 20. Before this visit we had a number of important talks.

Just before leaving New York I had a long talk with Kofi Annan. We discussed the timetables of the two Security Council resolutions and noted that it was the Council, more than UNMOVIC, that was faced with the different pace of the clocks. My January 27 report on unresolved disarmament issues, illegal imports and the state of Iraqi cooperation would not mark the end of the commission's work.

It was for the Council to consider our reports and its own options. I told Annan I thought these options were disarmament by inspection *or* disarmament by war. Continued inspection backed by military pressure and followed by long-term monitoring might squeeze the truth out of Iraq, lead to assured disarmament, and prevent any resumption of weapons programs. There was the difficulty of maintaining over time a pressure that was sufficient to keep Iraq contained. There could obviously be a risk that Iraq would one day throw out the inspectors, which would be dramatic and visible, or curtail the inspectors' activities, which could be gradual. Long-term Council fatigue would increase these risks. The U.S. administration did not like containment. The choice between inspection and armed action was not only for the members of the Security Council but also for Iraq. ElBaradei and I would tell Baghdad that it must act now and not continue to raise petty obstacles like those about espionage.

I also took up with Annan on this occasion my wish to make Dimitri Perricos my deputy. I wanted his agreement and support. Dimitri had tremendous experience from the 1991 inspections in Iraq, from the inspections and controversy with North Korea and from the dismantling of South Africa's nuclear program. He was the head of our operations division and now responsible for all the staff that planned operations from New York and all the staff that ran those operations in the field. He had performed superbly and with tremendous vigor. He was no easygoing fellow, not infrequently scaring people with his sharp arguments. Dimitri did not hesitate to contradict me, though he was usually gentler with me than with others. No one had ever seen him lacking in competence, judgment and drive. I used to say that he made up for any impatience I lacked. I not only respected him, I also liked him and still like him, and I was glad that Annan went along in making him my deputy. He fully deserved the position and he needed it, in particular in his relations with the Iraqi side. When I left in the summer of 2003, Annan rightly made Dimitri UNMOVIC's acting executive chairman.

6

To Baghdad and Back

On the morning of January 17, escorted by a swarm of police on motorcycles, Mohamed ElBaradei and I went to the Elysée Palace to see President Chirac. My image of the man, who had become known as a major opponent of armed action against Iraq at this time, was that of a forceful professional politician steeped in the rhetoric of principle and in the somewhat less principled day-to-day dealings of the French political world. I did not come with any surplus of admiration but left with a feeling that the French president's attitude on the Iraqi issue perhaps was dominated neither by a wish to stand as a symbol of peace nor (understandable in a politician in any country) as a response to the strong majority opinion of his voters. Rather, his thinking seemed to be dominated by the conviction that Iraq did not pose a threat that justified armed intervention.

In my briefing, I said the situation was tense. Iraq's cooperation—prompt access, etc.—had regard more to process than to substance. So far there had been little genuine effort by Iraq to solve outstanding disarmament issues. A number of intelligence services, including the French, were convinced that weapons of mass destruction remained in Iraq, but we had no evidence showing it. It was possible that mobile laboratories and underground facilities existed. This needed to be explored. It was also conceivable that relatively few weapons of mass destruction were retained. In any case, more time was needed to bring clarity on a number of issues.

Chirac said France did not have any "serious evidence" that Iraq retained proscribed weapons. Having met people from French intelligence and listened to them, I registered with keen interest that Chirac did not share their conclusions on Iraq. The intelligence services sometimes "intoxicate each other," he said. Personally, he did not believe that Iraq had any weapons of mass destruction. In his view, inspections up to 1998 had revealed a lot and had, in fact, disarmed Iraq. This proved that inspections could be an effective method. War was now the worst solution. It would fuel anti-western feelings in the Muslim world, and France was not ready to be drawn into a war. Only the Security Council was entitled to decide on any military action.

Mohamed ElBaradei noted that the presence of inspectors constituted deterrence for Iraq to resume any weapons programs. The institution of international inspections was in danger if inspections were now brushed aside in Iraq and not given time to achieve success. There could be no presumption of innocence in the case of Iraq, but the need was for carrots, not just sticks. Iraq needed to be more positive and provide full and active cooperation. This might be a bitter pill for Iraq to swallow, but it was necessary. ElBaradei was concerned that Iraq had called inspectors "spies," had not allowed private interviews and had not yet enacted national legislation prohibiting the production of proscribed weapons.

Before we went down to meet the press, Chirac said that Saddam Hussein was "locked up in an intellectual bunker." His entourage did not dare to tell him the truth. War would inevitably lead to his elimination. He would need to make some positive gestures. This might be unpleasant, but far less so than war.

On our way down to a lively press conference I noticed in one hall a short, temporary pillar which on one side advertised Coca-Cola! In the presidential Elysée Palace! I could not resist asking President Chirac if it was a piece of modern French pop art. He seemed totally relaxed about the presence of this thoroughgoing American symbol and explained that it had something to do with a children's fair. During the press conference he seemed equally relaxed when listening to answers I gave in French, but I could not tell whether his attitude was feigned or real.

After a short meeting with Foreign Minister Dominique de Villepin at the French Foreign Ministry, Mohamed and I parted. He was going to Larnaca via Vienna, his base, while I was to go via London, to see Prime Minister Blair. I got nervous when I discovered that my pickup time in the center of Paris was only forty minutes before my flight, but was amazed how fast we moved through Paris and on the turnpike, with police on motorbikes behaving as if they were in a circus arena. In general I am not enamored of the idea that VIPs should be able to push through at high speed, inconveniencing others, unless it is for security, but this time it was necessary.

When we arrived at Heathrow, British intelligence personnel led us through quick channels to a car and we were briefed by them during the ride to Checkers, the country residence of the prime minister. There, Tony Blair greeted us cheerfully and insisted on changing out of his jogging suit before our meeting, despite my protests that it was totally unnecessary. There was afternoon tea and with it something I had not had since I was a student at Cambridge nearly fifty years before: crumpets! They are like knighted muffins. A good beginning, somewhat less formal than my encounter with President Chirac.

I began with a briefing similar to the one I had presented in Paris. There was a need for more active Iraqi cooperation. The voluminous declaration of December 8 had not contained information that solved any disarmament issues. It had not yet been possible to set up interviews without the interviewees feeling at risk. We had found illegally imported missile engines and, very recently, eleven empty warheads designed for chemical weapons and a stash of nuclear documents in a private home. These were facts we had to look at more closely. Before we had done so, I did not want to make huge affairs of them. We did not go into specifics, except that the prime minister said he thought the issue of private interviews with Iraqis was important. I wondered to myself if he genuinely thought this was an important and realistic way to getting information, or whether he—and the U.S.—thought this was a case in which the Iraqi regime might balk and might be pinned to a violation of the resolution, a material breach?

Blair noted that he was concerned about an "elongated timeline." If there was no specific incident and if the findings of the inspectors were of a "lower order," there would be a dilemma. The military pressure was important to get Iraq to cooperate—a concept with which I agreed—but the U.S. could not keep troops idling in the area for months. Iraq had a duty to cooperate actively, and to reveal. A period of Iraqi reluctance could not be tolerated. Besides, what message would it send to a country like North Korea if, after some months of less than fully satisfactory Iraqi cooperation with the inspectors, the world backed away from the clear signal it had sent via the Security Council and amplified with a credible military threat? If there were to be a continued lack of "honest cooperation," serious decisions might have to be taken around the first of March.

I was not sure whether this reflected a U.S./UK understanding or if the prime minister thought that my awareness of this thinking would lead me to present a sufficiently ominous picture to my counterparts in Baghdad a few days later—a picture that might move the regime into more active cooperation. It further struck me from comments he made that his awareness of the horribly brutal, evil nature of the Baghdad regime weighed heavily in his thinking.

The terror exercised by the Saddam regime was, indeed, notorious and well documented, not least in official reports before the General Assembly of the UN. However, the reason that had been given by both the Clinton and the Bush administrations for "regime change" had never been that such a regime could not be tolerated on the earth, but primarily that such change was the best way to become confident about the eradication of any weapons of mass destruction. If they had leaned more on the terror of the regime as an impetus for armed action, they would have encountered the question of whether they intended to change *all* terror regimes. However, perhaps Blair and Bush, both religious men, felt strengthened in their political determination by the feeling that they were fighting evil, not only proliferation. In the absence of finding weapons of mass destruction in occupied Iraq, the two leaders have not surprisingly focused on the terror argument, about which they may have felt strongly but did not much rely on before the armed action.

In responding to Tony Blair, I did not reference the terror nature of Saddam's regime but said simply that the risk of a long period of "insincere cooperation" by Iraq could not be excluded. If, on the other hand, Iraq extended full and active cooperation, progress could be made fairly quickly—in a matter of months.

After our exchange, Blair very kindly took me and Torkel Stiernlöf, my personal assistant, on a tour of some of the rooms of the mansion. He showed us a Rubens painting which Churchill had tried to improve with some brushstrokes, a fact that was discovered only when it was sent for restoration. It was a warm and focused meeting. The question of intelligence did not come up this time. It would do so in later talks.

Through Larnaca to the Baghdad Meeting

On Saturday, January 18, the day after my talk with Tony Blair, we flew to reunite with ElBaradei in Larnaca in Cyprus, the starting point for our own shuttle to Baghdad. I stayed at the modest but nice Flamingo Beach Hotel, where we had set up a regional office and where we were in convenient reach of the airport. The name of the hotel was most appropriate as there were lots of flamingos in a shallow lake nearby. I learned that the birds get their color from the shells of cochineal beetles, which the birds eat. While I had not known this, I did know, as a lover of oriental rugs, that the shell was used to provide the strong red dye used for many rugs.

The owner of the Flamingo Beach Hotel hit the jackpot first with the Iraq inspections and, thereafter, the war. The winter season usually provided few tourists. Yet, from October 2002, UN officials and inspectors had simply been raining on his hotel from the sky. The period of large numbers of inspectors flying to and from Baghdad lasted only a little beyond the suspension of inspections in

March, but our office in the hotel remained and the officials maintaining it continued to turn up. In addition, lots of other UN organizations active in Iraq after the war had people at the Flamingo.

Mohamed ElBaradei and I arrived at Baghdad on Sunday, January 19. We rode into the dusty, worn city and checked in at the comfortable Al Rasheed Hotel, trying not to step on President Bush Sr., who looked up at you from a carpet deliberately placed at the entrance. We held our first meeting at the Ministry of Foreign Affairs the same afternoon. The Iraqi delegation was headed by Dr. Amir Al Sa'adi, well known to us from our previous talks.

In my introduction at the meeting I said we came with fresh impressions from the UN in New York, the EU in Brussels, and visits to Moscow, Paris and London. We could report that all perceived the situation was tense. We had instructions to update the Security Council on January 27 and much attention would be devoted to what we had to report. I said further that I did not think war was inevitable but it was a clear possibility. Credible disarmament verified by inspection was an alternative to war, not a prelude to it. The Security Council needed to become confident through the inspectors that Iraq was disarmed, and for the inspectors to become confident, transparency and evidence were required. We presumed neither guilt nor innocence. We needed active—or, with the modern term, *proactive*—sincere cooperation. No chess play! Inspection was not a penalty but provided an opportunity that Iraq should seize. There were several practical problems that needed to be resolved urgently. We needed to be able to fly helicopters freely into the no-fly zones and to use U-2 planes. The number of minders present at inspections must go down. In some cases there had been five Iraqi minders for one inspector! This was practically harassment. We needed some understanding ensuring that media would not disturb the inspections.

Mohamed ElBaradei said that much impatience had been built up during the eleven years since 1991. We needed to come to conclusive results within the next month or so. There had been progress, in particular prompt access to sites, but we needed specific evidence, documentation, interviews in private. He asked why the question of implementing national legislation had not yet been acted upon and said that some public Iraqi statements, like those calling the inspectors spies, sent the wrong signals to the world about Iraq's attitude to the new inspections.

Dr. Al Sa'adi brought up the question of the burden of proof. How could Iraq prove that it had no mobile units with forbidden biological activities, and how could it prove that it had not imported any natural uranium (yellowcake) from Niger? He voiced a good deal of complaints about my assessment of Iraq's December 8 declaration and argued that although the declaration showed that some missiles had exceeded the permissible range of 150 kilometers in test flights, they did not contravene the guiding resolutions. A lengthy special briefing on the missile issue was provided, as part of our talks, by one of the leaders of the program. During a tea break I talked to Al Sa'adi about our need to find a method to check trucks on the road, including the alleged existence of mobile production units for biological weapons. We had received some advice from police authorities, but we needed some form of control on the roads. The Iraqis would have to be part of these operations. Al Sa'adi was positive but added that the allegation about mobile germ factories was somewhat silly. The mere risk of collisions would be enough to sink any such idea.

The meeting went on for about two and a half hours on Sunday afternoon and the same amount of time on Monday morning. In the end we were able to resolve some of the outstanding issues, while others were left aside. It was understood that a normal ratio of minders to inspectors would be 1:1. Our helicopters could fly for inspections in the no-fly zones and would take on board Iraqi minders, as they could not use helicopters in the zones. However, no journalists would be taken on board. There was no breakthrough on the issue of provision of new evidence (e.g., more documents), nor was there any solution of the U-2 issue.

Mohamed had sent signals through several channels that we ought to be invited for a visit with Saddam Hussein, but only a visit to

Vice President Taha Yassin Ramadan was set up after the talks on Sunday. We went over many of the same issues with him as we had done in the talks: urgency, alleged espionage, implementing legislation.

After the meeting with Ramadan we called all inspectors and other staff from UNMOVIC and IAEA in Baghdad to our offices in the Canal Hotel to tell them about our talks with the Iraqis, to make them feel that we were all one team and to stress how important and delicate their jobs were.

After the meetings of the delegations on Monday morning we drafted a list of ten points with the Iraqis and presented it at separate press conferences before we left. We avoided having a joint press conference, as this could have given a false impression that all was going well, when in fact the result was meager. Before I stepped into the room full of media, Dimitri Perricos suggested that I should preface the points of agreement by mentioning some non-agreed point, so in my opening remarks I said that, regrettably, there were several points on which we had not been able to agree, notably that of the use of U-2 planes.

In the ten points it was recorded that the Iraqi side would "encourage" persons to accept access by inspectors to private sites (homes) and accept interviews in private, without minders. The Iraqi appointment of a commission to look for unreported munitions, following our discovery of some chemical warheads, was announced. We noted that the technical discussions with the IAEA would continue to clarify outstanding nuclear issues, including that of the aluminum tubes alleged to be for centrifuges, and the alleged attempt to import raw uranium.

This was our first trip to Baghdad since the start of the renewed inspections. We had warned the Iraqi side that time was running out and that we felt the need for spectacular progress. Yet the Iraqi side had spent much time voicing their resentment. I could understand some of it, but this was not the time for long complaints, nor for attempts to play chess with us on the U-2 surveillance flights, helicopters going into the no-fly zones, or private interviews. We had not been given the opportunity to see Saddam and tell him how serious the situation was. He evidently considered such a meeting beneath his dignity. Was he not sufficiently well informed, or did he believe that he could, once more, sneak out of a difficult situation? We left somewhat disappointed. An opportunity had not been used well.

On Monday afternoon we let our UN plane fly us directly to Athens to enable us to meet with the Greek foreign minister, George Papandreou. He was at this time the chairman of the EU foreign ministers, Greece having just taken up the EU presidency. There was no heating in the huge maw of the plane, and we arrived in Athens frozen stiff. However, the reception was nice and warm, and I immediately felt a good rapport with Papandreou. It was not only that he spoke fluent Swedish, having spent part of his youth and school years in Sweden, where his family had fled from the military junta that took power in Greece at the end of the 1960s. It was also his unassuming style and intelligent and constructive approach that appealed to me.

We had no difficulty concluding with Papandreou that Europe's contribution to the issue of non-proliferation would have to be more than just showing reluctance to use force. The U.S. had long been the most ardent and active voice against proliferation. European states' current opposition to the use of force against Iraq had to be complemented by a more active interest and role in other cases, like Iran and North Korea. Papandreou, Swedish foreign minister Anna Lindh (who was tragically knifed to death later in the year) and their European colleagues brought about such a development, leading in June to a declaration in Thessaloniki and the adoption of a paper on basic principles and a European Union action plan against the proliferation of weapons of mass destruction. The Europeans, like the U.S., did not exclude the use of force as a means of last resort. The question was *when* other means should be deemed exhausted.

Preparations for the Security Council on January 27

On our return to New York we began to prepare for the January 27 updating of the Security Council.

We were aware that many governments would examine our statements in the Council for any lines they might be able to use in support of their arguments. This was natural. But did any government exert pressure on us to make particular statements? I was often asked that question later and the answer is no. Governments and their ambassadors in New York were perfectly correct. No one came to me and urged me to say this or that. Another matter was that governments and officials pleaded their cases between themselves and in public. The U.S. did not defer going public with their assessment to await ours on January 27.

A few days before the meeting, the White House issued a document with the title "What Does Disarmament Look Like?" The familiar line was taken that the test was whether Iraq "had made a strategic decision to give up its mass destruction weapons." The document failed to register that Iraq had so far invariably provided prompt access to any sites and argued instead—plausibly, but without evidence—that Iraq was still running "highly organized concealment efforts." It noted that numerous quantities of weapons were "unaccounted for," which was correct but led the reader to the conclusion that the unaccounted items existed—which was uncertain. It further relied on several contentions which later proved unfounded or erroneous, including the allegation that Iraq sought to procure uranium from abroad, which presumably was based on a document later proved to be a forgery.

The U.S. positions laid out in the document were supplemented at about the same time by Deputy Secretary of Defense Paul Wolfowitz. In a speech before the Council on Foreign Relations he alluded to the line, expressed by both the Clinton and the Bush administrations, that there would have to be a "regime change" in Iraq. This was a demand that had never figured in UN resolutions and which, indeed, had been criticized since it left the regime no incentive to comply. With an admirable semantic somersault, Mr. Wolfowitz now managed to find a way of reconciling the U.S. and UN positions. He said that the only way to avoid regime change would be for the regime to change its nature. In plainer language: The elimination of Saddam was not an absolute condition, only that he would have to show a "massive change of attitude." It may be assumed that Mr. Wolfowitz was convinced that there would be no such change and no strategic decision.

There was not a direct advocacy of war. Rather, the U.S. was asserting on two major lines of argument that Iraq was violating Resolution 1441, which a few months earlier had afforded Iraq "a final opportunity" to comply with its disarmament obligations.

The first ground of the U.S. argument was that the Iraqi declaration of December 8 had been "inaccurate and incomplete." This could be true, but it depends in large measure on whether there were, in fact, more weapons to report. Without a doubt there were a great many proscribed items unaccounted for and suspicions that documents were withheld, but what if, in fact, there remained no weapons and no additional relevant documents, as Iraq asserted?

The second and main ground of U.S. argument was that Iraq had failed to provide the immediate, unconditional and active cooperation with UNMOVIC and the IAEA that was required by the resolution. This was obviously a much more general accusation and one that was somewhat harder to pin down. It was true that the Iraqis had dragged their feet as regards aerial surveillance and interviews in private. The U.S. further explained that you recognize disarmament when you see it, and referred to the three cases of South Africa eliminating its nuclear arms under IAEA supervision and Ukraine and Kazakhstan similarly doing away with their nuclear capacity. I had, myself, several times referred to South Africa as an example for Iraq, and it was obvious that while cooperating tolerably on procedure, the Iraqi regime did not exactly show enthusiasm for disarmament.

Yet the Iraqi government was worried about the Council meeting. In a long letter to Kofi Annan, Iraqi foreign minister Naji Sabri cited the UN inspectors under Richard Butler as having said in April 1998 that "not much is unknown about Iraq's retained proscribed weapons capabilities." The minister further referred to the full access that Iraq had given to our inspectors even though, as he said, some of them "have committed unacceptable acts." Despite the growing accumulation of U.S. troops on its borders, the Iraqi government had not lost its stridency.

January 27 Meeting

The expectations for the Council meeting were high. Was disarmament through inspection working or would there be war? This was no routine briefing by the Secretariat. The foreign ministers of most of the Council members would be there and the meeting was to be public. The UN, we were told, had never in its history experienced such media attention.

Having returned to New York from Baghdad and Athens on the afternoon of Tuesday, January 21, with the Security Council meeting scheduled for the following Monday, I had little time to prepare my speech. I had set down a few notes on the plane from Athens, and back in the office on Wednesday morning I immediately asked some staff members to draft pieces on specific inspection results and technical assessments. During that afternoon, evening and night I got down to my own writing. The whole of Thursday was devoted to UNMOVIC's advisory group, the College of Commissioners. The main work on the speech was done between Friday afternoon and 10:00 in the evening on Sunday, January 26. It involved half a dozen staff members: my closest advisers plus technical experts and a lawyer. At home in my apartment I worked on a diskette, which I then brought to the office for copying and printing for the rest of the team. Not really being computer literate, I was always scared that I would lose some text on which I had spent hours of scarce time. During this week, fortunately, no such calamity occurred.

The last corrections were entered Monday morning and a sufficient number of copies were made for the interpreters. The Council chamber was packed and there was literally electricity in the air with all the television cameras and microphones peering down on the arena and the horseshoe-shaped table at which the representatives of the fifteen state members of the Council were seated—most of them, this time, foreign ministers. Mohamed and I had reserved seats at the side until we were invited to sit at the table by the president of the Council, this month the ambassador of France, Jean-Marc de la Sabliere.

I had sometimes said that inspection was an opportunity and not a penalty—an opportunity to become credible. It seemed to me that unlike South Africa, Iraq had not, sadly, seized the opportunity that was offered to it, and I said bluntly in the early part of the speech that "Iraq appears not to have come to a genuine acceptance—not even today—of the disarmament which was demanded of it and which it needs to carry out to win the confidence of the world and to live in peace."

Using a distinction that Mohamed ElBaradei had made between cooperation on process and on substance, I noted that it appeared from our experience that Iraq had decided in principle to provide cooperation on process, notably access. A similar decision on substance, I said, was indispensable to bring the disarmament task to completion through the peaceful process of inspection. In effect, I was concurring with the American view that a "strategic decision" was needed. It seemed to me that half of such a decision had been taken, and I pleaded that the other half should be taken urgently.

On substance, I registered deficiencies. The resolutions of the Council talked about "unresolved disarmament issues," and I felt there had been almost a touch of arrogance when the Iraqi side had asserted that the "so-called 'outstanding disarmament issues' have no tangible significance." I commented in my speech that the outstanding issues deserved to be taken seriously rather than being brushed aside as "evil machinations," and I regretted that the 12,000-page declaration did not seem to contain any new evidence that would eliminate the questions or reduce their number.

I noted that our reports neither asserted nor excluded that weapons of mass destruction existed in Iraq, but pointed to lack of evidence and question marks which must be solved if the dossiers were to be closed. I illustrated this by going through a number of concrete issues, like that of the chemical agent VX. I said that there were "strong indications" that Iraq had produced more anthrax than it declared and that some of it might still exist. I did not go further than that. An expert briefing I had had on this matter had strongly suggested that a quantity of anthrax had been retained when anthrax was being destroyed in 1991, and could still be effective if the Iraqis had succeeded in drying the agent. However, the evidence, although impressive, had not been compelling.

I referred to our finding four empty chemical warheads at a declared site and a stash of nuclear-related documents in the home of a scientist. I also registered that the Iraqi side had set up a committee of investigation, which had found four more chemical rockets.

I mentioned the obstacles to flights by the U-2 planes. The Iraqi side had not denied that we had the right to send the planes, but had tried to make the propaganda point that there would be no risk for "our" U-2 planes if only the U.S. and the UK stopped their bombings in the no-fly zones. These and various other responses were unwise for a country that needed desperately to match its decision to give free and prompt access with "proactive" cooperation on all fronts. It was not, I said in the Council, enough for Iraq to open doors. Inspection was not a game of catch-as-catch-can.

I concluded the speech by telling the Council about the rapid buildup of the inspection operations, of our deployment in Iraq of 260 staff members from sixty countries, all serving the United Nations and reporting to no one else. In the past two months we had conducted about 300 inspections at more than 230 different sites. Of these, more than twenty were sites that had not been inspected before.

I said, finally, that the capability which had been built up in a short time was now operative and at the disposal of the Security Council. UNMOVIC, I said, shared the sense of urgency felt by the Council to use inspection as a path to attain, "within reasonable time," verifiable disarmament of Iraq. It was for the Council, not for me, to decide how long was "reasonable." However, I knew that time was running out, and I did not want anyone to believe that the inspectors were of the view that years of inspection were a tolerable option.

Mohamed ElBaradei had fewer and smaller problems in his nuclear dossier and did not hesitate to ask the Council for more time for inspections. In his speech he recalled that by 1992 the IAEA had largely destroyed, removed or rendered harmless all Iraqi facilities and equipment relevant to nuclear weapons production. By 1994 the agency had removed all fissionable material from Iraq. In 1998, when inspections were brought to a halt, the agency found no indications that Iraq had retained any physical capability to produce weapons-usable nuclear material. He also noted some difficulties. The agency had sought unsuccessfully to undertake private interviews. As recently as three days before, a request had been turned down. He further appealed for more actionable information from member states and urged Iraq to shift from "passive support" to voluntarily assisting inspectors by providing documentation and other evidence.

Mohamed concluded by noting that the agency's work was "steadily progressing and should be allowed to run its natural course." Provided there was to be sustained, proactive support by Iraq, the agency should be able "within the next few months," he said, to give credible assurance that Iraq had no nuclear weapons program. These few months would be a valuable "investment in peace, because they could help us avoid war."

To be sure, Mohamed had relatively few problems of substance on the nuclear side and could and should be less critical than I had been. Yet, I doubt I would have brought myself to directly plead for a few more months unless I felt I could guarantee satisfactory results in such time.

Reactions after the Meeting

The big public meeting adjourned right after our speeches, and at the following closed meeting there was no discussion but only a few questions to Mohamed and me. Nor did we encounter any immediate expressions of satisfaction or displeasure in our private contacts with ambassadors and other representatives. They were reporting, not reacting.

While I had hoped that my frank speech would jolt our Iraqi counterparts to stop foot-dragging and further petty bargaining, I had not foreseen that hawks in Washington and elsewhere would be delighted with the rather harsh balance they found in my update. I had not gone along with the U.S. and UK assertions that there existed weapons of mass destruction in Iraq or suggested that there were glaring breaches of the November resolution, but I had confirmed that the unresolved disarmament issues remained and that there were troublesome limitations in Iraq's cooperation on substance.

In the days after the meeting I was asked by journalists if I realized I had played into the hands of the hawks, and I replied that I had not been playing at all. My intention had been only to render an accurate report. That was what we were asked to provide and could contribute. It was for the Council to assess the situation and draw conclusions whether there should be continued inspections or war.

Raghida Dergham, the sharp, engaged and knowledgeable correspondent whom we used to call "the Druze missile," wrote in the Arabic-language newspaper *Al Hayat* that my report could be seen as "a service to the American position and ammunition to the hawks." However, she continued, "a second reading reveals that Blix may in fact be offering a service to Iraq by mounting the pressure, just a few weeks before the beginning of military operations, in the hope that Baghdad would fill the gaps in the declarations and encourage scientists and officials to be interviewed." Yes, although my main ambition had been to give an accurate report, this had certainly also been a hope I nourished.

I feared that the Iraqis might, again, do too little too late. They could have accepted inspections in the summer rather than the autumn of 2002. If they had, they would probably have got inspection conditions that were much more lenient than the draconian ones given to us in Resolution 1441. Their present attitude, even though a vast improvement on what they did between 1991 and 1998, incurred great risk. I suspect that the intrusion inherent in any inspection, however correctly pursued, combined with a strong sense of pride on the Iraqi side and made it difficult for them to imitate what I once jokingly suggested to Dr. Al Sa'adi the patient in the dentist's chair should do: cheerfully open the mouth wider and convince himself that it does not hurt, but only feels that way.

The official Iraqi reaction to my speech was perhaps predictable: Naji Sabri, the foreign minister, wrote a letter to Kofi Annan complaining about it. However, on Thursday, January 30, Mohamed ElBaradei and I received a letter from Dr. Al Sa'adi inviting us for a new round of talks in Baghdad. Had they realized that time was running out and that there was a need to change gears? Was this a last chance for a turnaround?

I felt the urgency of the new visit and the last-minute chances it might offer. We could not, however, allow ourselves to look naïvely eager to rush to Baghdad and risk coming out empty-handed. The Iraqis were the ones who should be eager to convince us and the Security Council that they were shifting gears and moving forward on the substance of disarmament.

Mohamed and I discussed whether we should try to secure a change by placing some conditions on our visit—such as Iraqi green-lighting of the U-2 flights, or solving some other problems we were facing. We did not consult anyone and decided to state our expectations for the visit rather than propose conditions. In contact with Mohamed, I wrote an affirmative reply to Dr. Al Sa'adi stressing that "the many questions which remain open . . . must be taken seriously and be resolved promptly."

7

Approaching the Brink

In the days between our updating the Council and our departure for Baghdad, more important actors appeared and policies were discussed at high levels within and between countries. The splits in the world and in the Security Council grew wider.

On Tuesday, January 28, President Bush gave his State of the Union message to Congress. I watched it on TV and was struck by how different it was in style from any European parliamentary affair. Despite the intense partisan politics in the U.S. Congress, the president was interrupted every few minutes as supporters and opponents alike, it seemed, stood to applaud. I could not imagine that such a thing would happen if Chirac had spoken before the French parliament or Blair before the British. It seemed like a patriotic feast, with the nation rallying around the head of state even though he stood for the policies of one party only. The president devoted most of his speech to the economy, apparently to avoid the impression that he was mainly interested in flexing the nation's military muscle. However, toward the end of the address the focus shifted to Iraq and North Korea, and this was the part the media registered most, including the statement that later became famous—or infamous: "The British government has learned that

Saddam Hussein recently sought significant quantities of uranium from Africa." The intended implication was that Iraq was seeking nuclear weapons. As I have mentioned before and shall describe later, the source of the claim made by the U.S. president before the U.S. Congress was a forged contract between Iraq and Niger.

Many interpreted President Bush's speech as meaning that the decision to go to war had been made. For months the U.S. had been following a plan preparing for an invasion of Iraq, but I believed, as before, that it could be stopped, modified or delayed, depending upon circumstances. I thought that the U.S. administration, or some of it, still hoped that Saddam Hussein would crack under the increased military, political and diplomatic pressure. Clearly, however, the president was turning up the heat on the Iraqis and, at the same time, preparing the U.S. Congress and public for war.

At a Bush-Blair meeting in Washington on January 31, my upcoming trip to Baghdad with Mohamed ElBaradei was described as meaningless or worse. President Bush had construed the mission as being one of "negotiation" and had said that "the idea of calling inspectors in to negotiate is a charade." While Bush did not welcome our mission, his scorn seemed chiefly directed against Saddam Hussein. The U.S. government did not want to raise the hope that there was any way out but war, nor did it wish to directly criticize the inspectors.

During February 2003, the U.S. military buildup in the Gulf continued and was expected to reach around 200,000 troops by the end of the month. It was evident that the actual use of this force against Iraq could only be avoided through some spectacular development that assured the U.S. and the world about disarmament in Iraq. The U.S. could not scale down its military presence or withdraw simply because Iraq opened its doors to the inspectors and let them in anywhere. The U.S.—and much of the rest of the world— was convinced that Iraq retained substantial quantities of weapons of mass destruction. At UNMOVIC we thought this was entirely plausible but, examining all material with a critical mind, we could not in good conscience say that there was any conclusive evidence. Even less could we see that there was any other urgency than that being created by the U.S. itself to bring the matter to a conclusion.

In order to change the U.S. attitude there would have to be a tangible surrender of Iraqi weapons or rock-solid evidence that they had been destroyed. The troops could not sit in the desert and wait for long. Just how long, we wondered at UNMOVIC. Like others, we suspected that a deadline was set for somewhere before the spring. If the U.S. soldiers would have to wear protective suits against chemical weapons, the fighting in hot weather would be horrible. When I had met Tony Blair in London in January he had mentioned that if there were a continued lack of "honest cooperation" from the Iraqis, serious decisions might have to be taken around March 1. At their meeting on January 31, Bush and Blair said the issue of Iraq was coming to a head in a matter of weeks, not months.

On the U.S. side there seemed to be little expectation that the inspection process would bring the decisive results needed. They had no comments on the fact that UNMOVIC had been inspecting for only two and a half months, preferring to note that UNSCOM inspections had gone on between 1991 and 1998 without producing decisive results.

We do not know what Saddam thought. He had had narrow escapes from difficult situations before, notably in 1991, when he survived Iraq's defeat in the Gulf War and retained power. Perhaps he was briefed by his lieutenants only about what they thought he wanted to hear—about the growing antiwar feelings around the world. Perhaps he thought that if he simply stepped up Iraq's cooperation with the inspectors one notch, world public opinion would prevent armed action against him.

At UNMOVIC we could speculate about U.S. and Iraqi intentions, but the speculations did not influence our work. We were in full swing with analysis and inspections, visiting more sites, trying to get meaningful interviews with relevant Iraqis, seeking anything concealed or clarifying why nothing was found.

Is a Security Council Resolution Needed for Armed Action?

The U.S. administration was not indifferent to getting a UN Security Council endorsement of the armed action. Opinion polls clearly showed that U.S. public support for armed action would be stronger with such an endorsement. Although my updating of the Council on January 27 had praised Iraq's cooperation on process, it had contained the comment that Iraq did not appear yet to have come to a genuine acceptance of disarmament. Some on the U.S. side seemed to have expected that this statement would be followed, almost as a matter of course, by a report in a similar vein at the next briefing of the Council. This and a hoped-for change in European attitudes would help to bring the Council to a desired second resolution endorsing armed action.

Nevertheless, although the U.S. would have welcomed a Security Council resolution, it did not want its plans to be dependent on any decision by the United Nations. On the legal side, it was gearing up to defend a unilaterally decided war. The official position was that armed action against Iraq did not require any endorsement by the Council. First, it could invoke Article 51 of the UN Charter, which allows states to act in individual or collective self-defense "if an armed attack occurs." The U.S. did not, it was said, need to delay action in its self-defense until Iraq had completed all its preparations to attack the U.S. The presence of weapons of mass destruction necessitated a reading of Article 51 allowing preemptive action. We do not have to sit and wait for the mushroom cloud, Condoleezza Rice said, and President Bush said the U.S. must deal with threats before they hurt the American people. Neither mentioned that any nuclear capability by Iraq would be years off, nor was it yet public that the famous uranium contract was a forgery.

Secondly, it was argued that Iraq had been in breach of a long series of Security Council resolutions and some of these—notably the latest, November's Resolution 1441—gave the U.S. the authority for armed intervention. Perhaps it was believed that these legal stands would make it less difficult to get a resolution through the Council—unnecessary though it was claimed to be. If members of the Council went along with a resolution authorizing armed force, they and the Council would be relevant and could influence the text. If they refused, no resolution would be placed before them to vote on. Armed action would take place and the Council would have been irrelevant.

If such reasoning were, indeed, followed, it ignored the possibility that other members of the Council might be unwilling to become relevant only by saying yes to the U.S. It was surely not this kind of relevance that the Council of European Foreign Ministers had had in mind when, in a statement on January 27, they had stressed the role of the Security Council. They did not rule out that force might have to be used at some stage, but they saw the Council as the forum in which the world should come together, pool its thinking, adjust to one another and decide on a joint course of action and the timing for it.

The U.S. legal position that there was no need for Council endorsement of armed action was rejected by many. It conflicted, in particular, with an understanding that the French had carried with them from the negotiations on the November resolution: that there would have to be a report by the inspectors on non-compliance by Iraq before any serious action would be considered, and that the use of armed force required a Council decision.

To the UK government, with a large part of its public opinion opposed to armed action, endorsement by the Security Council had high priority, though it was not stated to be indispensable. Not surprisingly, the UK was the Council member that tried the hardest to create a consensus and get a resolution endorsing armed action.

At UNMOVIC we were aware that a "war of necessity"— responding to a case of clear-cut aggression, like that of Iraq's occupation of Kuwait in 1990—can be launched individually or collectively without prior approval of the Security Council. Would the U.S. claim that it had slowly prepared for a war of necessity, or would it assert that it had unfettered freedom to make a "war of choice" against potential, uncertain and perhaps distant threats?

How distant and dim could the mushroom cloud be that Condoleezza Rice talked about? A U.S. assertion of a broad license for
itself to decide unilaterally on preemptive strikes would certainly
lead other states to claim the same right and result in an erosion of
the UN Charter's restriction on the use of force.

What Constitutes a "Material Breach"
of the UN Resolutions?

Regardless of the significant political-legal questions about the need
for Security Council endorsement of armed action against Iraq,
there was a need for those who wanted to take action to demonstrate concretely to the public that Iraq actually violated the resolution in which it had been given a "last opportunity." The resolution
itself pointed to two main categories of violations, or "material
breaches": namely, omissions or false statements about its weapons
programs, and failures to comply with and fully cooperate "immediately, unconditionally, and actively" with UNMOVIC and the
IAEA. In both regards the Council could look to the inspectors for
reporting any non-compliance immediately. However, on no occasion did UNMOVIC or the IAEA submit any special report to the
Council.

Once on a TV program I was asked what in our view would
merit a report. Although it was clear to me that we would not submit special reports about trivial matters, I did not want my answer
to send the Iraqis any reassuring message that they could obstruct
even in minor ways without consequences. I answered that if an
inspection team en route is delayed by a flat tire on one of the minders' cars, it is an accident, but if there are two or three flat tires on the
same trip, it may be serious. But, said the TV anchor, where do you
draw the line? And I answered, "Somewhere between one and two."
It was a flippant response to a question which had no good short
answer, especially not one that the Iraqis could hear.

Of course, any number of things could have triggered a report
from us, but we did not want to try to define them in advance, nor

do I think that the Security Council would have liked to have special reports about the various hitches that could and did occur. Our difficulties in getting Iraqi cooperation were described without drama in general reports to the Council—written and oral, formal and informal. Now that we feel nearly certain that there were no weapons to hide in Iraq, the explanations for the Iraqi reluctance on these two categories of violations, as on many others, must be sought elsewhere than in a wish to hide weapons. At the time when we encountered and reported on the reluctance, it undoubtedly hurt the claim of the Iraqis that they were providing immediate cooperation. Why were they reluctant in these matters? Self-respect? Pride?

In January, the U.S. seemed to have concluded that any focusing on "smoking guns" was risky. In an article in *The Washington Post* on January 19, 2003, David Kay, who later in the year was appointed by the CIA to head the U.S. Iraq Survey Group, wrote:

When it comes to U.N. inspections in Iraq, looking for a smoking gun is a fool's mission. That was true 11 years ago when I led the UN inspections there. It is no less true today.

And:

The answer is already clear. Iraq is in breach of U.N. demands that it dismantle its weapons of mass destruction.

And:

Let's not give it more time to cheat and retreat.

These statements were amazing coming from someone who, as team leader for some IAEA inspections in 1991, aggressively looked for and proudly held up "smoking guns"—trucks with nuclear equipment and telling documents. Little did David Kay know in January 2003 that later in the year he himself would be frantically looking for more smoking guns.

It was further argued—by Paul Wolfowitz—that the inspectors were not investigators and that they could only perform spot checks. Iraq should declare everything and the inspectors should only have to verify. This was true in the sense that Iraq had the duty to present all sites, facilities and data for the inspectors to verify, but the point was also disingenuous. It underestimated the capability of well-prepared inspections and interrogations, carried out by professionals with state-of-the-art equipment, supported by intelligence and entitled to go anywhere. Limiting inspections to spot-checking would not make use of their capability to verify the correctness and the completeness of what is presented to them through analysis of satellite pictures and other overhead images, surprise visits to non-declared sites identified by intelligence, and analysis of soil, water or biota samples using the most advanced methods.

Two other interlinked lines of argument had been pursued by the U.S. ahead of the January 27 update: Iraq did not provide the "immediate, unconditional and active cooperation" required. Iraq had not taken a high-level "strategic decision" to disarm as South Africa once did; it had not shown a "change of heart." The incomplete and allegedly inaccurate declaration of December 8 was used as an illustration. Nevertheless, while rejecting any need for a "smoking gun" to find Iraq in "material breach," the U.S. and UK realized that to convince the public and the world that Iraq deserved to be brought to order by armed action, they needed to show concrete cases of violations—preferably smoking guns.

Colin Powell's Presentation of Intelligence in the Security Council

It fell to U.S. secretary of state Colin Powell to present concrete cases of Iraq's violations and continued cheating to the Security Council and the world. There were precedents for such a presentation. The pictures which Adlai Stevenson, then U.S. representative to the UN, had shown the Security Council in 1962 during the Cuban missile crisis had been a great success and had convinced the world. Another case—with which I was very familiar—had played out in the Board of Governors of the IAEA in 1994, when we showed American satellite images revealing concealed installations at the North Korean nuclear center in Yongbyon.

It has been reported that Colin Powell struggled several days with the CIA about what material to include in his presentation, and that he had rejected a great deal as not sufficiently convincing. What remained must have been the best that they could release. It was delivered with bravura by a man who during a long and distinguished military career must have had many more opportunities than ambassadors do to use PowerPoint when briefing demanding audiences.

Almost a week before his day in the Council, Colin Powell was kind enough to phone me about the briefing. He said he would show what we needed to see. It was not a "determinant" briefing, however, and there would be no targets for inspection. The U.S. continued to support our work. They would judge the reaction in the Security Council and ask the UN for a time limit. I took this to mean an ultimatum to Iraq to come clean or face armed intervention. His words to me were similar to messages sent to the public, intended to downplay expectations for his briefing. These signals were all in vain. On February 5 the Council chamber was packed with diplomats and media watching Powell and two huge screens and waiting, once again, for smoking guns.

As I listened to Powell (with the CIA chief, George Tenet, sitting behind him) and as I watched the pictures and heard the tapes he played, I did not feel the discomfort that I later realized would have been natural. I thought the cases he described were interesting and that they would all need to be examined critically by our experts. There were some taped conversations alleged to be of Iraqi officials, illustrating how items had been removed and how telling instructions were to be eliminated—all intended to convince us that Iraq still possessed nerve agents. I found myself wondering about the authenticity of the conversations. Where did the tapes come from? From U.S. electronic eavesdropping? From the Iraqi opposition?

Before I accepted any of it as evidence of the existence of weapons of mass destruction, I felt I would need to know more. Since the occupation of Iraq, I have not seen any discussion of these tapes.

I felt more like an impartial judge looking at evidence submitted than like a junior prosecutor who has failed to find the evidence that his senior has laid his hands on. What blissfully did not occur to me during Powell's presentation was that although he had kindly said to me that the U.S. supported the inspections, the administration was now using him and drawing on his credibility to show the world what it "needed to see"—and what the inspectors had purportedly not seen. I had stated our conclusion that Iraq had not yet "genuinely accepted disarmament" but, at the same time, I had said our reports did not assert that weapons of mass destruction definitely remained in Iraq. The U.S. now made that assertion and hoped it would be accepted in the U.S. and around the world, together with a time limit after which armed action could be taken. If this was the "discrediting" of the inspectors, which Vice President Cheney had talked about to me and Mohamed ElBaradei, it was delivered implicitly and in a courteous manner.

The Russians wrote in an analysis that the American information did not square with the picture they had from years of UN and IAEA inspection work in Iraq. They suggested that the information needed detailed study, in the first instance by UNMOVIC and the IAEA. They further questioned the validity of a number of the cases, including the allegation that Iraq had mobile facilities for producing biological weapons. They knew from their own experience about the difficulties of such mobile units. I note that after the war some trucks were seized and it was first declared that they could not be anything but the suspected mobile bioweapons units. Soon that claim collapsed and most experts agreed that the function of the trucks was to produce hydrogen for weather balloons—which was what the Iraqi officials had been saying.

Much of the material in Powell's presentation had been made available to us by the U.S. and other countries. We had inspected most of the sites he described and taken samples from them for analysis that could detect traces of chemical or biological agents, if there were any. We had examined records and interviewed people at these sites. In no case had we found convincing evidence of any prohibited activity. The "decontamination" trucks which U.S. image analysts thought they had identified and had linked to the movement of chemical weapons shortly before an inspection could, in the view of our experts, just as well have been water trucks, which we had seen at the same site. Moreover, they could have been on the sites many days before our inspectors came, not just before the inspectors' arrival.

A "truck caravan" near a "biological weapons related facility" two days before inspections resumed could, in the analysis of our experts, have been connected with a seasonal delivery of vaccines, which we knew were stored in large quantities at this site for use throughout Iraq. The site had not in the past been associated with the production of biological weapons agents but with the storage of seed stock. Our inspections at the site showed there were no fermentors, which would have been indispensable to the production of biological agents.

One picture showed a ballistic missile factory where, two days before inspections began, five large cargo trucks had turned up to move missiles. UNMOVIC had visited this site four times since November 2002. It was the place where Iraq assembled its Al Samoud 2 missiles, and the activity reported by the U.S. appeared consistent with what Iraq had declared. Had we been asked by the U.S., we could have requested to see the shipping records for the relevant time. UNMOVIC concluded later in February that the Al Samoud 2 had a range that exceeded the limit set by the Security Council and ordered their destruction. At the time when the satellites had seen them being moved onto cargo trucks, they had not yet been declared proscribed.

Colin Powell did not include the allegation that President Bush had made only a few days earlier before Congress, that Iraq had sought to buy uranium from Africa. Had he been warned about the suspicions—later confirmed—that it was based on a forged document? He did, however, mention the case of aluminum tubes alleged to be intended for the construction of centrifuges for the enrichment of uranium. After analysis in the U.S. and by the IAEA there remained very little, if any, credibility in this case.

How solid was the evidence presented by the secretary of state to prove that Iraq retained weapons of mass destruction and thus was in material breach of the Council resolution calling for "serious consequences"? Some skeptical voices were heard almost immediately, and nearly a year later it is hard to avoid the reflection that Colin Powell had been charged with the thankless task of hauling out the smoking guns that in January were said to be irrelevant and that, after March, turned out to be nonexistent.

The Value, Use and Weaknesses of Intelligence

Several countries, including the U.S., had given us a good number of sites for possible inspection, and at none of the many sites we actually inspected had we found any prohibited activity. The sites we had been given were supposedly the best that the various intelligence agencies could give. This shocked me. If this was the best, what was the rest? Well, I could not exclude the possibility that there was solid non–site related intelligence that was not shared with us, and which conclusively showed that Iraq still had weapons of mass destruction. But could there be 100-percent certainty about the existence of weapons of mass destruction but zero-percent knowledge about their location?

I had not jumped to a conclusion that no WMD existed, but experience from the inspections and the examination of Colin Powell's cases made me feel obliged to say some words of caution in the Security Council about the evidence that had been coming from intelligence.

I recognized that there is a risk that intelligence agencies read more into the material than there is. If they fail to report something that later turns out to pose a danger or result in disaster, they will be faulted. If they overreport, on the other hand, they are not likely to be criticized. There is a further risk that the intelligence reports will not be read with sufficiently critical eyes by the policy- and decision-makers. A court will closely scrutinize the evidence supplied by a prosecutor before it sentences someone to jail. Could one be sure that governments would examine intelligence as critically before armed action was ordered against some target? There had been troubling mistakes. The U.S. bombing of the Chinese embassy in Belgrade in May 1999 had been one. Another was the U.S. cruise missiles fired in August 1998 on a Khartoum chemical factory that was erroneously thought to be linked with Al Qaeda. Was there not a risk in the current situation that governments convinced—for not implausible reasons—about the existence of elusive weapons in Iraq would identify some on the slightest of grounds?

I recognized, in all humility, that while inspectors only have to find out, analyze and report factually, governments often have to take action and cannot always allow themselves the luxury of waiting until the factual and analytical basis for decisions is complete and certain. If they do, their action might come too late, as Condoleezza Rice had said in a speech. Nevertheless, when the decisions are about war and peace, one would expect the governments of the most powerful and best-equipped states to have mechanisms and procedures in place to ensure some quality control over the material that experts prepare for them. One would expect that these governments themselves, at the very least, would examine the material with critical minds and common sense.

New York–London–Vienna

In our joint letter accepting the invitation to Baghdad, ElBaradei and I had written that the meeting would be of value if Iraq used it as an opportunity to show us and the Security Council that it was determined to tackle the unresolved disarmament issues. We made our view clear that outstanding questions of process, like the unimpeded use of U-2 and other surveillance planes, really ought to be solved even before we arrived.

Quickly meeting our known requests rather than bickering over them and grudgingly going along with them would have been the best course of action for the Iraqi side. Regrettably, it was not taken.

The day before Colin Powell presented his intelligence brief to the Security Council, I had told the UN Press Club that it was five minutes to midnight. His presentation made the clock tick louder. Having listened to it in the morning of February 5, I left New York for London in an increasingly charged atmosphere. With me were three people: my special assistant, Torkel Stiernlöf; our manager of media relations, Ewen Buchanan; and our UN security man, Eric Brownwell. We were now governed by security and so much in the spotlight that British Airways checked us in at their Concorde lounge. This enabled us to have dinner on the ground and use more time in the plane for sleeping. We got five hours sleep before we landed at London Heathrow, where I could shave and change. We were then taken via the Foreign Office to Downing Street, where I joined ElBaradei.

In our meetings with Tony Blair and Jack Straw, the British foreign secretary, I could not detect any trace of the critical tone about our trip to Baghdad that had come out of the recent Bush-Blair meeting in Washington. We were all aware of the need for Iraq urgently to do more to present any remaining weapons and/or provide evidence accounting for them. It was too late in the day for the Iraqis to practice brinkmanship and bazaar bargaining. I thought one reason why Blair had invited us to stop for a few hours might have been to strengthen our hand in Baghdad by showing that we had political support for our mission, as well as to convey to the English public some sense of restraint before committing to a military solution.

At the luncheon that followed with Foreign Office and intelligence people, we learned that the British were drafting a resolution that would demand action by Iraq before a specific date. In case such action was not forthcoming, the resolution would implicitly—but not directly—authorize armed force.

After lunch Mohamed took a plane directly for Cyprus while I took one for his city of residence, Vienna. Despite the time pressure, I wanted to give a lecture to the participants in our seventh general training course for inspectors, which was taking place there. I had addressed all the prior courses and I did not want to miss one. By stopping in Vienna and spending two hours with our trainees at this critical time, I wanted to impress upon them how vital I felt the role and conduct of the individual inspector was and how important it was that they acted in such a way as to be both professionally effective and correct. I reminded them that they would work for the Security Council of the United Nations, and not for any individual state.

On the flight from London to Vienna I happened to meet and have a long conversation with the foreign minister of Iran, Dr. Kamal Kharrazi, mainly about the idea of a Middle East zone free of weapons of mass destruction. He said Iran had launched the concept of a nuclear-weapon-free zone long ago and was still in favor of it. I said I thought that the zone, which had been explicitly included in several resolutions about Iraq, should be on the political agenda of peace in the Middle East. The region needed to move to détente and a regime with very effective inspection. I also said that it was in the interest of Iran to accept the additional protocol to the agreement on nuclear inspections.

Our conversation gave me a wild idea. Iraq was asked to be "proactive." Rather than appearing to accept disarmament reluctantly, which did not help them, should it not be in the Iraqis' interest to embrace disarmament in a positive, dynamic way? Of course, the most important and central act would be to present any weapons that might exist, or else evidence of their absence. Could there not be some other visible steps in the disarmament sphere? Could Iraq not come up with a package comprising, say, the long overdue Iraqi legislation prohibiting all citizens from engaging in any production, storing or acquisition of weapons of mass destruction; ratification of the Chemical Weapons Convention, which Iraq had not yet accepted; and acceptance of the IAEA Additional Protocol to the nuclear safeguards agreement? As the Security Council inspection regime was far more rigorous on nuclear and chemical weapons than the additional protocol and the regular inspections under the Chemical Weapons Convention, the Iraqi steps would not for the time being create any new obligations, but they might show goodwill and would constitute a voluntary acceptance of lasting treaty regimes. I talked to my assistant, Torkel, about it and decided to test the idea on Mohamed.

Vienna–Larnaca–Baghdad

After my stopover in Vienna and my meeting with our inspectors-in-training, I arrived late Friday evening at Larnaca and went to see Mohamed at his hotel, where I shared my wild thoughts with him. He promptly shot down the whole beautiful package. It would all look like diversionary maneuvers to distract from the main task, he warned. Perhaps he was right. In the current charged atmosphere such a package might be greeted with scorn, and it might be said that it was no business of inspectors to delve into such schemes. I dropped the idea and agreed with Mohamed to tell the Iraqis that they needed to do drastic things—not so much assuming obligations for the future as implementing existing ones.

On two occasions later I have wondered whether the idea was so terribly wrong. The first was in the early days of March, when, on the brink of war, the British suggested in informal Security Council talks a resolution demanding that Saddam Hussein make a televised speech in which he wholeheartedly embraced disarmament and agreed speedily to fulfill five concrete disarmament tasks. The second occasion was in December 2003, when Colonel Qaddafi of Libya declared with some fanfare that his country would do away with all efforts to acquire weapons of mass destruction and accept inspection and disarmament commitments to which it had not up till then committed itself. The negotiations with Qaddafi about this package, it was said, had started already in March, with the British taking the lead. I asked myself what would have happened if I had had the idea about Iraq a little earlier and tested it on Tony Blair and Jack Straw in London. Perhaps they, or someone like Amr Moussa, the secretary general of the League of Arab States, could have made use of it. Mohamed had probably been right that I would have been criticized if I had taken it up in Baghdad, but it could conceivably have been a scheme at the governmental level. Considering that Iraq nearly certainly did not have any weapons and that Saddam might have felt that a spectacular scheme could give him a dignified way out of his corner and a feather in his cap, he might have gone along. Who knows?

Baghdad Talks, February 8–9

We arrived in Baghdad midday on Saturday, February 8, and spent the whole afternoon at the Iraqi Foreign Ministry, in talks with Dr. Al Sa'adi, who was assisted by a large delegation including General Hussam Amin, the head of the National Monitoring Directorate.

At our opening session we said that the clocks of Resolution 1441 were ticking fast and loud. A "no" to war must be based on a firm "yes" to inspections. While there were differences in the Security Council, all members wanted to see more cooperation by Iraq. The U.S. was convinced that Iraq retained not only chemical but also biological weapons. On the suspicion that Iraq might have smallpox agents in its arsenal, the U.S. was now making plans for the vaccination of U.S. health workers. The French were suggesting a drastic increase and broadening of inspections.

For our part, we continued our buildup of inspections—e.g., by setting up field offices. We reminded the Iraqis that we had not asserted that there were still weapons of mass destruction in Iraq but also had not excluded it. Iraq had to stop belittling the unresolved disarmament issues as they had done in January, and start addressing them seriously. They knew what the most important issues were and they knew that they would need to submit evidence on them and discuss them with our experts. Our high-level meeting was not for such discussions, but we had brought experts who would be ready to listen. Perhaps the December declaration, which had not given very much, should be given a supplement?

I think Dr. Al Sa'adi understood that we were at a critical moment and did what he could, but was restrained by his instructions. He probably also felt that his team was not being treated fairly, that we had not taken in all the information they had supplied. He began the talks with detailed oral explanations on some of the central issues: anthrax, VX and missiles. He also presented documents with new analysis—but no new evidence. He noted correctly that it had been recognized by UNSCOM that Iraq had disposed of chemical and biological agents by pouring them into the ground in the summer of 1991. Unwisely, he said, this disposal had been undertaken without the presence of international inspectors, and all the records had been destroyed. This was why they had been deemed "unaccounted for" by UNSCOM and UNMOVIC. The Iraqi side had given much thought to how one could now scientifically try to assess the quantities of the agents disposed of. There existed modern techniques that could be employed for this purpose, but they required sophisticated equipment Iraq did not possess. Some preliminary investigations had nevertheless been undertaken by the Iraqis and were promising. Could we help to procure the equipment needed and make a joint effort? His teams were ready to speak to our experts.

Al Sa'adi's suggestion this time did not sound like the request for modern radar, which had been made earlier, ostensibly to facilitate safe U-2 flights. The new suggestion could be discussed with our team of experts, which comprised the three key disciplines of biology, chemistry and missile technology. They had been following our talks from the back benches. In the evening, when the Iraqi foreign minister, Naji Sabri, invited the front-benchers for a traditional dinner of grilled Tigris fish, Baghdad kebab and—for the infidels—wine, our experts studied the new documents. The following morning they met for discussions with their Iraqi counterparts, who included the famous Dr. Rihab Taha—nicknamed "Dr. Germ" and wife of Iraq's oil minister, General Amer Mohammad Rasheed. Before we sat down for our plenary session, our experts gave us a rather favorable report. The discussions had been very professional and had shed some new light, but had not really brought any new evidence. Our experts did not want to decline the suggested methods of assessing quantities of agents disposed of, but they were not hopeful. I had my doubts, too. If you pour one hundred liters of milk into the ground, is it likely that ten years later any sophisticated instruments can help you to assess and confirm that quantity by analyzing samples of the earth? Were the Iraqis desperately trying to find answers to open issues or were they just throwing dust in our eyes?

On other fronts the questions were more straightforward. Thus, we were given more extensive briefings than in January about the production of Al Samoud 2 and Al Fatah missiles. Iraq had itself reported test flights exceeding the range limits set by the Security Council, and we had already ordered that the test flights be stopped. The Iraqis probably sensed that we might proceed to order the destruction of missiles as violating the UN restrictions and wanted to supply us with their best arguments against destruction. They also proposed joint testing. We did not respond to the idea.

The special Iraqi commission appointed to search for any remaining chemical weapons warheads had had its mandate expanded to cover any prohibited items, we were told. A second commission, with the task of searching for documents and headed by General Rasheed, had now been added. It was welcome and of potential importance—if the action was serious and not cosmetic. In retrospect I note that it never reported any findings.

We discussed the issue of interviews of witnesses and experts and were given new assurances that the Iraqi authorities would "encourage" people to appear for interviews without minders and tape recorders. I repeated that if they could not come up with documents, interviews could be of great value, provided they were made in circumstances which allowed them to be credible. I also told Dr. Al Sa'adi during a tea break that we were planning to ask people to come for interviews outside Iraq and that we were making arrangements for these to be held in Larnaca.

Amazingly, the question of the U-2 flights, rather than being solved before our arrival, remained unsolved during and even after the meeting. It had been on the table since October. Dr. Al Sa'adi clearly had no instructions allowing him to move.

Mohamed ElBaradei had again suggested through various channels that we should meet with President Saddam Hussein. I never asked him which channels he used—whether it might have been the Iraqi ambassador in Vienna. I always felt somewhat ambivalent about the idea. Saddam regarded himself as the emperor of Mesopotamia and probably saw us as insignificant international civil servants, whose requests he might or might not assent to. But we were there neither to plead with him nor to negotiate. What could we do? Read the Security Council resolutions to him? I did not like the idea of meeting him and perhaps coming out empty-handed. The problem did not arise as Mohamed's request was, again, ignored.

We were received instead by Vice President Ramadan in the drab and dull reception room of a huge palace. A short man in uniform with a revolver in his belt and a beret on his head, Ramadan gave the impression of an old revolutionary, hardly intellectual but clear-headed and self-controlled. He thought my updating of the Security Council on January 27 had been unfair, but his tone was civil all the way through: "You must do what you think is right," he said. He seemed to believe that Iraq had reason to complain about the visit of our inspectors to a mosque (discussed in chapter 4) and he asserted that inspectors were asking inappropriate questions. Yet, Iraq would continue to cooperate. I said the situation was very tense. We needed results urgently. Our inspectors were no spies, and the Iraqi authorities ought to know this.

ElBaradei addressed him in Arabic and said Iraq should show eagerness about inspection, which was the peaceful way to disarmament. It was incomprehensible that they had not yet adopted the internal legislation that was required. Ramadan replied that legislation takes time. Mohamed noted that they had had thirteen years. I did not have the feeling we were dealing with a man of power. Dr. Al Sa'adi clearly looked to him for instructions and authorizations, but the vice president acted and argued on the instructions of Saddam Hussein. Ramadan gave us no indication that Iraq could or would do anything new. They had no weapons. They suspected some inspection work was linked to espionage, but they would continue to work with us. If they were attacked, they would defend themselves.

We also met with a group of officials sent by the South African government to talk to the Iraqis about the successful experience they had had of carrying out internationally verified nuclear disarmament. This was friendly advice, but it did not seem to change anything in the Iraqi attitudes.

What was there for us to report at the press conference? We had not agreed with the Iraqi side on any joint statement to the media. That could have looked like a "crisis solved," and this was certainly not the case. We did not want to appear naïve. We had obtained much less than we felt was needed and had to be careful in our summing up. Our overall impression from the meeting was that our Iraqi counterparts across the table were genuinely rattled. If, in fact, they had no weapons or evidence to deliver, they had at any rate realized that most of the outside world thought they had both and that they simply looked defiant talking about "so-called disarmament issues." They had focused on the central issues and provided further oral and written explanations about them. They had not supplied new evidence but they had proposed new (though not very hopeful) scientific methods to verify their declared past unilateral destruction of chemical and biological weapons.

The two Iraqi commissions appointed could prove of value—if they had not been set up just to create an impression. The U-2 and national legislation were matters that had been on the agenda for a long time and which we had thought Iraq should have been able to thrash out before our arrival. Yet, on these we could only report expectations for early action, not results. That was miserable. The Iraqis continued doing too little, too late.

We reported the specifics, such as they were, to the media. Like last time there were hundreds of journalists, but unlike the unorganized and chaotic encounters with crowds of Iraqi journalists, this one was orderly and kept under control by our press officers. The questions did not, I thought, reflect a sense that the game was over, but dealt rather with what progress had been made. We mentioned some but were careful to sound neither very optimistic nor in despair. ElBaradei put it well when he said that we needed "drastic change" and that we'd begun to see a "change of heart." I voiced "cautious optimism," but in reply to a question I said there had "not been a breakthrough." I took the opportunity to correct a mistake we had made: When we had found the twelve chemical warheads discussed earlier, we had said they were in a bunker built after 1991. The implication was that the warheads must have been moved there at a time when they were prohibited by the Security Council and so should have been surrendered. We had since learned, I said, that the store in which the warheads were found was actually from the pre–Gulf War period and the possibility was not excluded that the warheads had been there since then. I thought it was necessary to clarify our mistake, not only out of fairness but also for our own credibility.

We left Baghdad for Larnaca on the morning of February 10. There we got the latest press surveys and read them on the plane to Athens. We saw that Ari Fleischer, the White House press secretary, had said that time was running out. From Athens, Mohamed went back to IAEA headquarters in Vienna while I caught a direct Delta flight to New York. During the flights from Baghdad and Athens I realized that all the publicity was making my face known. The flight attendants asked for my autograph. I was also called to the cockpit during the Delta flight to receive a call through which we set up a meeting with Condoleezza Rice in New York for the next day.

The captain told me that he had flown U-2 planes. He was sure the Iraqi air defenses could not reach them. If this was right, why did the Iraqis delay green-lighting the U-2 flights and allow themselves to appear uncooperative? Did Saddam Hussein have such difficulty swallowing his own pride, or had his advisers not been able to tell him that it was too late in the day for any foot-dragging? My report to the Council was due only four days later. As I arrived in New York the green light for the U-2 flights flashed from Baghdad, at long last.

Condoleezza Rice, February 11:
The Issue Is Quickly Coming to an End

On the day after my return to New York I went first to the Pierre Hotel to brief the Australian prime minister, John Howard. He'd come from Washington and agreed with the U.S. administration's line of reasoning regarding Iraq. He listened kindly to my briefing and the hope I voiced for assurance of Iraqi disarmament through inspection, but appeared convinced that the Iraqis were cheating.

From the Pierre I walked down to the U.S. mission where, like last time, I met Condoleezza Rice in Ambassador John Negroponte's office. He, too, was in attendance, as was John Wolf, the assistant secretary of state for non-proliferation. The conversation lasted about an hour, and we began with the U-2. I told Rice that it was my understanding that the acceptance was without conditions, and that we would like to start the flights as soon as possible. From the Baghdad meeting I reported that we detected a more serious effort to cooperate actively, but we could not exclude that it was part of a dilatory tactic. The documents we had received were of interest, but they did not constitute evidence.

I went on to say that I had not been "terribly impressed" by the intelligence that had been provided by member states so far. By now UNMOVIC had been to a number of the sites indicated by intelligence tips and only one had proved of relevance to the commission's mandate. I said I planned to mention this fact in my presentation to the Security Council at the end of the week. Rice responded that intelligence quickly goes cold. The U.S. was not withholding any intelligence from us, but intelligence was no substitute for what Iraq needed to do voluntarily. It was Iraq that was on trial, not intelligence. She said further that the aim of Resolution 1441 had been to force Iraq to make a strategic decision to disarm, but that Saddam was continuing a "process game." He could not be allowed to get away with that. The Security Council had an obligation to uphold its own resolutions. Regrettably, the Council showed signs of a weakening resolve. The issue was "quickly coming to an end." It was now three minutes to midnight. In response to my question whether there would be a new resolution in the Council, Rice said it was being considered and had not been excluded. In conclusion, she said the U.S. was well aware of the need to protect UN personnel in Iraq—a signal that advice about the withdrawal of inspectors, at least American inspectors, might come.

Rice did not seek to influence me in respect to the report I was to give four days later. Nor did she in any way discourage me from talking about the shortcomings in intelligence which I had mentioned. I was therefore surprised when, one day after our talk, *The Washington Post* carried an article which contained the following:

> National security adviser Condoleezza Rice flew to New York this morning to press chief U.N. weapons inspector Hans Blix to acknowledge in a Security Council briefing Friday that Iraq has failed voluntarily to scrap its prohibited chemical, biological and nuclear weapons programs, according to U.S. and U.N. diplomats. . . .
>
> Rice's unannounced meeting with Blix underscored the Bush administration's concern that the Swedish diplomat's report to the Council on Friday, while critical of Iraq, may not be decisive enough to persuade wavering Security Council members to support an immediate move to war.
>
> Sources said Blix's report will be much briefer than the one he gave to the Council on Jan. 27 and that, as of today, will not contain a declaration that Iraq is in clear violation of its obligations, which the United States has sought.

I had not talked to media after our meeting, but it is quite possible that some people in Washington worried that my statement to the Security Council three days later would not do anything to tip the hesitating members toward a resolution authorizing armed force. The article did not actually say that Rice had pressed me, only that she had flown to New York *to* press me. If she did have that intention or someone thought she had it, she did not carry it out. Did the article perhaps express what some other people in Washington wished her to do? Did it knowingly ignore what had happened and deliberately seek to create a false impression to somebody's liking? Was this manipulation? Spin created by someone in campaign mode? How could the paper say anything about the length and contents of my speech when not even a first draft of the statement had been written? I wrote some parts of it in the afternoon after my meeting with Rice, but most of it was written on Thursday and was not ready until 11 p.m., less than twelve hours before it was delivered in the Council.

That *Post* article had also contained some statements from Colin Powell to the Senate Budget Committee. Maybe he had even said what in the paper was attributed to him and put within quotation marks:

> It is clear that a moment of truth is coming with respect to Iraq and with respect to the Security Council, as to whether it will meet its responsibilities. This is not just an academic exercise or the United States being in a fit of pique. We're talking about real weapons. We are talking about anthrax. We are talking about botulinum toxin. We're talking about nuclear weapons programs.

Rereading the statement many months after the war, one can still agree that the affair was not academic. But while a "fit of pique" may not be an appropriate label, it's clear that the U.S. determination to take on Iraq was not triggered by anything Iraq did, but by the wounds inflicted by Al Qaeda. The assertive references to "real weapons," "anthrax," "botulinum toxin" and "nuclear weapons programs," which were perhaps effective rhetoric when they were made, today—after the "moment of truth"—are sad reminders of failed intelligence. One might also wonder whether the Security Council did not, in fact, "meet its responsibilities" when, despite tremendous political pressure, a majority of the members showed that the Council was against the draft resolution that was being prepared to give a green light to immediate war. They showed this so clearly that the sponsors chose not to put the resolution to the vote.

Other Signals

Other actors on the world stage sent other signals at this juncture. The French circulated a so-called non-paper, which is the diplomatic term for a proposal tossed up in the air to see if it has a chance of flying. The French foreign minister, Mr. Villepin, had advanced most of the ideas of the non-paper already in earlier discussions in the Security Council. As an alternative to armed action, the non-paper advocated a further beefing up of the inspection regime. The number of inspectors could be doubled. New security units could monitor certain suspicious sites. Convoys of trucks could be stopped systematically and aerial surveillance could be increased. The flow of intelligence from national agencies to a new inspection center could be stepped up. UNMOVIC and the IAEA could list all unresolved disarmament issues in order of priority, and there could be a coordinator for disarmament in Baghdad reporting to myself and ElBaradei.

On one point I courteously and sincerely expressed support for the French non-paper: inspections of road traffic. We needed to do something about the allegations that Iraq was moving weapons of mass destruction around the country and that it had mobile biological weapons production units. We were, in fact, trying to develop concepts for such inspections, but the advice we had received from police organizations had not been practical.

I saw the French ideas chiefly as a desperate effort to avoid just saying no to the U.S. drive to war, and instead to introduce something that might look like a positive alternative. We had built up our organization very fast and had ignored U.S. suggestions two months earlier to double the number of inspectors. The U.S. was scornful about the French proposals, although they went in the direction the U.S. had advocated earlier. Time had passed. For the U.S., the inspection phase was coming to an end.

Kofi Annan's Plea

On February 8, while Mohamed and I were still talking in Baghdad, UN secretary general Kofi Annan had made a reasoned plea for a continued multilateral approach to the Iraqi issue. All, and foremost the leaders of Iraq, had a duty to prevent war if we possibly could, Annan said. The UN founders were not pacifists. They had given the organization strong enforcement rights and those had, indeed, been used when Iraq invaded Kuwait in 1991. This lesson remained relevant. Iraq had not yet satisfied the Security Council that it had fully disarmed itself of weapons of mass destruction. However, this was an issue not for any one state but for the international community as a whole.

Almost as if he foresaw the debate that would come soon about "wars of necessity" and "wars of choice," Annan went on:

> When states decide to use force, not in self-defense but to deal with broader threats to international peace and security, there is no substitute for the unique legitimacy provided by the United Nations Security Council. States and peoples around the world attach fundamental importance to such legitimacy, and to the international rule of law.

As an example of such a broader threat he mentioned the horror posed by weapons of mass destruction—by no means confined to Iraq—and said that only a collective, multilateral approach can effectively curb the proliferation of these weapons. Under Resolution 1441, Iraq had been given a last chance. If it failed to make use of it and continued its defiance, the Council would have to make another grim choice, "based on the findings of the inspectors." He was not, as I read him, advocating a passive line, nor even opposing preemptive action, but rather speaking against *unilateral* action and in favor of common action and some patience: "When that time comes," he said, "the Council must face up to its responsibilities." I could not have agreed more. As a servant of the Security Council I could not say these things, so I was glad that Kofi Annan stood up and did so, and put it so well. I was also no pacifist and did not want to see the inspections go on year after year in the way that had happened in the 1990s, but it was, in my view, too early to give up now. When I had been asked by the press in Baghdad about a statement by Bush that "the game is up," I had replied, "We are still in the game." That was true, but the president was the one who called the shots.

Preparing the Statement for the Security Council Meeting on Friday, February 14, 2003

My schedule was so full during the days before the meeting that I hardly had time to be awed by the increasing tension and attention. During the three days between my return from Baghdad on Monday afternoon and the Council meeting on Friday morning, there were the meetings on Tuesday which I have mentioned, with Prime Minister Howard of Australia and with Condoleezza Rice. I also had to chair a special half-day session of UNMOVIC's advisory group, the College of Commissioners, to which we reported about our discussions in Baghdad and to attend a meeting of outside experts which we had arranged in New York to assist us in the assessment of the Iraqi missile program. That meeting gave us assessment and advice that led us to request that Iraq destroy its Al Samoud 2 missiles.

The drafting of what would possibly be the most important statement of my life to the Security Council had to be done between these various commitments and during late evenings.

It was true, as the London *Times* correspondent James Bone reported, that I had begun some drafting in longhand on the plane on the way back from Baghdad, but it was more a list of points than a text and was not, as he wrongly guessed, in Swedish. The heavy work was done during the three days we had in New York. Mr. Bone rightly guessed that I would avoid uttering the words "material breach," which, in his assessment, would "spell the end for President Saddam Hussein." He knew from many comments I had made to the media that I insisted it was up to the Security Council to make that determination. Indeed, the Council had instructed me to "report immediately" any "interference by Iraq with inspection activities" and any "failure" to comply with its disarmament obligations. It had quite naturally and clearly reserved for itself the task of assessing whether the interference or failure reported amounted to a "material breach."

As we had not submitted any special reports about Iraqi interferences or failures, it was not surprising that with the hardening positions for and against armed action, the principal parties in the Council examined my reports in detail for any support they could find. The more nuanced these reports were, the more credibility they had—but the less they lent themselves as support for categorical judgments.

8

Search for a Middle Road: Benchmarks?

Security Council Meeting on February 14, 2003

At the special meeting of the Security Council on Friday, February 14, almost all member states were represented by their foreign ministers, including Colin Powell of the U.S., Jack Straw of the UK, Dominique de Villepin of France, Russia's Igor Ivanov and China's Tang Jiaxuan. The German foreign minister, Joschka Fischer, chaired the meeting. It was open to the press and the public, which also meant that it was open for the members of the Council to address the whole world, including their domestic constituents. Probably all governments represented knew in what direction they wanted events to go and were eager to present arguments to justify their positions and, if possible, influence others.

The Council chamber was packed with diplomats from the missions. The world's media were all there, and the sidewalks outside the UN were filled with trucks that carried huge discs for transmitting to every corner of the planet. To avoid being caught by the media, who would ambush me anytime they got the chance, I was taken into the building by car through the garage. Our press officer, Ewen Buchanan, had not had much sleep for all the media phoning him during the night. He now received an e-mail, call or fax every minute or so and tried to be evenhanded between countries and between big and small media. On the ground floor I walked between lines of press people on my way to the Council chamber and told them that I would speak in the Council—not before.

It was as if the decision whether there would be war in Iraq was to be taken in the next hour in the Council, and as if the inspectors' reports on Iraq's cooperation were like a signal of red or green. Although neither was the case, it was a very important meeting.

Mohamed ElBaradei and I were called by the president to take our seats at one end of the horseshoe-shaped table and to introduce the discussion. I have often been asked if I was nervous, with the whole world listening and watching. I was not; nor, I believe, was Mohamed. You do not feel the cameras or microphones in the distant glass boxes but concentrate on the president who gives you the floor and the participants whom you address. In informal meetings of the Council I would often have to speak without a written text, but this was a public meeting with records, and I did not plan to digress. It was the writing of the speech, not the delivery of it, that was difficult. In a Swedish interview I was later asked why my suit was wrinkled, when the whole world was watching. It took me a while to find the answer: that it would have been worse if the speech had been wrinkled.

I began my statement by describing the inspection capability we had built up and how we were using it. I thought the members of the Council should know about the inspection tool that was at their disposal and which they could continue to deploy or decide to discard. I then told the Council that UNMOVIC had not found any weapons of mass destruction, only a small number of empty chemical munitions. There were no smoking guns to report. Another matter—and one of equal significance, I said—was that many prohibited weapons and other items were "not accounted for."

I went on to say:

One must not jump to the conclusion that they exist. However, that possibility is also not excluded. If they exist, they should be presented for destruction. If they do not exist, credible evidence to that effect should be presented.

Many national intelligence agencies were convinced, I said, that prohibited weapons and programs existed in Iraq, and I would not take issue with their conclusions. They had many sources of information that were not available to us. I noted the good working relations UNMOVIC had with various intelligence services but also noted, significantly, that UNMOVIC had not found any prohibited item at any of the sites suggested by intelligence agencies.

As the inspection authority of the Security Council, we would only base our reports on evidence that we could, ourselves, examine and present publicly. "Without evidence," I said, "confidence cannot arise." This remark was primarily directed to the Iraqis, who had failed to present credible evidence in support of their contention that items unaccounted for had been destroyed or had never existed. It was equally relevant, however, to the U.S., UK and others who had affirmed that Iraq retained weapons and other prohibited items—affirmations which have been the subject of a melting process that began long before the Council meeting and has continued ever since.

I went on to comment on one of the cases that Colin Powell had talked about in his presentation to the Council. It concerned a site that was very familiar to us. As I described earlier, we had not drawn the conclusion from the material presented that there had been chemical weapons on the site just before the inspectors came to it. I had told Condoleezza Rice that I would voice reservations about intelligence, and she had not tried to discourage me from doing so. Colin Powell, to whom I spoke during the lunch break, did not seem at all offended by my comment. To judge by some media reactions, however, it was almost as if I had insulted the United States. They had wanted me to contribute arguments for war. Instead I had poured cold water on the U.S. case.

My major message to the Council was that Iraq had taken some steps that could be the beginning of active cooperation to solve substantive open disarmament issues. Even though my language was very guarded, my tone was less critical of Iraqi cooperation than it had been in my January 27 speech. I was often asked later why there was such a change in tone between the two speeches, and I used to explain that if you are asked to report about the weather, your reports must be different when the weather changes.

I ended my statement by responding to the question of how much more time we needed to complete our task in Iraq. I said that the resolutions envisaged two major tasks: inspection aimed at eliminating all possibly existing weapons and programs that had been prohibited in 1991, and monitoring as a means of detecting and deterring any revival of the weapons programs. Monitoring was open-ended in time. If Iraq had cooperated fully in 1991, I said, disarmament could have been achieved in a very short time through the process of inspection, sanctions could have been lifted and monitoring would have remained. Regrettably, this had not been the chain of events. At this juncture, three months after the adoption of the November resolution, the period of disarmament could still be short, I said, if immediate, active and unconditional cooperation were offered UNMOVIC and the IAEA.

Mohamed ElBaradei was less guarded than I had been. For the IAEA, he said, some technical questions remained—but no "unresolved disarmament issues." He concluded by reporting that the agency had found no evidence of ongoing nuclear or nuclear-related activities in Iraq. His comment was a stark contrast to Colin Powell's assertion a few days earlier of a "nuclear program" as a fact.

The Foreign Ministers Locking Horns in the Security Council

The debate which followed the reports by ElBaradei and myself seemed like a pitched battle in which the participants had only seven minutes each to send their words and arguments like colorful tracer bullets through the room. A rare feature was the amount of extemporization. For important public discussions, ambassadors will mostly have their speeches cleared with their ministries and will avoid deviating or digressing from their instructions. Here, though, were the persons who *gave* those instructions. They knew what they could allow themselves to say. Even though they did not change the policy lines of their governments, their departures from the texts written in advance made for a very unusual debate. With the foreign ministers in the chamber, the countries and their different profiles came alive.

On the one hand the U.S., the UK and Spain were holding that Iraq had evidently not had any change of heart and that time must be nearing for a serious decision—a euphemism for authorizing military action. On the other hand were the many who felt that the inspection process was not going badly and that it was premature to raise the idea of the use of force. Despite the polarization—or perhaps due to it—there was a wish for a middle road and, in the days after the meeting, one began to take shape.

Colin Powell said that Iraq had failed to comply with the November 2002 resolution, that its December 8 declaration had been "an early test of Iraq's seriousness," and that Iraq had answered, in effect, that it would see what it could get away with. The process of inspection could not be "endlessly strung out." Powell did not ask for immediate action or decision but urged the Council to consider "in the very near future" the issue of "serious consequences."

Jack Straw reminded the Council that in 1991 Iraq had been given ninety days to disarm. What had it done in eleven years, seven months and twelve days? The diplomatic process had to be backed with a credible threat of force; shying away from using force and giving unlimited time for little cooperation would make disarmament in Iraq and elsewhere much harder. In making that point, Mr. Straw was advancing an argument that probably had a lot of support also in Washington. Action in Iraq would send a signal to other potential proliferators. Did he have Iran, North Korea and perhaps Libya and Syria in mind? He joined the U.S. in making a "strategic decision" by Iraq the central point, but spoke more in terms of the need for it than the lack of it:

> I hope and believe that a peaceful solution to this crisis may still be possible. But this will require a dramatic and immediate change by Saddam.

Straw might have envisaged the dramatic change occurring as a result of Iraq cracking in the face of U.S./UK military determination and an ultimatum threatening war, preferably embodied in or endorsed by a Security Council resolution. That such a resolution was being considered had been confirmed by Condoleezza Rice in our talk a few days before this meeting. If the resolution did not result in a dramatic change, it would, at least implicitly, authorize the armed action that was being prepared. Aware of this, doubting that there would be a "dramatic change" and reasonably satisfied with the inspection process, the majority in the Council was unwilling to support a resolution of the kind expected.

The drive for a resolution had not been helped by the presentations which Mohamed and I had made in the Council. Quite to the contrary, our statements had probably strengthened the Council's aversion to armed action against alleged Iraqi threats, which appeared to most capitals to be far from manifest and imminent.

The French foreign minister, Dominique de Villepin, said that inspections were not at a dead end. On the contrary, we were beginning to see progress, and France wanted to further strengthen the inspection regime. The option of war might seem swifter, but once the war is won, the peace must be built, and no one could be certain that the path of war would be shorter than the path of inspections. France did not exclude the possibility that force might have to be resorted to one day. However, the assessment of whether force was justified and the guarantee for its effectiveness rested with the international community, acting together.

Ending his speech, Mr. de Villepin said he represented "an old country," and all in the chamber remembered that Donald

Rumsfeld had recently spoken somewhat contemptuously of the "old Europe," which did not agree to armed action in Iraq, while the "new Europe"—by which he meant the Eastern European countries—looked more favorably upon such action. Mr. de Villepin's comment drew laughter, and his speech ended with applause.

Mr. de Villepin's repartee stimulated several of the foreign ministers to follow his line and discover the age of their countries. The Chinese minister reminded all that China was "an ancient civilization." Jack Straw said he spoke on behalf of "a very old country, founded in 1066, by the French." Mr. Powell admitted that the United States was a "relatively new country" but noted that it was the "oldest democracy" represented at the table. These were the light touches in an otherwise rather tense exchange.

The Chinese foreign minister said that, like the majority in the Council, he believed that the inspection process was working and should be given the time needed to implement the November 2002 resolution. The German foreign minister asked why we should now halt the inspections. He agreed with the French ideas to strengthen the inspections and said that the long-term monitoring regime should be developed to prevent any future revival of Iraq's weapons program. The containment had to be on a permanent basis.

The Russian foreign minister, Mr. Ivanov, joined those in the Council who wanted the inspections to continue and said that an overwhelming majority of states in the world were of that view. He then brought up an idea which became central in the weeks following the meeting, reminding the Council that Resolution 1284 (1999) instructed UNMOVIC and the IAEA to submit their work program to the Council, including lists of "key remaining disarmament tasks." Evidently critical of the non-specific argument that Iraq had failed to implement the November 2002 resolution and had not shown the will to disarm, Mr. Ivanov noted that the adoption of a work program for the inspections would provide some objective and specific criteria against which Baghdad's cooperation could be measured.

Iraq Attaining Benchmarks of Disarmament
Could Prove There Was a Change of Heart

The idea of measuring Iraq's actions against precise requirements—rather than judging whether it had had a "change of heart" or had taken a "strategic decision"—had a good deal of appeal. However, it was understood that leaving such a measurement to the end of July, as would have been the case under the 1999 resolution, would be totally unacceptable to the U.S. A way out, it seemed after the Council meeting, might be to require Iraq to solve a few specific issues—to attain some "benchmarks"—within a limited time.

When I left the Council chamber after the February 14 session, I told Jack Straw about a document UNMOVIC had been preparing as a basis for selecting key remaining disarmament tasks for the work program. This document contained "clusters" of unresolved issues and indicated precisely what was required of Iraq in each issue. Perhaps these could be of use in a "benchmark" approach? He was most interested. So was Colin Powell, when I presented the idea to him over sandwiches in the Council lobby, after the meeting. He asked me to phone him to talk about it during the upcoming weekend.

It seemed the exploration had begun as to whether it might be possible to reconcile the requirement of a "change of heart" or "strategic decision" (ostensibly based on the November 2002 resolution) with the requirement that Iraq fulfill precise "benchmarks" as evidence of such a decision, which had its roots in the December 1999 resolution. Perhaps such fulfillment could supply proof of a strategic decision? The idea of requiring attainment of precise benchmarks had been in the air at the Council meeting, but not on the table.

There was disappointment in Washington at the outcome of the Council meeting and the statements ElBaradei and I had made. They had not been helpful to the U.S. drive toward a resolution containing an ultimatum and implicitly authorizing force. The disappointment was not voiced at the official level but was soon reflected in some media. Under the circumstances, there was, understandably, an interest in at least exploring the idea of benchmarks.

The French and many others would maintain that armed action required an explicit authorization by the Security Council. Even though this argument was not accepted by the U.S., it would clearly be less difficult to obtain an authorization if inspection reports pointed to Iraqi conduct that could reasonably be characterized either as "material breach" or as non-attainment of some benchmarks set by the Council. At present the inspectors' reports simply painted Iraqi conduct as gray, not black, and much of the U.S. dossier on Iraq constituted circumstantial evidence, with references to Iraq's record of deceit and past use of chemical weapons and long-range missiles. There was a lack of smoking guns that would impress the public. Defending the adequacy of such evidence to prove Iraqi guilt, the U.S. assistant secretary for non-proliferation, John Wolf, was quoted as saying that if something walks like a duck, swims like a duck and quacks like a duck, it probably is a duck. The problem was, as someone remarked, that the public wanted to see "a smoking duck." Surely this was why Colin Powell had presented his intelligence cases to the Security Council. Perhaps non-attainment of specific benchmarks could be helpful.

The British, who were the most fervently in favor of a UN resolution embodying an ultimatum and had felt the resistance to it stiffening, came to think that a change of focus might help. The new resolution could demand a declaration by Saddam showing that he had had a change of heart. To demonstrate that the declaration was genuine, there could further be a requirement on Iraq to attain a number of benchmarks within a limited time.

At UNMOVIC we had a well-documented catalog of unresolved disarmament issues, each concluding with clear and precise indications of what Iraq could do to resolve them. Interrelated issues had been clustered together. This was the document I had mentioned to Jack Straw and Colin Powell after the February 14 Security Council meeting. I had registered their immediate interest.

Behind the categorical positions the U.S. and UK took in the Council, there appeared to be also an interest in finding a way to bring the Council to consensus.

On Saturday, February 15, the day after my conversation with Colin Powell at the UN, Condoleezza Rice phoned me at my apartment in New York and asked about the document. Outside, there were huge antiwar demonstrations moving up the avenues. I felt a bit encouraged by her interest and explained that UNMOVIC had nearly finished work on the document and would soon submit it for discussion in our College of Commissioners. At Rice's request I promised that the following week I would show the current draft to John Wolf, who was a member of our College of Commissioners.

On Sunday I phoned Colin Powell, as he had suggested, and explained again the nature of our "cluster document." It contained precise demands regarding what Iraq would have to do to solve the various disarmament issues. If the Security Council wanted to set benchmarks, this document could be of use. Mohamed ElBaradei had told me he thought the remaining questions in the nuclear field could be cleared up by April 15 if Iraq cooperated fully. The problems in the fields of biological and chemical weapons and missiles were much greater, but I asked Powell whether the U.S. could accept April 15 as a deadline for these as well. He said it was too late.

Public Opinion Against War Makes Some Governments Look for a Middle Way

The Security Council meeting on February 14 had been followed by high-profile demonstrations the day after. Broad and vocal public opinion against the war turned out millions around the world, including in the United States itself. Indeed, in New York, protesters marched on Second and Third avenues near my apartment house, and I had been in the midst of them when I went out to buy milk. In fact, I had worried a little that I might be recognized as the chief inspector and risk being hoisted to some demonstrator's truck as a mascot. (Later, the Swedish ambassador, who lived in the same area, gave me a poster that he had picked up on the avenue after the demonstration. On one side it proclaimed BLIX—NOT BOMBS! It hangs on my wall now.)

The government in Washington appeared completely impervious to antiwar opinion. *The New York Times* reported President Bush commenting that leadership sometimes involves "bucking public opinion" and that "the role of a leader is to decide policy based upon security." It further reported that he was pushing ahead with a strategy "to persuade reluctant allies that United Nations inspections would not secure the disarmament of Iraq," and that he was planning "to reach a decision on the use of force against Iraq within weeks, whatever the Security Council does."

It is conceivable that the tough U.S. public posture was designed to make Iraq chicken out and prevent it from having any illusion that the Bush administration would give in to antiwar opinion. However, I am more inclined to think that the U.S. leadership was planning for war at full steam ahead, with an option for calling it off in the unlikely event that Iraq cracked.

Other countries and their governments responded in various ways to antiwar opinion. The antiwar demonstration in England was the largest protest in the country's history. Italy and Spain saw massive antiwar majorities in opinion polls, but their governments stayed firmly with the U.S. The French government—while not ruling out the use of force as a means of last resort—espoused the dominant antiwar opinion and represented it. The prime minister of Canada, Jean Chrétien, told his parliament that he would oppose military action that was not explicitly authorized by the Security Council. His view was shared in many UN-committed countries, including my own, Sweden. In Germany, a poll registered some 86 percent as rejecting war and the German foreign minister, Joschka Fischer, said that war was not a way to bring about disarmament.

Several of the members of the Security Council, like Mexico and Chile, were active in the search for a middle ground. Their governments were under increasing pressure from Washington to get on the war wagon, but public opinion in their countries was against armed intervention. To Mexico, the situation must have appeared as paradoxical as it was painful. Mexico had for many years deliberately refrained from seeking a seat in the Security Council and had only recently decided that it wanted one in order to exercise its responsibilities as an important Latin American country. It now found itself rewarded for its ambition to become a world citizen by being squeezed between the need and wish to develop good relations with its big neighbor and the public opinion of its own citizens, which was distinctly against war. Chile was in a similar situation.

I could not see any direct impact from the public demonstrations on the international scene. However, the insistence by many states on continuing inspections and on the search for a middle ground and the benchmark approach did coincide with the growing antiwar opinion demonstrated on the streets around the world.

My Own Ideas for How the Specific Demands in the Cluster Document Could Be Used as Benchmarks

Monday, February 17, was Presidents' Day in the U.S., and the UN was closed. This was lucky because New York had just been through a blizzard. Coming from Stockholm, where snow-clearing is standard, mostly quick and noisy, I enjoyed the quiet inefficiency that descended on Manhattan with the snow. My wife and I walked down Second Avenue, which had a thick white layer and was empty of cars. Occasional skiers enjoyed a brief spell of comparative advantage over pedestrians and cars.

It was a good day for work at my office in the deserted UN Secretariat building, when I finalized my own ideas for how our work on clusters might be used. I put down my ideas in the form of a draft resolution for the Security Council and a background paper, and I decided to show it to Sir Jeremy Greenstock, the British permanent representative to the UN, who was to visit me later in the day to talk about the cluster document. I knew Sir Jeremy well and both liked him and appreciated his skill and judgment. He would see if I was onto something that could be made use of. If so, he, occupying a seat in the Council (unlike myself, who was its servant), could take the matter forward. If he thought it futile, there was a wastebasket nearby. He refrained from any immediate reaction and I gave him both my background paper and draft resolution as food for thought—no more. He gave both to the Americans. In the weeks that followed, the Brits came to make important use of the benchmark idea, while after a short period of interest the Americans grew cool to it. Perhaps the U.S. reasoned that the attainment of precise benchmarks and verification thereof would inevitably take some time and might not prove a consensus avenue to authorizing armed force. Declaring that Iraq had shown no change of heart could be quicker—and be done unilaterally, if need be.

The Blix Paper and Draft Resolution, February 17, 2003

In my background paper I tried to identify the premises: Military pressure was and remained indispensable to bringing about Iraqi compliance; many delegations felt that not enough time had yet been given to inspections; eleven weeks was a rather short time to allow the final conclusion that disarmament could not be achieved through the inspection path and would have to be abandoned. It would not seem unreasonable, I then suggested, to set "an explicit time line" within which satisfactory cooperation and resolution of unresolved disarmament issues and key remaining disarmament tasks would be demanded. It was a political judgment, I wrote, to decide how much time should be given.

It would be for the Security Council to judge—after a report by the inspectors—whether there had been adequate cooperation and resulting disarmament. One could select a number of benchmarks to be attained by Iraq within the time given rather than ask that the whole catalog of open issues be solved. The UNMOVIC cluster document, with its explicit demands on Iraq could be made available soon, if requested in the Council.

My draft requested that UNMOVIC/IAEA submit by March 1 a list of "key points" (currently remaining disarmament issues and questions), along with indications of what Iraq should do to resolve them (the benchmarks). It further spelled out a number of demands for Iraqi actions, including the elimination of all missiles identified as proscribed by UNMOVIC. It requested UNMOVIC/IAEA to report to the Council before a specific date (which was left open) as to whether Iraq had done what was asked of it. Last, it stipulated that if the Security Council were to conclude that Iraq had not fulfilled what was demanded and had thus "not made use of the inspection process," the inspections would be terminated and the Council would "consider other measures to solve the disarmament issue." This draft provision reflected my opinion that inspections offered Iraq an opportunity that was not open endlessly, and that it was for the Council—but not individual members of it—to consider and decide on the alternative to inspection.

Destruction of Al Samoud 2 Missiles Requested

The issue of missile destruction was included in my draft because UNMOVIC was about to request that Iraq destroy more than one hundred Al Samoud 2 missiles. A special group of international experts called by UNMOVIC had unanimously concluded that these missiles were capable of exceeding the range limit of 150 kilometers set by the Security Council, and we had discussed the issue early in the preceding week with our College of Commissioners. As I had mentioned in the Security Council on February 14, we had concluded that Iraq was prohibited from having the missiles. However, I was not completely sure that Iraq would comply with the request for such a massive destruction. It would, in fact, be a test of Iraq's readiness to cooperate on a matter of substantial disarmament, as distinguished from cooperation on matters of process, like unlimited access. In this sense it fit very well into a resolution on benchmarks.

I cannot say I felt indignant that the Iraqis had somewhat

exceeded the permissible range. In fact, I was more concerned that Iraq might have prepared designs for missiles of much longer range, and that we had not yet found them. After a talk with one of our outside expert consultants, I was also concerned that, like India, Iraq might prepare to give its Al Samoud 2 missile a substantially longer range by fitting it with two engines rather than one.

I thought reports on the destruction of so many missiles would impress governments and the world, showing that disarmament by inspection would go beyond picking up some minor quantity of mustard gas or overlooked empty chemical warheads. Indeed, I told myself quietly, if war were avoided because the inspection process appeared promising, perhaps the destruction of the missiles would have been the best possible use that could have been made of them. In this expectation I was to be disappointed.

In retrospect, I note that Iraq did comply with our request, although Saddam Hussein's first reaction in a televised interview with Dan Rather on February 24 had sounded defiant. It was no small affair to destroy these big machines. The Iraqi side asked us in Baghdad not to publish pictures of the operation, saying it was painful to them. This might have been true. There was certainly a pride that they had succeeded in designing and producing these missiles and a corresponding pain in destroying them. Conceivably this could contain a clue as to why the Iraqis chose to destroy biological and chemical weapons without inspectors present in 1991, as they claimed. They might have felt it hurt their pride. We had always assumed that this unobserved unilateral action had been undertaken to enable Iraq to retain some weapons secretly. On the occasion of the Al Samoud missile destruction our inspectors were present. We did not publish any pictures.

The destruction was not given much international attention, and the U.S. attitude toward it seemed somewhat vacillating. In a letter of January 3, 2003, Assistant Secretary John Wolf had urged me to take forceful action on any prohibited items: destroying rather than removing or rendering them harmless. On February 28, Condoleezza Rice said to me over the telephone that she worried that Iraq was dragging its feet in the destruction operation. However, on March 5 she said the destruction, which was taking place, was just to mislead. I then asked her if she would have preferred that the Iraqis reject the order. She did not answer, and it occurred to me later that she might indeed have preferred a rejection as it would have constituted a clear-cut violation of the November 2002 resolution.

Bearing Rice's comment in mind, I took the opportunity two days later (March 7) to present the destruction to the Security Council as "a substantial measure of disarmament." "We are not watching the breaking of toothpicks," I said. "Lethal weapons are being destroyed." To this Colin Powell retorted, "I know they are not toothpicks, but real missiles. But the problem is that we do not know how many missiles there are and how many toothpicks there are. We do not know whether or not the infrastructure to make more has been identified and broken up."

All in all, some seventy Al Samoud 2 missiles were destroyed under our supervision, and we calculated that there were some thirty more deployed. We had a rather good idea of the infrastructure, based on Iraqi declarations and inspections on the ground. I have little doubt that the U.S., preparing for the invasion of Iraq, was genuinely interested in the destruction of these missiles, and that the belittling of our operation came only as part of the overriding effort to portray Iraq as refusing to disarm.

Next Steps on the Benchmark Path

The day after my February 18 talk with Sir Jeremy Greenstock, I had lunch with U.S. Ambassador John Negroponte, Assistant Secretary Wolf, and the director of counter-proliferation on the U.S. National Security Council. My deputy, Dimitri Perricos, was with me. I explained the approach of my cluster paper and said it was not my task to push the Council but only to call their attention to uses that could be made of the paper. After the lunch John Wolf joined me in my office, and I let him leaf through the draft cluster document, as it then stood. I had the distinct feeling that he was not enthusiastic.

While *The New York Times* could hardly have seen my drafts, the idea of benchmarks was in the air, and on February 18 it carried an editorial in which it was stated that President Bush needed to work with the Security Council and that Washington should spell out the steps Baghdad needed to take to stay the threat of war—in short, benchmarks. The news pages of the same issue carried a report that U.S. and UK officials hoped that a statement by the European Union not ruling out the use of force against Iraq, "in combination with possible critical statements about Iraq's cooperation over the next several weeks by Hans Blix . . . could ultimately provide the basis for backing of force by the Security Council members, including France." It went on with the following curious lines:

By early March, the administration expects that Mr. Blix will be prepared to make a more negative appraisal of Iraq's cooperation than he did before the Security Council on Friday. Officials said Mr. Blix gave them that impression in private.

Mr. Blix is being pressed by the United States to set "benchmarks" over the next several weeks, demanding that Iraq fulfill its obligations in at least three specific areas: allowing unimpeded interviews with scientists, destroying illegal rockets and allowing unconditional overflights by reconnaissance planes.

The lines could not have come from my luncheon guests because they were printed the same day as the luncheon, nor had I said anything that would justify the comment—indeed, *any* comment—about future appraisals. Perhaps some policy architects in Washington thought they could influence me to come with a more negative appraisal of Iraq next time around. However, that time was scheduled only for March 7, nearly three weeks later! And did Washington really want to make use of the benchmark idea? The three that were mentioned were eminently do-able. It was all rather puzzling and suggested there were possibly different lines of thinking in the great capital.

The Canadian Attempt to Find a Middle Ground

I was far from the only one looking for a middle ground. At a meeting on February 19 at which all members of the United Nations could address the Iraqi issue, Ambassador Paul Heinbecker of Canada voiced some support for the U.S. position but urged that UNMOVIC should define those tasks on which evidence of Iraqi compliance was most urgently required. That was, in effect, setting benchmarks. There would be "an early deadline"—not 120 days—before which Iraq had to comply by providing evidence. Such a process, the ambassador said, would provide the Council a basis on which it could assess Iraqi compliance.

He ended by placing the burden on Saddam Hussein to act even at this late hour, but added two lines which echoed the mood of the government in Ottawa but hardly the one in Washington: namely, expressing the conviction that a peaceful resolution was still possible and that multilateral institutions are essential to managing our ever more integrated world.

A Conversation with Tony Blair on February 20

On February 20, using the secure telephone line in Ambassador Greenstock's office, I had a long conversation with Prime Minister Tony Blair about his initiative. The prime minister said that the Americans had been disappointed with my February 14 report. It had undermined their faith in the UN process. Well, yes, I thought, their faith that the UN process would lead to the authorization of the military route might have been undermined. The Americans, he said, were attracted by a second Security Council resolution, up to a point, but did not feel they needed one. There was a risk of the UN being marginalized and the international community split. He wanted to offer the Americans an alternative strategy, a type of ultimatum that would include a deadline for attaining the resolution of some disarmament issues and impose a duty on Saddam to cooperate actively. Failure to do so would constitute a breach of the November resolution.

The conversation suggested to me that Blair was positive both to the position that a clear change of heart was the only way Saddam could avoid armed action and to the idea that benchmarks could be set which would show that change of heart. He said we needed to define cooperation, perhaps by listing categories by which it could be assessed. The Americans were talking of taking action by the end of the month.

I said I was attracted by the concept of a timeline—an ultimatum. Indeed, I had included it in the papers I had given to the UK ambassador. Full cooperation, I told Blair, could be defined—or as he had just put it, listed by categories. I mentioned, as examples of issues that had already been resolved, interviews outside Iraq, noninterference with surveillance flights by U-2 and other planes, and destruction of Al Samoud 2 missiles. I further mentioned that UNMOVIC would by the following week have a catalog of actions required of Iraq—the cluster document. I also said that the Iraqis had become much more active. I was receiving a "flow of half-promises." Maybe the Iraqis were starting to panic. I said I needed more time. Condoleezza Rice had assured me that weather was not a factor in the American planning. I said there should be some room for compromise in the American position; they were going ahead too fast.

Tony Blair said that the Iraqis could have signaled a change of heart in the December 8 declaration, but had not done so. The U.S. did not think Saddam would cooperate. Nor did Blair. But, he said, we needed to keep the international community together.

I said that I had asked Colin Powell about setting a deadline of April 15 and that he had responded this was too late. I thought it really too early. Blair said he would pursue the ultimatum/deadline route and try to get me as much time as possible. It should be possible to assess whether Saddam was cooperating. I replied that the demands for cooperation had to be related to what was realistically do-able. By this I meant that benchmarks should be something that the Iraqis could accomplish, if they made an effort. The speedy destruction of Al Samoud 2 missiles was a good example.

Part of my conversation with Blair touched on the role and quality of intelligence. I said—as I had to Condoleezza Rice—that while I appreciated the intelligence we received, I had to note that it had not been all that compelling. Only at three sites to which we had gone on the basis of intelligence had there been any result at all.

Personally, I tended to think that Iraq still concealed weapons of mass destruction, but I needed evidence. Perhaps there were not many such weapons in Iraq after all. Blair said that even the French and German intelligence services were sure there were such weapons; the Egyptians, too. I said they seemed unsure, for instance, about mobile biological weapon production facilities. I added that it would prove paradoxical and absurd if 250,000 troops were to invade Iraq and find very little. Blair responded that the intelligence was clear that Saddam had reconstituted his weapons of mass destruction program. Blair clearly relied on the intelligence and was convinced, while my faith in intelligence had been shaken.

9

Deadlock

On Friday, February 21, the day after I had talked to Tony Blair, Condoleezza Rice phoned me and we had a short talk. She began by saying she had heard that after our conversation on February 11 I had been displeased that wildly misleading stories had been in the press, which asserted inter alia that she had "admonished" me to say this or that. She wanted me to know that she, too, was displeased. I had the feeling that she meant what she said.

If, as I have come to suspect, information might have been passed to the media on what some policy hub wanted or expected her to say—without caring to check what she actually *did* say—I could see why she would be displeased. They were creating their own virtual reality! Only much later has it occurred to me that this would have been a very minor piece of virtual reality compared to the vast and ominous story about Iraqi weapons that was woven by statements at the highest levels, out of thin threads.

I thanked Ms. Rice for her comment and, keeping her posted from my side on what we were doing, I told her about the letter we had just delivered to Iraq, requesting the destruction of all Al Samoud 2 missiles.

Maybe the comment she had made was the main purpose of the call. However, she went on to impress upon me that whatever we might say about cooperation from the Iraqi side, we could not say that it had been "immediate." I realized that she was looking for grounds for holding Iraq in violation of Resolution 1441, which required "immediate" cooperation. Her point was valid. While in recent weeks the Iraqis had become much more active—even frantic—in their cooperation, the start had not been "immediate." I said I would not forget the point, and I actually made it when I spoke in the Council on March 7. I think this was as far as Rice ever came to telling me what she thought I ought to say. I did not think that encroached on the independence I should have. I always found our talks straightforward. She had come from a university world demanding empirical knowledge, critical thinking and logical argument, and entered the hot, bubbling pot of the political world with its mixture of emotional appeals, polemics, personal ambitions, media management and spin. I always felt she preserved a little cubicle of the unsentimental and rational academic world around her. For me, that made discussion easier.

On February 24, the UK, U.S. and Spain circulated a draft resolution "in blue," which is a proposal that is not given a document number and on which no action or voting is yet asked. It asserted that Iraq had failed to comply with November's Resolution 1441 in that it had failed to cooperate fully and because its declaration of December 8 had contained false statements and omissions. This non-compliance, it was further asserted, posed a threat to international peace and security. The operative part was short and might not have appeared singularly *in*operative to the lay reader. It simply "decided" that Iraq had failed to take the final opportunity afforded to it in Resolution 1441 and that the Council should "remain seized of the matter." It did not signal armed intervention. It was like a jury giving a guilty verdict deferring an immediate decision about punishment.

As UK Ambassador Greenstock said in introducing the paper, the sponsors were not asking for any instant judgments. The Council would express the view in the resolution that Iraq had so far made the wrong choice, but also that there was still time to make the right choice, to show a "change of heart." I should note that while his statement was very forceful and while it referred to 8,500 liters of anthrax, 2,100 kilograms of bacterial growth media, 1.5 metric tons of VX nerve agent and 6,500 chemical bombs, he avoided asserting that these quantities definitely existed, and prudently asserted instead that we did not *know* what happened to these quantities. Thus, Iraq was not accused of having them but of not accounting for them. I appreciated the nuance.

Although Tony Blair had told me that, like the Americans, he did not think the Iraqis would cooperate, he probably wanted to show more patience than the U.S. government cared to. *The New York Times* had reported about a week earlier (on February 18) that the resolution would be "straightforward" and state that Iraq "faces serious consequences"—again, a euphemism for armed action. This clearly reflected the U.S. impatience. President Bush was cited in the same report as having scornfully referred to giving Saddam Hussein "another, 'nother, 'nother last chance." Yet, the text actually tabled by the UK on February 24, with the U.S. and Spain as cosponsors, did precisely give that chance. The absence of any reference even to "serious consequences" might well have been tactical. It might have been feared that such a reference would cement the difference between the UK and the antiwar Europeans rather than softening the opposition to armed intervention.

France, Germany and Russia did not present their position in a draft resolution. Instead, they declared in a memorandum to the president of the Security Council that the priority should be to achieve the full and effective disarmament of Iraq peacefully, and that the conditions for using force had not been fulfilled. While suspicions remained, there was no evidence that Iraq still had weapons of mass destruction or even the capabilities to produce them; inspections had just reached their full pace and worked without hindrance.

The memorandum proposed that UNMOVIC and the IAEA should submit their work program on March 1, rather than simply before March 27. This would contain the list of key remaining disarmament tasks in order of priority, and would clearly define what was required of Iraq. The inspectors would report to the Council at any time if Iraq interfered with the inspections or failed to comply with its obligations. They were further to report on implementation every three weeks and submit an assessment after 120 days.

While the draft by the UK, U.S. and Spain had been premised on the "impatient" November 2002 resolution, the proposals of Germany, France and Russia were pretty much in line with the more "patient" resolution of December 1999. They urged that inspections should be given the necessary time and increased resources, but stressed—significantly—that "they cannot continue indefinitely."

February 24: A Clash at UNMOVIC's College of Commissioners

The College of Commissioners met in regular session on February 23 and 24 to be consulted on the quarterly report due to be submitted to the Security Council by March 1, and to be brought up-to-date on events. This session of the normally calm expert group heard some rather heated exchanges, notably between John Wolf and myself concerning the role and content of the cluster document. These meetings were informal and confidential, so the discussion was direct and unrestrained.

The draft quarterly report to the Council was a rather detailed compendium of UNMOVIC'S work in Iraq from December 1, 2002, to February 28, 2003. It also touched the more general and politically burning question of whether Iraq had cooperated "immediately, unconditionally and actively"—a question which the draft resolution circulated by the UK, U.S. and Spain answered in the negative. The assessment by UNMOVIC was, like my statement in the Council on February 14, more nuanced. Minor frictions notwithstanding, Iraq had been helpful on "process." On "substance," we wrote, Iraq could have made greater efforts to find any remaining proscribed items or provide credible evidence explaining their absence. Hence, the results in terms of disarmament had been limited thus far. We added that it was hard to understand why a number of the measures that were now being taken by Iraq could not have been initiated earlier. If they had been, they might have borne fruit by now. We concluded:

> It is only by the middle of January and thereafter that Iraq has taken a number of steps which have the potential of resulting either in the presentation for the destruction of stocks or items that are proscribed or the presentation of relevant evidence solving long-standing unresolved disarmament issues.

Our quarterly report to the Security Council described the cluster document that was now presented as a draft to the College for comments. The report noted that apart from serving as the basis for the selection of "key remaining disarmament tasks," the clusters might also provide yardsticks against which Iraq's disarmament actions could be measured—in other words, benchmarks.

At this stage, members of the Security Council knew about the existence but not the contents of the cluster document, and the Germans and Russians were keen that it should become public to show that precise requirements could be placed on Iraq, rather than nebulous demands for a "strategic decision" or a "change of heart." On the other side, neither the U.S. nor the UK was opposed to a declassification of what was still an internal document. As it turned out, both the U.S. and the UK foreign ministers got copies of the not yet declassified draft, presumably through the American and British members of our College.

The German and French foreign ministers, who had been eager to make use of the document but did not have such a channel of quick provision, only got copies—of the finalized text—at the Security Council meeting on March 7, and could not make use of it to show what concrete benchmarks might look like. Their U.S. and UK colleagues, by contrast, were therefore able to make extensive and preemptive use of the draft to show how unreliable Iraqi declarations and conduct had been in the past. Colin Powell, welcoming the compilation, said it demonstrated Iraq's "strategic decision to delay, to deceive." Jack Straw said he had gone through all 167 pages on the flight to New York and found them a very chilling read. He held up his heavily underlined copy for his colleagues to see and praised the painstaking work that went into compiling it. This was on the seventh of March.

The cluster document was an up-to-date factual analysis of all Iraqi weapons issues known to us. It had used reports prepared by UNSCOM in 1999 as a starting point but taken into account what had been learnt since then, e.g., through Iraqi documents submitted, satellite images, and—importantly—the results of our own inspections. The document examined category after category of prohibited weapons, identifying and lumping together related open issues in clusters. It indicated on each issue what Iraq could do to help resolve it, starting the enumeration of actions, wherever relevant, with the possible presentation by Iraq of any existing weapons or other prohibited items.

After the discussion, the members of the College agreed to supplement their oral comments with written ones by Monday, March 3, telling us which items they thought should have priority. Having had the advice from our College members, we would then be in a position to submit our selection of "key remaining disarmament tasks" to the Security Council, which some members of the Council wanted to occur early to help in a selection of benchmarks.

John Wolf's problems with the cluster document were not related so much to what it contained and analyzed as to what its relevance was at this stage, and what it did not contain. In his view, Resolution 1441 had demanded immediate disarmament (actually immediate cooperation), which required a "strategic decision." We needed a report card, he said. The document provided only a readable historical account testifying to Iraqi deception. Moreover, it spent only a few pages on events after 1998. What had the Iraqis done since then? There was also no adequate account of the question of UAVs (or drones), about which Colin Powell had spoken. There was no sign of any change of the Iraqi mind, which was all that mattered.

I sensed that Wolf—and presumably the U.S. government—was now throwing overboard the approach we had been asked by the Security Council to follow and had, in fact, followed for several years, with the Council's approval. Despite Wolf's reference to the

question of UAVs, he clearly took the view that individual disarmament issues now were of secondary, if any, interest and relevance. I
was puzzled that the Americans did not afford the smallest window
to the benchmark approach, which Washington saw London working on. I could not imagine that Wolf would have come out so cate-
gorically if he had not had direction from Washington. Even so, the
tone of his comments could have been more courteous. The disdain
shocked and surprised the other members of the College. I felt
indignant and I did not hide it. We had worked hard and long on a
line that had had the full approval of the Council, including the U.S.
government. Now that government seemed to abandon the line
altogether. OK, but was it fair to combine this abandonment with
criticism of our work for irrelevance and inadequacy?

The heated exchange was one thing. The concrete points Wolf
had raised about the drones and the period after 1998 were another.
The nearly four-year gap between the end of 1998 and the return of
inspectors to Iraq was, indeed, a problem. We had little solid information about the period apart from satellite images showing a variety of refurbishments and new buildings, most of which we had
checked in inspections without finding anything proscribed. We
would have to admit, as it has been aptly put, that "you don't know
what you don't know."

Like other members of the College, John Wolf supplemented his
oral comments with a letter. He noted that the cluster document
was an excellent recapitulation of issues outstanding at the end of
the UNSCOM period, updated through later material. It did not,
however, provide an adequate basis for resolving the totality of outstanding issues, as stipulated in Resolution 1441. Reliance on "secondary sources," such as documents or in-country interviews, could
not provide adequate reassurance. Rather, he went on,

> the genuine "dramatic change" by Iraq would have necessi-
> tated that it admit openly, not under pressure, that it had
> and has WMD and WMD programs. This change would
> have had Iraq voluntarily take inspectors to the secret hide
> sites. Iraq would have shown the facilities where production

has/is taking place; Iraq would have elaborated the illegal procurement networks. . . . That is not what Iraq did. That is not what Iraq is doing. Trying to discern a set of benchmarks, or tasks, will only dilute the full disarmament stipulated in Res. 1441.

As I went through his formulations I understood them to say, *The witches exist; you are appointed to deal with these witches; testing whether there are witches is only a dilution of the witch hunt.*

An article in *The New York Times* on March 2, describing the disappointment in some circles in Washington that I was not helpful to their cause in the Security Council, had some interesting comments on how the benchmark issue was seen in the same circles. The article claimed—erroneously—that there had been extensive discussions between me and the U.S. administration on the benchmark approach. In reality, as I have shown, the extensive talks were with the British. The article went on to explain:

> Some administration officials said they hoped that effort might still highlight Iraq's many failures to disarm. Others said they wished the idea of "benchmarks" had never been introduced.
>
> "The benchmarks have become a diversion from the key issue of whether Saddam Hussein is meeting his obligations," said a State Department official.

It was evidently this attitude that John Wolf expressed in his letter, which I read the day after the article was published.

Wolf appended some comments on individual issues that were discussed in the cluster document. On biological weapons, he noted that the document failed to cover "shared information" about activities after 1996. On mobile labs he noted, in particular, that "we have provided you information that Iraq not only has these mobile plants but also produced agent recently." Similarly, he noted that on chemical weapons the cluster document did not draw on "shared information that demonstrates the continuation of a program beyond the Gulf War."

I have no doubt that Wolf was convinced about the validity of the findings of U.S. intelligence, which had been kindly "shared" with us. We tried in our inspection work to verify such findings. However, we would not present claims by intelligence agencies as *our* findings unless we found that there was credible evidence supporting them. For instance, the claim that there were mobile labs for the production of biological agent had been made by several intelligence agencies. We took it seriously and looked for the labs, investigating various places where they might have been linked to water and electricity. However, without finding evidence we would not assert, as Wolf evidently wanted us to do, that they existed. After many months of occupation, claims that certain trucks that were found were the famous biolabs have been recognized as "embarrassing." I am not aware of any other intelligence "shared" with us that has been substantiated by credible evidence.

Condoleezza Rice on February 28 and March 5: We Are Coming to a Crossroad

When Condoleezza Rice phoned me on February 28, it was not to talk about benchmarks. She had probably left that idea to John Wolf, who turned out to be vehemently against it. Rather, she wanted to voice a concern that Iraq might try to use human shields, especially U.S. and UK citizens, to deter attacks. The risk might increase as we got closer to a vote on a resolution. I replied that if the draft UK/U.S./Spain resolution implied that the inspection effort was to be abandoned—the text circulated would only state that Iraq had failed to take the "final opportunity"—perhaps it should have a clause about the withdrawal of inspectors. I had the operational responsibility, but the Security Council had the political responsibility

Rice said we were not there yet. However, we were coming to a crossroad. Resolution 1441 had required immediate, unconditional and active cooperation. Iraq had missed the opportunity. I interjected that UNMOVIC's quarterly report, which we had discussed in the College, would say that the Iraqis could have done things earlier. They were now very active, and by the time I would present the quarterly report to the Council there might be more to say, e.g., about the destruction of Al Samoud 2 missiles. Rice said she was worried that Iraq was dragging its feet in the destruction of the missiles but, even if they did blow them all up, it might be only the tip of the iceberg. We agreed that it should be in Iraq's interest to start the destruction promptly and go on without delays.

Rice also noted the difficulty in keeping an army sitting. She was clearly also concerned that I might specify precisely to the Council how much more time UNMOVIC would need for inspections. She had no reason to worry. How could I honestly tell how much time would be needed to resolve remaining disarmament issues? I told her I would say that if there was to be full Iraqi cooperation it would be a matter of months—not years, nor weeks—to reach results. I later did say precisely that.

Rice phoned me again on March 5. She again voiced concern about the safety of U.S. and UK inspectors, who might be particularly vulnerable if armed action were taken. The UK's ambassador Greenstock had made the same point two days earlier. I had responded that withdrawing any inspectors while intense efforts were being made to find a peaceful way forward would look like a recognition of the inevitability of war. I said that all inspectors were UN civil servants and that we could not distinguish between them.

A few days later we found that some Americans whom we had trained and hired as new inspectors and who were to go to Baghdad had been advised by U.S. authorities not to go. We did not advise any staff to leave Baghdad on the basis of their nationality. (They were all in the end flown out—with active assistance from the Iraqi side.) On the other hand, we never prevented any staff member from leaving Baghdad before the expiry of contract. Few did, and in fact some U.S. and UK staff insisted on going to Baghdad or staying there against advice from their countries.

The main point Rice wanted to make on March 5 was to voice the hope that I would keep Resolution 1441 as my guidepost in measuring Iraqi compliance: "immediate, active and unconditional." I said this referred to cooperation, not disarmament, which could never be immediate. I told her further that I would refer not only to Resolution 1441 but also to Resolution 1284, as my quarterly report was required under that resolution and the cluster document was produced under it and would be released under it. Our conversation ended this time by my noting that a U.S. general had said that the U.S. objective in Iraq was disarmament, not the elimination of Saddam. Did they know where the weapons of mass destruction were? No, she said, but interviews after liberation would reveal it. I am sure she was speaking in good faith. I only said it was odd that no tips had been given to us that had led us to sites with weapons of mass destruction.

Things had evolved considerably in Washington since my conversation with Colin Powell on February 16. Had it been the British interest in benchmarks that led the U.S. to look at this path? Whatever the reason, it became clear to me that the administration now felt the simplest route would be to declare that Iraq had not cooperated as it should have. The benchmarks approach might drag the matter out and take too much time. I just wonder what the discussions had been like with the British, who were trying hard to pursue the idea. Despite the negative U.S. attitude, the British continued to work on the concept.

Intense Diplomacy before the March 7 Security Council Meeting

Every day the U.S. seemed more determined to abandon the inspection path. An invasion force of some 250,000 was now sitting on the doorstep of Iraq and the only big hitch that seemed capable of causing delay was not getting permission to move troops through Turkey. Despite billions offered to Turkey to secure this permission, and the Turkish government favoring it, the country's legislature did not go along. It was a bit paradoxical to hear some U.S. policymakers talk about the future blessings of democracy for Iraq while not showing much understanding for the qualms of the democratically elected Turkish parliament.

As much as the U.S. was bent on invasion, the French, Germans and Russians were bent on inspection. Their foreign ministers met in Paris on March 5 and declared that disarmament of Iraq through inspection was possible and that the inspections were "producing increasingly encouraging results." However, they also said that "these inspections cannot continue indefinitely." Their declaration seemed to aim at the benchmark approach: The work program of UNMOVIC should be presented without delay, and the remaining disarmament issues should be prioritized, with detailed time lines being set for each issue and progress reports submitted to the Council enabling it to evaluate the results.

There was already speculation whether a resolution declaring Iraq in non-compliance could attain the requisite nine votes for approval, and Angola, Cameroon, Chile, Guinea, Mexico and Pakistan were the subject of much attention by the Council's great powers. There were reports about intense economic and diplomatic pressures on these countries and even about the U.S. eavesdropping on their missions in New York. Bulgaria was to get the advantageous economic status of "market economy" while Chile would have its free-trade agreement with the U.S. delayed. The story was told how in 1991 the U.S. had withdrawn $24 million in annual aid to Yemen when that country failed to support the resolution authorizing the Gulf War. U.S. diplomats had told the ambassador of Yemen that he had just cast the most expensive vote of his life.

The point in the Paris declaration that attracted the greatest attention was that the three countries would "not let a proposed resolution pass that would authorize the use of force." Although no veto was demonstratively flashed, the text stated that "Russia and France, as permanent members of the Security Council, will assume all their responsibilities on this point." These two states, but not Germany, have the power of veto, so the innuendo was there.

That same day, Colin Powell said on Russian television that although he was skeptical, peace still had a chance if Saddam did everything he was asked and adopted a "strategic decision" on voluntary disarmament. He said the Iraqis were only doing the minimum in order to ease the pressure on themselves. The U.S. would await the reports of the inspectors on March 7 and thereafter decide with its cosponsors whether or not to push for a vote on a resolution. The *Times* in London reported Powell as saying that the missile destruction was a sham and that in early February Iraq had started to move sensitive materials every twelve or fourteen hours. It was not explained whether these materials related to weapons of mass destruction or whether they were conventional arms being moved in face of the risk of war. Reuters reported that the U.S. and the UK did not yet have the nine votes needed and that the UK was exploring modifications in the existing draft to attract more votes.

This was the political climate as we approached the Council meeting.

The day before the meeting, on March 6, a delegation from the League of Arab States visited Secretary General Kofi Annan, and I was invited to join, along with Mohamed ElBaradei. They were planning to go to Baghdad and wanted to hear our views. Annan explained the situation with customary clarity. There were various options: the U.S./UK/Spain resolution declaring Iraq noncomplying; the French/German/Russian line of defining key disarmament tasks, having frequent reports from the inspectors, and making an assessment after 120 days; and the Canadian idea of key tasks as benchmarks, and a deadline for compliance at the end of March.

The Iraqis needed to be proactive, Annan said. They needed to show a change of heart, allow interviews outside Iraq, etc. I agreed with him and said that Saddam could make a speech presenting the "strategic decision" that was asked. ElBaradei noted that we had had four years of hiatus and now only four months of inspection. He said a "change of heart" was a subjective criterion. To identify key remaining disarmament tasks was to provide objective criteria. There was a U.S. clock ticking fast, and Saddam was ignoring it and speaking about inspectors as spies.

Friday, March 7: The Security Council Meeting at Foreign Minister Level. Reports by Mohamed ElBaradei and Myself. A Long Day.

I had worked in the office with my advisers until 11 p.m. on Thursday, March 6, to finalize the speech by which I was to introduce UNMOVIC's twelfth report to the Council. I was now a delicate piece on the chessboard and had to be moved with protection, not least from media who were eager to ambush me. On the morning of March 7, I was driven down to the UN garage together with my nice UN security man, Eric Brownwell. We walked past the garbage cans and factory crates to a basement level of elevators I had never seen before. There was even an elevator waiting for us! However, as we reached the thirty-first floor, the privacy was over. The corridor was full of journalists and cameras. They were there not so much for me as for the German foreign minister, Joschka Fischer, who'd come for a courtesy call before the meeting. Mohamed was already in my office, and the three of us talked briefly while the cameras buzzed and clicked. Mohamed asked me if I had noted in my speech that inspections were going full swing and could give results. I said the notion was there.

Mohamed and I went up to the secretary general's office on the thirty-eighth floor, then we went down together with Annan to the Security Council chamber, which was packed with people. The Guinean foreign minister was to preside, wearing spectacular African garb. Most member countries were present at the foreign minister level: Colin Powell, Jack Straw, Igor Ivanov, Dominique de Villepin, Joschka Fischer . . . Television cameras and radio microphones stood ready to beam the speeches around the world. Mohamed and I were invited to take seats at the table, and I was asked to speak first. It was not a very long speech. I had reported so much and so often to the Council before, and now I was formally presenting UNMOVIC's quarterly report, which lay before the members and which described our inspection work for the period from December 1 to February 28. I needed to supplement the report with information on what had happened since it was drafted.

Friends in Washington told me later that what the U.S. administration would have liked to hear—and missed—in my speech was some general judgment regarding lack of cooperation by Iraq. However, the picture was now much more complex than it had been when I reported on January 27. American U-2 planes and French Mirages were now performing surveillance flights over Iraq for UNMOVIC, and Russian planes and German drones were coming next. There was a continued disappointing dearth of documentary evidence, which I regretted: "When proscribed items are deemed unaccounted for, it is above all credible accounts that are needed—or the proscribed items, if they exist." I discussed how we tried to get some clarity on the issue of the alleged existence of mobile laboratories and how inspection work continued regarding remotely piloted vehicles (RPVs). I highlighted the destruction of Al Samoud 2 missiles. Against the belittling of this operation that we had seen, I repeated my earlier statement that, "we are not watching the breaking of toothpicks." It was "a substantial measure of disarmament—indeed, the first since the middle of the 1990s."

I also noted that progress had been made in the field of interviews. In the preceding week we had done seven interviews "on our conditions"—i.e., without any Iraqi official attending and without any tape recorder. I said that Iraq was making a major effort to allow an objective assessment of the quantities of chemical and biological weapons that were unilaterally destroyed in 1991. In this, as in other matters, I said (making a point that my friend Mohamed thought essential), "inspection work is moving on and may yield results." I made the point a bit more specific—but not less guarded—by saying:

What are we to make of these activities? One can hardly avoid the impression that, after a period of somewhat reluctant cooperation, there has been an acceleration of initiatives from the Iraqi side since the end of January. This is welcome, but the value of these measures must be soberly judged by how many question marks they actually succeed in straightening out. This is not yet clear.

Against the not infrequent but exaggerated suggestions that the inspectors were holding the keys to peace and war in their hands, I stressed that it was for the Council to assess, on the basis of the factual descriptions I had provided, whether Iraq had cooperated "immediately, unconditionally and actively" as required under Resolution 1441. I noted nevertheless that although Iraq had become "active" or even "proactive," these initiatives three to four months into the new resolution could not be said to constitute "immediate" cooperation. The Council, not I, was to make the overall judgment.

I later said to a very seasoned American political friend that it would have been presumptuous of me to pass such judgment, and he commented, "Hans, they wanted you to be presumptuous." Well, yes, if it went their way, but not if it had gone the other way!

At the end of my speech I informed the Council officially about the existence of the cluster document and said we had declassified it and were making it available on request.

Many would have liked me say that I needed only a few months more to solve the disarmament issues. Mohamed had said this. However, he had few question marks. I said that even with a proactive Iraqi attitude, "induced by continued outside pressure," verified disarmament would take not years, nor weeks, but months. I added that "neither governments nor inspectors would want disarmament inspection to go on forever," but reminded the Council that, after verified disarmament, a sustained inspection and monitoring system was to remain in place to strike an alarm if there was any sign of revival of forbidden weapons programs.

Mohamed, who spoke after me, said that after three months of intrusive inspection, the IAEA had found no evidence or plausible indication of the revival of a nuclear weapons program in Iraq. He presented two stark pieces of information on matters that had recently emerged: First, the IAEA had concluded after extensive investigations that the much-publicized aluminum tubes Iraq had attempted to import were not likely to have been related to the manufacture of centrifuges for the enrichment of uranium. Second, the contract alleged to have been made between Iraq and Niger for the import of raw uranium—yellowcake—was not authentic. This was, if the expression is allowed, a blockbuster. In its uncontrolled eagerness to nail Iraq to a continued nuclear weapons program, the U.S. administration had allowed its president to use the yellowcake contract in his State of the Union address, despite knowledge within its own cadres that it was a questionable piece of evidence. Now it would have to live with Mohamed's revelation and suffer from its own poor quality control of information.

Mohamed concluded that the IAEA should be enabled in the near future to provide the Council with an objective and thorough assessment of Iraq's nuclear-related capabilities. He also referred, as I had done, to long-term monitoring as providing the international community with ongoing and real-time assurances in the future.

The discussion which ensued in the Council and at the following luncheon did not bring the parties closer. A basic and significant point made by both the German and the Russian foreign ministers was that their differences lay not in the aim—preventing proliferation—but in how to attain it: They were not fighting each other, they were fighting over how to treat a third party! While several of the ministers joined the United States and Colin Powell in making a "strategic decision" the criterion for fulfillment of Resolution 1441, the foreign minister of Mexico asked how one would identify such a decision, while the German and Chilean ministers asked what was the value of a strategic decision made by someone who was not trustworthy.

The French, German and Russian ministers advocated the concepts they had declared in Paris some days earlier. What was the point, the German minister asked, of preparing for inspections for two and a half years and then giving inspectors only two and a half months to work? The French minister said that setting a deadline of a few days for inspection would merely create a pretext for war, but that he was ready to shorten his own proposed deadline of 120 days. He also suggested that a meeting should be held at head-of-state level, an idea which was rather mercilessly shot down during the luncheon when two ministers said it was bad enough to demonstrate the existing rift at foreign-minister level.

Colin Powell confirmed what we had heard through John Wolf: that definitions of unresolved issues, whether clustered or not, were not of interest. All that mattered was the strategic decision, and this could be identified by the kind of enthusiasm that had been seen in the cases of South Africa and Ukraine. The statement thus confirmed that the U.S. considered that by adopting Resolution 1441, the Council had abandoned the approach taken during the 1990s. Powell belittled the steps that Iraq had taken (e.g., the destruction of missiles) and sought to reduce the credibility of the IAEA. He did not accept the agency's stand on the aluminum tubes—a stand which had, in fact, been accepted by the experts of the U.S. Department of Energy, which runs enrichment facilities. He said further that, "as we all know," in 1991 the agency had been just days away from determining that Iraq did not have a nuclear program. As I shall show, neither this claim nor subsequent claims by other senior U.S. representatives to the effect that the IAEA had failed to see Iraqi nuclear programs in 1995 and 1998 have been backed up by any explanations or evidence. Powell ended by urging an early vote on the resolution.

Jack Straw, the UK foreign secretary, received applause for his forceful, off-the-cuff speech and thereby evened the score with his French colleague, who'd received a similar reception at the Council meeting on February 14. Mr. Straw announced an amendment to the UK/U.S./Spain draft resolution of February 24. The preamble of the old draft was left unchanged but the operative paragraphs were new. The old draft had simply "decided" that Iraq had failed to take the final opportunity afforded to it in Resolution 1441 and that the Council remained "seized" of the matter. As I noted, it declared guilt without meting out punishment. The new text called on Iraq immediately to "take the decisions necessary in the interests of its people and region"—no doubt the "strategic" decisions. The next operative paragraph declared that Iraq would be considered to have "failed to take the final opportunity" unless on or before March 17, 2003, the Council concluded that Iraq had demonstrated full, unconditional, immediate and active cooperation and was yielding possession of *all* weapons and other prohibited items and information regarding prior destruction. There were no benchmarks: "all" weapons were to be turned in. It did not sound realistic. However, the time limit was there. In theory, it seemed possible to give mercy in return for urgent penitence.

More troublesome was the sixth preambular paragraph of the draft resolution. It noted, as before, that Iraq's declaration of December 8 had contained "false statements and omissions" and that Iraq had "failed to comply with and cooperate fully in the implementation" of Resolution 1441. Not surprisingly, the French whispered that this was declaration of war "by preamble." Nevertheless, I thought, here on March 7 there was something new: a theoretical possibility to avoid war. Saddam could make a speech; Iraq could hand over prohibited items. It was only a little later in the process, when at long last the benchmark notion made its appearance, that it occurred to me that the Iraqis would be in greater difficulty if, as they had been saying, there truly *were* no weapons of which they could "yield possession." Who would believe them? Certainly not the U.S. administration, which sounded more and more convinced of the existence of weapons of mass destruction, and more and more irritated at the inspectors who did not join them in this—mistaken—belief.

10

Bashing Blix and ElBaradei

On March 7, I did not answer the question whether or not Iraq had disarmed. I did not know. Rather, I gave a mixed picture based on our inspections. Cooperation had accelerated, but I noted that it had not come immediately, and while it was resulting in the destruction of missiles that we had judged proscribed, it had not straightened out any question marks. It was left to the Council to assess, on the basis of the detailed factual report I had presented, to what extent Iraq had complied or not complied with Resolution 1441, and to decide on what was to follow.

Now, many months after the armed action by the U.S. and its allies, I cannot but wonder how the world would have reacted if the inspectors had simply declared that they agreed with the U.S./ UK assessments—which were later shown to be wrong or highly dubious—about aluminum tubes, uranium contracts, mobile bio labs, drones, etc. What if the Security Council had then authorized the armed action and occupation only to find Iraq devoid of prohibited items?

Is Inspection Needed?

My refusal in my March 7 speech to assume that items "unaccounted for" might exist displeased some people in Washington. On

March 2 *The New York Times* reported "a senior administration official" as saying that "the inspections have turned out to be a trap. . . . We're not counting on Blix to do much of anything for us." And further: Blix had issued defiantly ambiguous pronouncements and was now "more interested in pleasing all sides than stating the facts" that Iraq had prohibited weapons, and that I did "not want to go back to Sweden and be the cause of a war." The criticism was evidently based on the conviction that U.S./UK evidence was conclusive and that my only reason for not swallowing it hook, line and sinker was that I would not want to be seen as easing a Security Council vote authorizing war.

The same article further reported that there was every hope in the Washington administration that the votes for the resolution could be obtained, "but decreasing hope that Mr. Blix will be a help in *rounding them up*" (my emphasis). Getting the UN votes authorizing war was the main U.S. preoccupation. That the professional inspectors, who had by then visited many hundred sites of the most varied kind, including sites based on intelligence tips, and analyzed many thousands of documents, had not come to confirm U.S./UK assertions was apparently not an overwhelming concern of the administrations.

Perhaps the British still felt a hope that Saddam Hussein would cave in and give evidence of his conversion by fulfilling some benchmarks within the ten days before the proposed March 17 deadline. On the U.S. side, the setting of benchmarks appeared either as a distraction or, at best (if Iraq rejected them), a means of highlighting Iraq's failures to cooperate and to disarm. Arguing against the French proposal to intensify inspections by tripling the number of inspectors, Donald Rumsfeld was quoted in the *International Herald Tribune* as saying that if you need inspectors to determine if Iraq is complying, then one or two would do. In other words, what was needed was a judgment, not inspection. The war was seen as certain and the adoption of the resolution endorsing it desirable but not indispensable.

Persuading Security Council Members to Vote for the Resolution

The U.S. administration had no easy task ahead of itself. It had to persuade enough members of the Security Council to get nine votes for the resolution. Opinion polls indicated that 86 percent of Germans rejected war in Iraq, so the German government was not likely to be swayed. Public opinion in Chile and Mexico was also negative. The governments of the African members of the Council were lobbied not only by the U.S. but also by antiwar France. The Angolan ambassador said in the Council that his country knew from experience what war was.

I have no documentary evidence of the pressures that the U.S. exercised on governments and ambassadors in this campaign, but it was easy to see that those members who were sincerely opposed to armed action at this juncture felt highly uncomfortable. It made me reflect on the grounds on which governments can legitimately base their votes in the Security Council.

The UN Charter obliges the members of the Council to assess and determine if there is a "threat to the peace, breach of the peace, or act of aggression," and they undoubtedly have the right to determine whether a state, like Iraq, has complied with Council resolutions that are binding upon it. Is it legitimate for a state member of the Council to allow its assessment and vote to be influenced by circumstances that have nothing whatever to do with the question of whether there is a threat to the peace or non-compliance with resolutions? Is a promise from another government that in return for a desired vote it will give generous aid or speed up the conclusion of a free-trade agreement a legitimate ground on which to cast such a vote?

In the U.S. Congress and perhaps in the legislatures of some other states, members—and, even more, groups of members—sometimes make their votes on an issue dependent on getting something in return on a totally different issue. When such horse-trading becomes too crude, the public reacts. I seem to remember such a reaction when a member of the U.S. Congress made his vote for higher compensation in the U.S. armed forces dependent upon a commitment that a squadron of planes would remain in his home state of Oklahoma. Are deals of this kind permissible in the UN Security Council?

The members of the UN—now 191 states—confer on the Council the "primary responsibility for the maintenance of peace and security." They further agree that in performing this responsibility the Council "acts on their behalf." Would, say, Ruritania be properly acting on behalf of the UN membership, which has elected it a member of the Council, if it were to allow an offer of foreign aid to influence it to vote in favor of a resolution declaring that Iraq was in non-compliance with its obligations? My answer would be no, and my advice would be that Ruritania should consult with the group of states to which it belongs and which nominated it to the seat in the Council to learn whether there is a common attitude on the question. If there is, it will be less difficult to ignore outside pressures. And if the common will of the group is followed, the weight and significance of the eventual vote will be greater.

We would properly react if a judge on a court allowed his vote for the death penalty in one case to be influenced by another judge's offer of support in a different case. Is this any different from one state urging another to vote for an authorization of the use of armed force which will inevitably lead to death and destruction?

When eventually the U.S. and UK decided not to put the draft resolution to a vote because they had concluded that it would not pass, this was, as I read it, testimony to the strong opposition in the public and in governments all over the world (perhaps with the exception of Kuwait) to armed action *at this juncture*. A formal vote was never taken but the informal conclusion of the Council was clearly no. A few saw this as the Council making itself irrelevant, and argued that only by supporting the U.S./UK draft resolution would the Council have participated in policymaking. My conclusion was the opposite: By withholding an authorization desired if not formally requested, the Council dissociated the UN from an armed action that most member states thought was not justified—at any rate, not at this stage.

Independent Inspection Becomes Impediment
to Vote on Intervention

I have no doubt that the position of the inspectors was of importance to the opponents of the armed action. Unlike the U.S./UK, the inspectors did not believe they had conclusive evidence that Iraq had weapons of mass destruction. This strengthened the widely held view that at any rate Iraq did not constitute a threat that had to be dealt with immediately by force. If armed action would be needed, it could be authorized later. The inspectors were not seen by the opponents of armed action as "defiantly ambiguous" but rather as doing an independent and credible inspection job on the ground, looking at the data with critical eyes and trying to report objectively.

The U.S./UK governments, while not even for a moment shaken by the cautious assessments of the inspectors, recognized that the inspectors' position had become an impediment to getting the war authorized by the Security Council. A news item from Washington on March 9 reported that "American diplomats acknowledged that their biggest challenge was in persuading the world, particularly the other Council members, that Mr. Blix and Dr. ElBaradei were incorrect when they suggested that the inspections were working so well that they needed more time to carry them out." How was this challenge handled?

First I should note that, as far as I know, only the U.S. government tried to claim that the inspectors were wrong in their assessments. The other governments sponsoring the resolution—the UK, Spain and Bulgaria—made no comments on this point. Secondly, I should further note that Article 100:2 of the UN Charter obliges member states to "respect the exclusively international character of the responsibilities of the Secretary-General and the staff and not to seek to influence them in the discharge of their responsibilities." This provision is aimed at creating a reliable international civil service, taking its instructions from the political bodies of the UN but not from individual members of the organization.

Thus, member states would not be free to exercise "pressure" on the UN inspectors.

Members are obviously free to criticize the work of UN staff, and under various Iraq resolutions they were asked to assist the inspectors, e.g., by recommending sites to be visited. Where is the border between inappropriate influence on the one hand and legitimate criticism and desirable recommendations on the other? Members of the U.S. government and administration did indeed voice criticism against the inspectors, directly and even more by feeding information to the media. As I shall show, the criticism was unfounded and unfair. Nevertheless, with the exception of one instance, I did not feel subjected to impermissible pressure by the U.S. or any other government. Was my skin too thick to feel it? I prefer to think that, despite the criticism issued in the heat of a campaign for votes, there was in various U.S. government quarters—perhaps not including the Pentagon—a good measure of respect for our professionalism and an awareness that we listened to advice but would ignore pressure.

Although Vice President Cheney had told ElBaradei and myself as early as the preceding October that the U.S. would not hesitate to "discredit" the inspections, the administration may have concluded that pressure on the inspectors was not appropriate and that high-level and direct criticism of them was not opportune. Whether the result of a joint consideration or of personal choice, public statements by Colin Powell, Condoleezza Rice and Ambassador John Negroponte about the inspectors' positions were mostly restrained and all contacts perfectly civil.

It is not difficult, however, to discern how the U.S. administration swung from seeing the inspection reports as potential assets in underpinning a future demand for armed action to identifying them as an impediment, the authority of which the U.S. needed to undermine.

Although Colin Powell's presentation of U.S. intelligence in the Security Council on February 5, 2003, was a show to the world of what U.S. intelligence—but not the inspectors—had found, there was no explicit criticism of the inspectors in his presentation.

Indeed, in an article in *The Wall Street Journal* which preceded his presentation, he wrote that the presentation would "reinforce what the inspectors told the Security Council" and that "together we must face the facts brought to us by the U.N. inspectors and reputable intelligence sources." Thus, he appeared to agree with the inspectors and only to go further and assert that Saddam was "concealing the evidence of his weapons of mass destruction, while preserving the weapons themselves."

The Criticism of UNMOVIC

John Wolf had certainly implied criticism when, at the February 23–24 College of Commissioners session, he'd questioned why our cluster/benchmark document hadn't referred to information offered to us by U.S. intelligence.

There might have been some disappointment even earlier that we did not simply adopt and report other intelligence information that had been given to us—e.g., about possibly hidden anthrax—or been made public. The atmosphere grew more heated as the hunt for votes intensified and reports from national intelligence were used to persuade states that armed intervention was indispensable to eliminate alleged Iraqi weapons of mass destruction. We had earlier been criticized for our reluctance to take Iraqi scientists abroad for interrogations. In this more charged atmosphere, UNMOVIC and I were criticized for not concluding, as the U.S. had, that an Iraqi drone and a cluster bomb we had inspected were intended for the dispersal of biological or chemical weapons.

The Cluster Bomb and the Drone

On March 6, the day before I was to speak in the Security Council, I was visited by U.S. Assistant Secretary John Wolf. He asked me in a rather discourteous tone why UNMOVIC did not conclude that the discovery of an Iraqi UAV drone and a cluster bomb for the delivery of chemical weapons were violations of Iraq's obligations. He tossed photographs of a drone and a cluster bomb on my table.

The drone issue was not new. Our inspectors had examined several of them and while Iraqi explanations had not been very satisfactory, we had not yet come to any conclusions about whether the drones were legal. Did any one of them have a range beyond the 150 kilometers permissible for missiles? Although the U.S. claimed they had identified a flight of 500 kilometers, it appeared to have been in racetrack mode, showing that the fuel was enough for this distance, though the effective reach might be limited by how far the guiding signal went. Was its body of drop tanks designed to carry and disperse biological or chemical weapons or only to contain photo equipment? These relevant questions had not yet been sufficiently explored. Accordingly, we had not drawn any conclusions.

I had not been briefed about the cluster bomb, and I said that Wolf could talk to our experts about it. He asked if I did not know what my staff was doing, and I replied that whenever there was something significant, they would tell me. I was confident that my deputy, Dimitri Perricos, would not fail to tell me about any significant discovery. In retrospect, I should like to believe that some of the rudeness in Wolf's approach could have been due to *his* being unaware of the weakness of his cases and, hence, of his démarche.

I asked him where he had got the pictures and he said he would not tell me. I said I resented it if he had obtained them through UNMOVIC staff. The pictures did not represent anything that needed confidentiality, and if the Security Council had asked to see them we would have circulated them. However, they were not in the public domain. I could not exclude the possibility that an UNMOVIC staff member had leaked them to the U.S., although it would have been a breach of duty.

I would resent, however, the U.S. seeking or even accepting information from us in such a way. I could also not exclude the possibility that the U.S. had managed to crack our secure fax, through which the pictures might have passed. The British newspaper *The Observer* had run articles claiming that the U.S. was bugging the offices and home phones of diplomats from Security Council member states. Whatever the explanation regarding our pictures being in Wolf's hands, his reply gave a bad taste.

In the oral presentation we had prepared for me to give at the next day's Security Council meeting (March 7), our inspections of remotely piloted vehicles were mentioned briefly with the comment that we were examining the range and capabilities of the various models. There was no reference to the cluster bomb and the empty spherical bomblets that had been found.

On the following Sunday, March 9, *The New York Times* had a detailed article in which Washington officials revealed that inspectors had recently discovered "a new variety of rocket [the cluster bomb] seemingly configured to strew bomblets filled with chemical or biological agents over large areas." The officials provided the information to reinforce the U.S. view that inspectors had found "incriminating evidence in Iraq." They also showed photographs of the weapons but, according to the article, "did not say how the photographs were obtained." The paper made the cautious comment that it remained unclear whether the cluster warhead was newly developed or from pre-1998.

From the UNMOVIC experts who subsequently briefed me, I learnt that the bomb and the bomblets—copies of South African munition imported by Iraq long ago—had been found in an old factory store and appeared to be scrap from the past rather than anything of current interest. There were no traces of chemical agents. The weapon had a short but intense political life span lasting from Thursday to Monday, when it was mentioned by U.S. Ambassador Negroponte in the informal consultations of the Security Council. Thereafter we never heard about it again, neither from the U.S. nor from anybody else. Presumably it remains in its store for old and discarded munitions, unless it has been looted for its metal value.

On the same Sunday, March 9, Colin Powell appeared on Fox TV. He said that I was "a decent, honest man"—which was nice of him at this juncture—but he thought I should have made more of the cluster/benchmarks document we had made available to the Security Council. As he had done in the Council, he stressed how the document showed year-long Iraqi efforts of deceit. He focused on the drone and said that the U.S. would "be making some news about it in the course of the week." They did.

This was not the first time that the drones were used for political effect. Already in a speech on October 7, 2002—before the vote on the "war resolution" in the U.S. Congress—President Bush had expressed concern that the Iraqis might use their unmanned aerial vehicles (UAVs) for missions targeting the U.S. Colin Powell had argued the same in his speech before the Security Council on February 5, 2003.

There was no doubt that this time the administration was set to inject the drone and cluster bomb as issues—indeed, even as "smoking guns, which the inspectors had deliberately chosen to belittle." Reuters reported on Monday, March 10, that the White House was aware that the resolution could go down in defeat. Seeking votes, Bush and Powell had worked the phones to leaders in member countries such as China, Pakistan, Angola and Mexico. The news agency also reported that the White House had "expressed annoyance" that Hans Blix had failed to mention to the Security Council "an Iraqi unmanned aircraft, whose existence was disclosed" in a declassified document circulated by the inspectors. Ari Fleischer, the White House press secretary, said that later on Monday U.S. delegates would ask at a closed Security Council meeting why the drone was not part of Blix's report. Colin Powell had only complained mildly that I could have "made more" of the drone. Now it was said—erroneously—that I had failed to mention it.

The story thus improved by the hour. It would get worse. A "fact sheet" purporting to summarize UNMOVIC's cluster/benchmarks document was issued by the State Department and sought, again erroneously, to describe our conclusions on the drone and several other issues as definitely incriminating Iraq.

James Bone, the UN correspondent of the London *Times,* easily outdid Washington. He now repeated the incorrect Washington assertion that I had not mentioned the drone in my Council presentation, and characterized this as "an apparent attempt by Dr. Blix to hide the revelation to avoid triggering war." He predicted—wrongly—that the discovery would make it easier for waverers to accept the U.S./UK line and quoted a senior diplomat from a swing vote saying, "It's a biggie." The drone, he wrote, was considered by British and U.S. officials to be a smoking gun, and the UK and U.S. would now "press" Blix to admit that he had found it.

I was wondering whether I would, for the first time, face a clash with members of the Security Council in the closed consultation meeting. I intended to defend UNMOVIC and myself against any unfair and unfounded criticism. I need not have worried. According to the notes I took—there are no official records from these meetings—the UK's ambassador Greenstock, who had many points to make about a possible compromise resolution, did not mention the two weapons issues. The drone and the cluster bomb were taken up in some detail by U.S. Ambassador Negroponte, albeit without any direct criticism of UNMOVIC or myself. He said the drone had not been declared and that this was a serious omission. It had, he said, a substantial range and could be used for the delivery of biological and chemical weapons. It could be a violation. What was UNMOVIC's strategy?

When by the end of the lengthy consultation I got the floor, I said that there was a lot of information flowing in and that all did not deserve immediate reporting, but could await periodic reports. We had publicly and separately reported our finds of warheads for chemical weapons and of nuclear-related documents, but we had not reported on finding the leftover cluster bomb and submunitions which were possibly once intended as a chemical weapon. We had judged this find to be of limited importance. I referred to the drone and said I had mentioned it without details in the Council. I now reported that it had a wingspan of 7.45 meters and that Iraq had described testing it for a range of 55 kilometers with a payload capacity of 30 kilograms and a flight time of 30 minutes. I said it had not been declared as it should have been. (The Iraqi side later claimed that they had provided a somewhat faulty declaration.) I reported that we continued to gather data on this and other drone models. Until now we had not found any links to weapons of mass destruction, but additional work was needed to verify the accuracy of the flight ranges declared. Iraq claimed the vehicles were intended for conventional purposes, such as surveillance, targeting and electronic communications jamming. If they were found to have a range longer than 150 kilometers or to be designed for the delivery of biological and chemical weapons, they would be illegal. UNMOVIC was investigating these points. There were no comments in the Council to my explanation.

As my colleague Dr. ElBaradei was not present at this informal Council meeting, I took the opportunity to state briefly that public comments that had suggested the IAEA had allowed itself to be misled by Iraq even after the end of the Gulf War had not been documented and, in my view, were not justified.

Although informal consultations without written speeches and official records—by far the greater part of the Council's proceedings—are, in principle, confidential, they are far from secret. As the Havamal, the old Icelandic book of Viking wisdom, tells us, the world knows what a threesome knows. Indeed, the members of the Council often have a political need to explain to the outside what they seek to do, and the media, of course, have a duty to cover the political process. After informal consultations in the Council chambers there is most often an opportunity for the UN correspondents to ask questions of the participants, who can hardly avoid passing the space reserved for the press. As on this occasion there was high tension in the air and UNMOVIC had a central role, they were eager to hear my comments.

I used the occasion to note the relevant fact that UNMOVIC's cluster/benchmarks document, which we had now declassified, nowhere asserted that Iraq had weapons of mass destruction but showed numerous discrepancies and deficiencies in Iraq's accounts of such weapons. I said that intelligence gathering was difficult and necessary. While we had great respect for it, we must soberly assess the results. We had done so when we prepared the cluster document. Mr. Bone, the correspondent of the London *Times,* tried to follow up on his own news report by asking me why we had not reported about the drones. I limited myself to simply saying that there was a lot about drop tanks in our report. When I was asked directly about the American criticism, I replied that "everyone tries to squeeze us to get as much mileage as they can."

If the Washington officials had failed to set the issue ablaze more generally, they had at any rate very successfully ignited Mr. Bone. The next day, March 12, the London *Times* had an article by him with the headline BLIX SHOULD TURN THE "SMOKING GUN" ON HIS OWN HEAD. He explained in the article that it was time for me to resign. I had, so he said, discredited myself and "betrayed the trust of all those many millions around the world who put their faith in the United Nations." Dr. Blix, he said, "is apparently determined that he will not be the man who triggers war. . . . Although he 'emphatically' denies he is keeping information from the Security Council . . . he has been burying it." He ended the column by saying that, "when history of this tumultuous time is written, Dr. Blix will be the man who tried to hide the 'smoking gun.' "

What Was the Truth about the Drones?

We were certainly not hiding anything. In retrospect the matter seems simple: The U.S. administration had concluded—almost certainly wrongly, it now appears—that the drone was a violation of the Security Council's resolution. At UNMOVIC we were not ready to make that assessment. This angered Washington, despite the fact that it must have been known that the U.S. Air Force itself did not believe the Iraqi drones were for the delivery of biological and chemical agents.

In Baghdad, meanwhile, they evidently got worried by the U.S. media blitz. General Amin, the head of the National Monitoring Directorate, called a news conference on March 11 where he showed the drone to the press. He explained that it was powered by a two-stroke motorcycle engine, had a ground-control range of eight kilometers and was used only for reconnaissance. He said its payload was twenty kilograms and it was designed to carry a video camera, not biological weapons. He claimed that Iraq had declared it but had made a typographical error, giving it a wingspan of 14.5 feet instead of 24.5 feet. An AP writer present at the show reported on March 12 that the wings were of balsa wood and held together with duct tape. *The New York Times* correspondent in Baghdad reported that it was "farcical" to describe this as something serious.

Even as Washington seized on the drone and the cluster bomb and criticized me and UNMOVIC for not highlighting the issues, *The New York Times* reported that some American officials were skeptical that the UNMOVIC cluster/benchmarks document pointed to Iraqi violations. A defense official had also said that the drones described might not be an effective means of delivering biological or chemical agents. It was made known several months later, in July, that the U.S. Air Force, the greatest repository of U.S. expertise on drones, had all along doubted that Iraq's drones were designed for attack and held that they were for reconnaissance. This view was strengthened by the examination of drones that became possible after the occupation. The CIA seems nevertheless to stick to its conclusion. Perhaps an effort is being made to ensure that the issue disappears from the screen as a matter of controversy rather than as error?

Undermining the IAEA and ElBaradei

Nothing could have given stronger political support for a preemptive strike than convincing evidence that Iraq had or was near acquiring nuclear weapons. The IAEA, which had been responsible for all nuclear inspections in Iraq, did not see any such evidence and openly questioned some of the evidence on which the U.S. and UK sought to rely in 2002 and 2003. To defend and bolster its own case, the U.S. administration sought to undermine the credibility of the IAEA. Although the postwar experience appears to have proved that the IAEA was correct in questioning some of the U.S./UK evidence, the unfounded points of criticism which were leveled—for the first time ever by a government—against the IAEA have, regrettably, not been withdrawn, and may cause damage that is not in anyone's interest. Here is the story of the roots of this disagreement, which probably reach down as far as 1991.

As director general of the IAEA at the time, I was responsible for the agency's 1997 report to the Security Council on nuclear inspections in Iraq. Dr. ElBaradei, who succeeded me as director general, was responsible for the report of 1998. The conclusions of the two reports were essentially the same: The agency had acquired a full understanding of Iraq's nuclear weapons program and had eliminated the whole infrastructure and removed all fissionable material from Iraq. Iraq no longer had any physical capability of producing any significant amount of weapons-usable nuclear material. There were no indications that further disarmament was required in the nuclear sphere, but various other questions remained to be clarified.

The Iraqi government was angry that the agency did not, in these circumstances, close the file and give Iraq a clean bill of health. When Dr. ElBaradei and I met with Dr. Dhia Jaffar, the central figure in the Iraqi nuclear program, in New York in May 2002, he got so worked up on this matter that Dr. Amir Al Sa'adi had to calm him down.

The view that Iraq's nuclear dossier was pretty much closed by the end of 1998 appears to have been shared by all members of the Security Council, including the U.S. The arrival of the Bush administration made no difference in this respect. Indeed, on February 24, 2001, Colin Powell—going beyond the nuclear sphere—was quoted as saying that Saddam Hussein did not have "any significant capability with respect to weapons of mass destruction."

The Impact of September 11 on U.S. Assessment of Iraq

The terrorist attacks of September 11 changed the vision of the Bush administration. Although no new evidence had become available, the history of Saddam's past use of chemical weapons and missiles, of his past nuclear ambitions, and of the difficulties his regime had caused inspectors throughout the 1990s were seen in a new, more ominous and incriminating light. As early as November 14, 2001, Richard Perle, the exotic superhawk connected with the Pentagon, said that the most compelling argument for going to war with Iraq was that with enough time Saddam would be capable of attacking the U.S. with a nuclear weapon. "Do we wait for Saddam or do we take preemptive action?" he asked. Half a year after the war began, in September 2003, President Bush confirmed that his administration still fundamentally embraced this view, saying that the attacks of September 11 had shown that "we have to deal with threats before they come on our shore."

Seen through this new prism, various events and reports came to be viewed as evidence that Iraq was moving toward a nuclear weapons capability that had not been suspected before. Early in September 2002, President Bush declared that satellite photographs of new construction at Al Furat, Iraq's former site for uranium enrichment by centrifuge, showed that the country's nuclear bomb program had been resurrected. "I don't know what more evidence we need," he said. But he would, in fact, need more. The Iraqis immediately invited the press to Al Furat, and dozens of journalists visiting the site under Iraqi escort saw no centrifuges. Subsequent reports by the U.S. and UK make no further mention of the photos.

UK and U.S. Reports on Iraq, September 2002

In the same month the Al Furat photos were released, both the UK and the U.S. issued reports listing their reasons for concluding that Iraq was violating the various weapons bans. The U.S. nuclear list was conspicuously shorter than the British, and did not cite the alleged attempted import of natural uranium (yellowcake) from Africa which President Bush later cited in his State of the Union message on January 28, 2003. Both pamphlets mentioned the Iraqi effort to import specially designed aluminum tubes which,

the U.S. text cautiously said, "*officials believe* were intended as components of centrifuges to enrich uranium" (my emphasis). Such
language, of course, is a way of renouncing or at least reducing
responsibility for what you publish.

There was a surprising discrepancy in the two reports' assessments of the time that would be needed for Iraq to develop nuclear
weapons. The British document was detailed on this point and
explained that as long as sanctions remained effective, Iraq would
not be able to produce a nuclear weapon. This did not differ from
the IAEA's assessment. If sanctions were removed or became inef-
fective, the British dossier said, it would take Iraq at least five years
to produce the required fissile material for a bomb; if Iraq was able
to obtain such material and other needed components from foreign
sources, it would only take a year or two. The US report avoided
making an assessment of its own but cited the International Institute of Strategic Studies' conclusion that Iraq could build a nuclear
bomb within months if it was able to obtain fissile material. Again, a
way of disseminating an alarming message to the public while limiting responsibility for its correctness.

The U.S. report noted further that Saddam Hussein had met
repeatedly with his nuclear scientists over the previous two years,
"signaling" his continued interest in developing nuclear weapons.
There is no effort here to place the responsibility for the statement
on someone else. One might wonder, however, how reliable a signal
this was. Since the war, we have learned about the miserable conditions in which the nuclear scientists worked at this time, and that
there was simply no possibility for a nuclear weapons program. Was
Saddam deliberately sending the outside world a signal designed to
mislead it into believing that, contrary to its declarations to the UN,
Iraq was continuing its nuclear efforts? Or was he merely trying to
keep the scientists' spirits up and feign to Iraq and its Arab neigh-
bors that scientific progress continued as usual? That the scientists
tried to keep Saddam's spirits up—and seek to ensure that some
flow of cash would continue to themselves—appears confirmed by
several reports.

The Aluminum Tubes

The aluminum tubes had a much longer career as evidence than the new Al Furat buildings which President Bush had thought made all further questions unnecessary. This is somewhat surprising, as even early in the discussion David Albright's Institute for Science and International Security, a Washington research group with a good reputation, voiced serious doubts that the tubes were intended for centrifuges. So did the IAEA, which had physically examined the tubes and had considerable knowledge on the matter. The tubes were illegally imported, yes, but all illegal imports did not necessarily relate to weapons of mass destruction. It was later revealed that the U.S. Department of Energy, which is responsible for centrifuge enrichment in the U.S., had dissented from the conclusion that the tubes were for centrifuges. However, the officials with political responsibility evidently wanted this conclusion.

In spite of the warning signals, Deputy Secretary of Defense Wolfowitz continued to cite the tubes as significant evidence. He admitted modestly that the U.S. might be mistaken—but then, he said, it could also happen that the IAEA was mistaken. The ironic turn of phrase showed who he thought was to be trusted. Colin Powell also invoked the tubes as evidence of an Iraqi nuclear weapons program during his presentation in the Security Council on February 5, but added a caveat that this views was not unanimously accepted. One month later, Dr. ElBaradei reported in the Council that Iraq had maintained that the 81-millimeter tubes had been sought for rocket production. The IAEA team had made a thorough investigation and had concluded that the tubes were "not likely to have been related to the manufacture of centrifuges." Although Colin Powell did his best to keep the issue unresolved, the IAEA's view seems to have been borne out. A report by Barton Gellman in *The Washington Post* on October 26, 2003, revealed that although not all in Washington had even at that late date abandoned the centrifuge theory, the postwar experts in Baghdad had discarded it and no longer showed any interest in the tubes. One expert volunteered the view that they might be looted to be used as drainpipes. . . .

The Yellowcake

The yellowcake story, which surfaced with the publication of the UK report in September 2002 (in time for the UN General Assembly session), has achieved as much visibility, not to say infamy, as the claim made by Prime Minister Blair in the same report that Saddam's planning "allows for some of the WMD to be ready within 45 minutes of an order to use them." The report asserted that Iraq had "sought significant quantities of uranium from Africa despite having no active civil nuclear power programme that could require it." As I noted previously, the U.S. report that appeared the same month did not mention the case, but in January 2003 Condoleezza Rice wrote about it and Colin Powell asked delegates at the World Economic Forum in Davos, Switzerland, "Why is Iraq still trying to procure uranium?"

Exhibit number one in the intriguing affair was a document that purported to be a contract between the governments of Niger and Iraq for the delivery of yellowcake, or natural uranium. This yellowcake achieved the high point in its career when President Bush mentioned it in his State of the Union message on January 28, 2003: "The British government has learned that Saddam Hussein recently sought significant quantities of uranium from Africa." Considering that the case had been explicitly included in the published UK dossier, the president's statement could be argued to have been incontrovertible. But, on the other hand, the fact that at this time there existed within the president's own administration knowledge that the key piece of evidence had been falsified, makes it a scandal that the sentence had not been purged.

The low point for the yellowcake came on March 7, when, as I recounted in chapter 8, Mohamed ElBaradei reported to the Security Council that the documents were false. While I did not even raise an eyebrow, my thoughts at that moment were essentially, "Wow." Mohamed had not told me in advance, so I had not known it was coming. I had, however, for many months thought it curious that Iraq would seek to buy yellowcake. Most people's thoughts jump to bombs as soon as someone mentions the word *uranium.* However, the uranium you mine in the ground and concentrate into yellowcake must go through long and very difficult industrial and chemical processes before it becomes the explosive for nuclear bombs. With their facilities for these processes destroyed, why should Iraq have sought to buy yellowcake? If they would be able one day to shake off sanctions, they could mine uranium in their own country, as they had done before the Gulf War. The yellowcake story did not appear to me to stand up to common sense. But then, it was not the only item in the Iraq affair that did not fit with common sense, and I never publicly voiced my doubt.

It appears that while it took considerable time for the IAEA to get a copy of the yellowcake documents from the CIA, it did not take the agency long to establish that they were forgeries—or, to use the gentler diplomatic language appropriate for an international civil servant, "not authentic." For one thing, it appears that they were signed with the name of a minister who was not in the government of Niger at the time the document was dated.

Unfair Criticism of the IAEA

Following ElBaradei's speech, Colin Powell refrained from comment on the forgery revelation, although it must have been rather painful. However, he did make an effort to undermine the agency's credibility by saying, "*As we all know,* in 1991 the IAEA was just days away from determining that Iraq did not have a nuclear program. We soon found out otherwise. IAEA is now reaching a similar conclusion, but we have to be very *cautious*" (my emphasis).

Perhaps Powell's line was derived from talking points shared within the administration and aimed at countering the IAEA's influence on the forthcoming vote. On March 9, Condoleezza Rice was interviewed on ABC television and said, "The IAEA, *of course,* missed the [nuclear] program in ninety-one, missed the program in ninety-five, missed it in ninety-eight." Her comment, and that which followed, was strikingly similar to Mr. Powell's: "We need to be *careful* about drawing these conclusions, particularly in a totalitarian state like Iraq" (my emphasis).

ElBaradei's statement on March 7 had also included the point that "we have to date found no evidence or plausible indication of the revival of a nuclear weapons program." On the television program *Meet the Press* on March 16, just before the war, it was Vice President Cheney's turn to tackle him: "I think Mr. ElBaradei frankly is wrong. . . . And I think if you look at *the track record of the International Atomic Energy Agency* on this kind of issue, especially where Iraq's concerned, they have consistently underestimated or missed what it was Saddam Hussein was doing. I don't have reason to believe they are any more valid this time than they've been in the past" (my emphasis).

More than two months later, on May 28, in a curious kind of defense of the U.S. occupying force having not yet found any illegal weapons in Iraq, Deputy Secretary of Defense Wolfowitz implied poor performance on the part of the IAEA. He said, "I mean, it took time in 1991, *if you recall.* I think it was three months after the war that the IAEA was prepared to declare there was no nuclear program, and it was about three to six months later that they discovered that, in fact, they were pursuing not one, but I think four different routes to nuclear weapons. . . ." (my emphasis).

These criticisms were the first and only ones directed against the IAEA by a government regarding its inspections in Iraq. They could perhaps be disregarded as peculiar to a momentary U.S. effort in the spring of 2003 to convince the world that Iraq had resumed its quest for nuclear weapons. However, it seems to me more likely that they had deeper roots, probably on the military side of the U.S. administration rather than in the Department of State and Department of Energy, both of which have considerable experience in working with the agency. I have described in chapter 2 the previous Bush administration's resistance in 1991 to the Security Council giving the agency any mandate to inspect Iraq after the Gulf War.

Toward the end of 2003, some U.S. government officials seem to have voiced criticism of the IAEA because the Agency Secretariat was not ready to conclude, from the clandestine Iranian enrichment program alone, that Iran was striving to make a nuclear weapon. In connection with Libya's declaration a little later about its readiness to abandon all efforts to develop nuclear weapons, U.S. officials seemed displeased that the agency's experts expressed the view, after visiting the country, that Libya had been a rather long way from a nuclear capability. In both cases, one may discern an effort to depict the agency's assessments as being too lenient.

Perhaps it would be useful to check whether the problem is not the opposite: that statements and assessments on the U.S. side sometimes have been too alarming or exaggerated. U.S. claims made in 2003 about Iraq and nuclear weapons would seem to point in that direction. However that may be, the account I have presented in chapter 2 regarding IAEA inspections in Iraq should show that while the agency "missed" the Iraqi nuclear enrichment and weapons program when it operated the traditional safeguards system under the Nuclear Non-Proliferation Treaty before April 1991, it did a perfectly creditable job as the Security Council's nuclear inspection tool after that date. The record needs to be set straight.

11

Diplomacy on the Brink: The Breakdown

The formal agenda item for the Security Council meeting on March 7 was the twelfth quarterly report of UNMOVIC, which covered the inspections in December, January and February.

Resolution 1284, under which the inspection regime was set up in 1999, required not only that quarterly reports should be presented but also that after a period of initial inspections we should submit a draft "work programme" for approval by the Security Council. The latest date for this submission was calculated to be March 27—still twenty days off. The draft program should list what we regarded as "key remaining disarmament tasks." If progress was made in resolving these tasks within 120 days, the road would be open for the Council to suspend—not lift—the sanctions. Thus, such suspension could happen by the end of July if Iraq cooperated fully. In the view of the Russians, the French and the Germans, there was nothing wrong with this perspective. They felt the inspections were going reasonably well: There had been no denials of access and a large number of missiles were being destroyed.

To the U.S. administration, the prospect of the work program stretching four months into the future must have appeared totally unacceptable. It had concluded—erroneously, and with some internal footnotes of dissent—that Iraq did possess chemical and bio logical weapons and could even produce them in mobile units, that it was making long-range unmanned aerial vehicles capable of dispersing them, and that it was reviving its past nuclear program. In its view, the items which the inspectors considered unaccounted for almost certainly still existed. The logical conclusion was that Iraq must have made false statements or omissions in the declaration it had submitted in December 2002, thereby committing a further material breach of its obligations and justifying armed intervention. Although Iraq had given inspectors unimpeded access, it had not, in the U.S. view, cooperated as required regarding interviews, U-2 flights and adoption of legislation prohibiting the production of proscribed weapons—again material breaches. As expected, Iraq had not seized the final opportunity given to it by Resolution 1441 but was trying to cheat and do the minimum it thought it could get away with.

It was time to consider action, *viz.* armed intervention. The official U.S. position was that no specific authorization by the Security Council was needed. At the same time it was felt that there would be an advantage to having the UN's blessing, and it was well understood that an endorsement by the Council was of great political importance to Washington's main ally, the British.

A "Smoking Gun" or the Absence of a "Strategic Decision" as Grounds for War

Although Colin Powell, Paul Wolfowitz and David Kay all in their different ways argued that a "smoking gun" was completely unnecessary, there is little doubt that the U.S. administration would have dearly wanted to find one and make it exhibit number one in the case for war. In the days after the meeting of the Council, the administration went to the media and voiced its displeasure that UNMOVIC had not held up either the drone or the cluster bomb as evidence of violations by Iraq. Presumably the aim was both to give publicity to the alleged smoking guns and to erode confidence in the inspectors, who had failed to sound an alarm about the items.

The U.S. administration's weekend information drive during the first days of March had the expected desired echo, at least in the conservative media. I learnt that I had been vilified, crucified and made to look like an imbecile, and I realized that I saved a lot of adrenaline by hardly ever watching TV and by limiting my reading to a few high-quality newspapers. However, both nasty and amusing messages penetrated my shield of convenience. One e-mail advised me that if I could not see the smoking gun I should turn to my optician—to which I answered with thanks for the advice and the comment that I wanted a pair of lenses without color. My comment triggered a new mail applauding my intention to get rid of the rose-colored glasses I was evidently wearing. I have not yet informed my correspondent that my imaginary optician later recommended a magnifying glass, and that I am thinking of buying two and donating one to the Pentagon. . . .

Another mail told me that I was not a watchdog but a French poodle. A tabloid headline proclaimed that BLIX TRICKS IRK U.S. I could not help admiring it. I would have bought a drink for the editor who drafted it.

By and large I was unperturbed by the sniping. We had not been trying to position ourselves somewhere between the U.S./UK and Iraq, nor, indeed, between any governments. We were not appointed mediators, but inspectors. However, the fact that Saddam Hussein's regime was one of the most brutal the world had seen and had long been a danger to the region did not justify any twisting of observations or uncritical attitude to evidence. I knew our inspections and reports were professional, honest and without any hidden agenda to absolve or indict. Nothing is perfect, and we could have been wrong on one point or another, but I was confident we had our feet on the ground and rendered and assessed the reality with a reasonable degree of correctness. I said on some occasion to the press that we might not be the brightest in the world, but we were at any rate in nobody's pocket.

Protesting that smoking guns were unnecessary, the U.S. administration asserted that Iraq had not taken the necessary strategic decision to disarm. This assertion was less impressive and persuasive than a demonstration of a smoking gun would have been, but it was harder to contradict.

Looking at the question in retrospect and knowing that it is possible that strategic decisions were, in fact, taken in 1991 (in all areas except missiles), I cannot help wondering *why* the Iraqi side did not try to convince us of this in 2002 and 2003. They could have pointed to the statement to this effect which Hussein Kamel, the son-in-law of Saddam, made in 1995 when he defected to Jordan. Had there really been no written orders issued in 1991? If there were some, why were they not presented? Why was the Iraqi side so late in presenting UNMOVIC with lists of people who they claimed had taken part in the destruction of prohibited items in 1991? Why did they not present these people for interviews in December 2002?

Key Remaining Disarmament Tasks, as Benchmarks

The idea of setting benchmarks which Iraq should attain to convince the world that it was disarming had been in the air for some time before the Security Council meeting on March 7. Like the smoking guns, it was almost an antithesis of the somewhat nebulous concept of strategic decision. It would identify precise, concrete goals that Iraq needed to attain. The U.S. administration appears to have been somewhat ambivalent on the idea. On the one hand, it might help the Iraqi regime to get through a critical period by tolerably fulfilling some early benchmarks in order later to stall and cheat. On the other hand, giving Iraq successive sets of benchmarks to fulfill could be said to take the weakness out of the concept of strategic decision by indicating concretely what would be acceptable evidence of such a decision. There appears also to have been an awareness that if Iraq were given difficult benchmarks and little time to fulfill them, a resulting failure could make it easier to obtain the desired authorization of force from the Security Council. The net result was halfhearted U.S. support for the British attempt to use the benchmark concept as a quick test of Iraq's will to cooperate.

It could be said that the demand in the 1999 resolution that progress should be made in the solution of "key remaining disarmament tasks" amounted to a benchmark approach, albeit one that could last 120 days or more. The key tasks selected could be seen as benchmarks and their fulfillment would be evidence of cooperation. The Russians, French and Germans felt the benchmark approach already existed in the resolution of 1999. Why should one devise new benchmarks—new "key tasks"—when UNMOVIC was very soon to propose a list in its work program? They were aware that the "key remaining disarmament tasks" were to be selected by UNMOVIC from the cluster document that was being finalized, and they had urged UNMOVIC to speed up its presentation of that document and of its work plan, no doubt with a view to boosting the benchmark idea and linking it into the procedure foreseen under the 1999 resolution. Neither the U.S. nor the UK objected to the German/French/Russian wish for a declassification of the cluster document.

Colin Powell and Jack Straw, who had had the opportunity to read an early draft of the cluster document given to UNMOVIC Commissioners, made extensive use of it in the Council meeting to demonstrate how Iraq had cheated and concealed—the implication being that inspection did not work. There was no early sign of the subsequently voiced U.S. disappointment that the document had not pointed to any smoking gun, nor any echo of John Wolf's acid comments in the UNMOVIC College that the document had little interest and that all that mattered was a conclusion that no strategic decision had been taken.

Dominique de Villepin, who unlike his U.S. and UK colleagues had probably not seen the edition of the document issued to the Commissioners, urged inspectors to present the work program and the list of key remaining disarmament tasks as early as possible. Like the Russians and the Germans, he sensed it was urgent that the Council espouse these tasks. March 27 was too far away. He declared that he was ready to ask the inspectors to submit progress reports every three weeks on the fulfillment of the key tasks and to ask the Council to assess Iraq's implementation of the work program within a shorter time than the 120 days prescribed in the 1999 resolution.

A Speech by Saddam Hussein Announcing the "Strategic Decision"

In Jack Straw's speech in the Council on March 7 he made it clear that Iraqi disarmament could not be expected in the short time the draft resolution left for Iraq to come into compliance (i.e., until March 17). He did not suggest that Saddam Hussein should simply announce the strategic decision, but at the informal Council consultations in the evening following the public session, Sir Jeremy Greenstock said that there was enough time for Iraq to *speak* and act to convince all of a strategic decision to disarm voluntarily. What Sir Jeremy had in mind was probably a speech by Saddam Hussein and a catalog of acts (benchmarks) that was shorter than the key remaining disarmament tasks that would very soon be listed by UNMOVIC.

On the day after the Council meeting I saw Amr Moussa, the secretary general of the League of Arab States and former foreign minister of Egypt. We were old friends. I had known him since we were both delegates in the Legal Committee of the General Assembly, years before. He was now planning a visit to Baghdad by a delegation under the aegis of the League, to see Saddam Hussein. I suggested to him that although the impact of a "strategic decision" declaration by Saddam would be uncertain at this stage, it seemed about the only path open—and the sooner it was tried, the better. I sketched points that I thought could be included in a televised address by Saddam. For instance:

- That he wanted to create absolute certainty in the world that no attack on Iraq could be justified by the fear that Iraq had weapons of mass destruction.
- That UN inspection had verified the destruction of many such weapons in the past but, since doubts still existed, he would declare that *whatever prohibited weapon or other proscribed item or activity might still exist, possession was yielded to the UN inspection.*
- That all Iraqi authorities—military or civilian, scientists, engineers or others—were requested to give the UN inspection organs all information that they possessed, in full and accurate disclosures. Citizens were to be urged to tell UN inspectors the truth, whether they were asked to do so in Iraq or to go for interviews abroad.

I said to Amr Moussa that this kind of declaration might not be enough to stave off the imminent danger of attack. There had been rumors in the past year that Saddam had thought of stepping aside. He might announce that he felt it was time for him to do that and to announce who was to be in charge. I said further that he might invite myself and ElBaradei to come and meet him and receive assurances along the lines described. Last, I suggested it might be helpful to convey to Saddam that if, in spite of all, the situation came to armed action, Iraq must refrain from any hostage-taking and any use of chemical or biological weapons. If it did not, the people in the world who now opposed armed action would say the action had proved justified.

In the end, the mission of the Arab League was canceled and Saddam never got to hear Amr Moussa and the points I had thought out—one of the more unusual speeches I have ever sketched.

The British Operating on the Brink

In the Council consultations, the UK was first a bit cautious as to whether "a list of defined tasks"—benchmarks—would be useful. In my private notes I recorded Sir Jeremy Greenstock as saying that "it would be blindingly obvious" if Iraq made a strategic decision. He implied, I suppose, that it was really unnecessary to specify what should be seen as evidence of a decision. Nevertheless, being aware that others did not think it was unnecessary and being anxious to gain support for the resolution, the Brits yielded another inch and proceeded to work out a paper defining what would be accepted as evidence of a strategic decision. In a solo performance, Sir Jeremy tried to persuade other members to go along. While the U.S. representatives did not seek to impede him, you could sense that they had instructions to tolerate the British effort for a few days, but not more. Perhaps Washington was even a little worried that Sir Jeremy might succeed in getting a majority for a benchmark resolution and that the Iraqis would succeed in complying? It was an interesting moment with a potential divergence between the Anglo-Saxon allies.

The paper, as it emerged, sought two kinds of evidence of a strategic decision. First, Saddam Hussein should pronounce the decision in a televised speech. In a most helpful manner, the paper contained a number of specific points to be used. Second, before March 17, Iraq should attain five benchmarks to provide the necessary evidence that the decision was real and genuine.

The points listed for Saddam to cover in his speech were not vastly different from the ones I had discussed with Amr Moussa. However, I had thought of transmitting the advice to Saddam orally through a high Arab official, in confidence. The UK draft would contain public instructions to Saddam regarding what he was to say. It would also force him to confess explicitly that Iraq had in the past sought to conceal its weapons of mass destruction. Requiring humiliation, I thought, would be a sure way of getting the emperor of Mesopotamia to reject the idea of a declaration. Perhaps this was the intention? The Syrian representative was the only one in the Council who commented on the points of substance. He said that it would be perceived as humiliating the Iraqi people, not only Saddam. Other representatives asked what purpose there was in asking for a declaration by someone who was regarded as a habitual liar.

A Talk with Tony Blair about the Benchmarks That Iraq Should Attain

At 8:00 in the morning on March 10, I had a call from a member of the British mission. He apologized for disturbing me at such an undiplomatic hour and asked if I could come to his mission in half an hour to take a call from his prime minister. I realized that was a civilized 1:30 p.m. in London, gulped a cup of tea, for once skipped making my bed and rushed down to 47th Street to take the call on the secure line in Sir Jeremy's office.

Tony Blair said they needed five or six items on which the Iraqis could demonstrate their compliance with UNMOVIC's work program. Along with the declaration by Saddam, items the Brits had been considering included accounting for anthrax, the chemical agents VX and mustard, SCUD missiles and remotely piloted vehicles; and promising genuine cooperation with UNMOVIC's plan to take scientists (along with their families) for interviews outside Iraq. The process could not go on until April/May but perhaps it could extend a few days beyond March 17. I sensed he found it hard to persuade the U.S. to go along. The Americans doubted, he said, that they had UNMOVIC's sympathy. I did not comment.

In retrospect, I think this view probably was taken by the U.S. administration when UNMOVIC did not brand the drone and cluster bomb as smoking guns. They had made a good deal of noise about this. It does not bother me that we had different views on the nature of these items, but I still find it insulting if they believed that our assessments were prompted by a wish to avoid finding incriminating evidence. I told Blair that none of the items he had mentioned would fall outside our list of unresolved disarmament issues. Whether they would all be among the key issues we would select, I could not yet say with certainty.

The final list of benchmarks on which the British settled included the items Blair had mentioned, with the modification that instead of accounting for mustard gas, Iraq was to account for and surrender mobile facilities for the production of chemical and biological agents. We had looked long and in vain for these facilities, which Western intelligence agencies were then very sure existed.

The Other Members of the Council

The French, Germans and Russians did not see a need for a set of newly chosen benchmarks, as UNMOVIC would come in a few days with a list of key tasks that had been selected after months of solid analysis. However, it was well understood by all that in a situation where early proof was desired of an unreliable client's will to fulfill all his obligations, the benchmark approach offered the possibility of a kind of "down payment" approach, with installments to be made successively at suitable intervals, the first being due, perhaps, as early as ten days after the adoption of the resolution. Gradually, confidence could arise that the "strategic decision" pronounced was genuine.

The French ambassador explained to me that France could accept a shorter time for the attainment of key remaining disarmament tasks than the 120 days stipulated by Resolution 1284. He was still talking about the whole list we would present rather than thinking of a shorter list of benchmarks that might be attained in a shorter time. How much time would UNMOVIC need for its list? he asked. I explained that we might select some seventeen key issues and that their attainment depended above all on the Iraqi side. Even with excellent cooperation, it would take months. Perhaps June 1 could be a set as the time limit. We would in any case have to submit a quarterly report by that date.

The principal problems for the French were not, however, whether there would be a short or a long list, or even how much time was given, but the stand of the U.S. that there would be no need for the Council as a body to assess whether a list of issues had been solved or benchmarks attained. The U.S. maintained it was free to make this assessment solo and to draw its own conclusions. The French disputed that right and so did many others, asserting that it was for the Council—not an individual state—to authorize war. I said I understood this well and agreed there was a risk that the U.S. could come on March 17, assess alone that Iraq had failed to take the last opportunity offered to it and commence armed action. However, I said, there was also the possibility that if Iraq made a declaration and clearly attained three of the five benchmarks by that date, there would be a new dynamic away from the use of armed force.

To complete the destruction of the missiles before March 17 should be do-able; to send thirty scientists and their families to Larnaca for interviews might not be practically easy but should also be do-able; and to give full information about the drones should be possible. I was more pessimistic about the accounting for or surrender of anthrax, VX and mustard. We had tried hard to get clarity on these issues and I could not be sure that there was anything left— nor, if there was not, that Iraq had documentation to that effect.

Nevertheless, was it not worth taking this chance? There did not have to be any concession that the U.S./UK had the right to make solo assessments and go to war without specific Council authorization. That question could remain as moot as it was when Resolution 1441 was adopted. However, I felt the French—and for that matter several others in the Council—were worried about a scenario in which they might accept the resolution and Iraq might tolerably attain a first batch of benchmarks, yet the U.S. would nevertheless launch its war. In such a situation, all who had accepted the resolution would be said to have joined in authorizing the war.

The French impression was that the U.S. administration had decided on war already in January, and they did not want to bless it. My view was a little different. I did not doubt that there was a decision to go to war, unless by a certain date important things— a declaration of the legendary "strategic decision" and attainment of benchmarks—were to happen. In that case, a decision could be changed, deferred or suspended, and the buildup could be slowed or stopped.

Within the Security Council, Chile and five other non-permanent members, sensing that time was running out and yet feeling that demanding the attainment of benchmarks before March 17 was not a serious proposition, looked for some compromise. For a short while they consulted members about a draft that would have a list of benchmarks similar to what the British had prepared, but would replace the televised speech by Saddam with a less humiliating letter from the Iraqi leadership and would extend the time given for the attainment of benchmarks to three weeks or thirty days (both figures appeared in the hastily drafted document). It was clearly a more "realistic" paper than the British—except that the time allowed went beyond what the U.S. would tolerate. There was another vital point: As President Ricardo Lagos of Chile had explained to me on the phone while his very able Ambassador Valdes was with me, and as was evident in the draft prepared by Chile, six elected members of the Council were of the view that it was for the Council collectively to assess whether Iraq had attained the benchmarks and to decide on further action. They were not willing to let the Council abdicate this prerogative. The U.S. on the other hand was not ready to drop the claim of a right to go it alone.

The End

In the informal Council consultations on Thursday, March 13, Sir Jeremy Greenstock tried desperately to win support for the British benchmark paper. If he got "traction" on it, he could be flexible on a number of points, even altogether dropping the draft operative in paragraph 3 or, indeed, the whole draft resolution, which looked like an ultimatum. Although this step was presented as a last concession, the political signal of the benchmark paper standing alone would probably also be seen as an ultimatum. It would be understood that if the declaration was not made and/or the benchmarks not attained, serious consequences could be expected.

By Friday, March 14, all efforts to reach an agreement in the Council had collapsed. The draft prepared by Chile and five other elected members was withdrawn, the European Union ambassadors met without any convergence, and a meeting of the five permanent members was canceled. There was no traction except under the tanks in Kuwait.

We were informed that the owners of the helicopters we had chartered and used in Iraq had decided to take the machines out. They did not want to see their hardware stranded in Baghdad, as Chilean helicopters had been in 1998. We had put an alarm system in place to enable our staff to depart at short notice. We were naturally concerned, however, that Iraq might try to take hostages among our staff or that staff might be stuck in Iraqi territory with hostilities going on. We had filled our headquarters in Baghdad with stocks of drinking water, food and other necessities. In a talk I had with Kofi Annan, he said that whenever a signal was needed about withdrawal of staff from Iraq, he would give it for all UN staff, including inspectors.

The Work Program That Survived the Withdrawal of the Inspectors

With the knowledge that the U.S. would not give Iraq even five days to attain a short list of five benchmark tasks, there was something surreal about finalizing UNMOVIC's work program, which was to identify key tasks to be solved hopefully within the next four *months*. Nevertheless, we did as the 1999 resolution bade us. Having had the advice of our Commissioners regarding which tasks they felt should have the highest priority, we had drafted a program and we finalized it on Monday, March 17.

I suppose Washington considered as wasted labor all the hectic activity that went into the resolution and into a procedure that they regarded as obsolete. However, that was not the view of the Germans, French and Russians. In a declaration on Saturday, March 15, they asked that UNMOVIC should present its work program on Tuesday, March 18, that the Security Council should meet at ministerial level to approve it, that there should be a prioritization of the key tasks, and that Iraq must cooperate in the attainment of the tasks. They reaffirmed their view that nothing justified a renunciation of the inspection process and that force should only be used in the last resort.

Even on Monday, March 17, after the U.S. had asked us to withdraw the inspectors, it was requested in the Security Council that the work program should be presented for approval, that the inspectors should be given a time frame and that the Council should meet to evaluate the result. The surreality was complete when I presented the program on Wednesday, March 19—the day after our inspectors had been withdrawn from Baghdad. The reason why many members of the Council wanted to have the program on the table was no doubt that they were keen for the world to see that the inspections were going on in the good order set by the Council itself, and that the interruption was not the result of any failure of the inspection regime. It was caused by an unjustified armed action by the U.S. and the UK.

Blix and ElBaradei Invited to Baghdad

Last-minute initiatives are natural in crisis situations. One such initiative was the British espousal of the benchmark idea, with which they sought to build a bridge between U.S. impatience to see quick and tangible results of a "strategic decision" and the measured pace of a work program. Other initiatives, not publicly revealed at the time, appear to have come from influential persons within the Baghdad regime, who unsuccessfully sought direct contacts at high level in the U.S. in order to offer measures designed to stave off invasion.

One last-minute measure was a letter sent to Dr. ElBaradei and me from our opposite number in Baghdad, Dr. Al Sa'adi. It arrived on Saturday, March 15, and proposed that we should come as early as possible to Baghdad to try to accelerate the inspection process and take note of the progress achieved. I immediately contacted Mohamed, who seemed rather eager for us to go. However, what was suggested by Al Sa'adi fell far short of the ideas before the Council regarding a Saddam TV speech admitting past cheating and proclaiming a strategic decision to accomplish a list of benchmark actions, providing some evidence of Iraqi seriousness. Mohamed and I had earlier concluded that any visit to Saddam would need to be preceded by a declaration on his part. We could then come and discuss the implementation. The great emperor of Mesopotamia would hardly stoop to negotiate with lowly creatures like us, and we could not allow ourselves, least of all at this critical juncture, to go there and listen to platitudes. The best we could expect to achieve at a personal meeting would be to convey some dose of reality, which those in his environment might not dare tell him about.

It had just been announced that Bush, Blair and Spanish prime minister Aznar were to meet in the Azores the following day. As I felt their advisers should be aware of our invitation to see Saddam in Baghdad, I informed not only Kofi Annan but also the British and American permanent UN representatives. Sir Jeremy called back quickly. The UK Foreign Office urged caution. One should not give Saddam a lot of room to play games. The bars should be set high for our going. There was a need not only for a declaration but also for some "down payment." London was alluding to the benchmarks. John Negroponte said the U.S. discouraged our going. Neither capital was categorical.

We had never before sought any prior approval from the Council before traveling to Iraq, nor did we have in mind to do so now. Yet, we were not acting in a vacuum. We could hardly accept the invitation before we knew what would be declared at the Azores meeting. Kofi Annan advised that rather than demanding some prior Iraqi declaration, we might ask Al Sa'adi to clarify more precisely what he thought could be attained, and we should inform the president of the Security Council. The Azores meeting came to show that the initiative had come too late.

The same was true for the speech Saddam gave suddenly, on his own initiative, on the very day of the Azores meeting. Perhaps the speech, broadcast over his son's television network, was intended to be a kind of response to the demand for the declaration of a strategic decision. Saddam said that Iraq had had weapons of mass destruction in the past but declared that it no longer had any. There was no reference to any benchmarks that he was willing to meet.

The Azores Atlantic Summit on Sunday, March 16

The Azores meeting was a rather curious gesture, perhaps designed to demonstrate the unity of the three states that had cosponsored the draft resolution, which was still before the Security Council. When I had talked to Sir Jeremy Greenstock on the Saturday before the meeting, he had ventured that it was about peace rather than about war. However, the declaration that came out, although nebulous, looked to me more belligerent than peaceful. It referred to Saddam's defying UN resolutions for twelve years. The responsibility was his. If conflict were to occur, the U.S. and its allies would seek the affirmation of the territorial integrity of Iraq. Any "military presence" would be temporary.

I watched the broadcast from the Azores at the ABC TV studios in Manhattan, where I was waiting to be interviewed by Swedish television. Later, sitting before the camera and listening through the earpiece to the questions from Stockholm, I said it seemed to me that there had been a difference in tone between Bush and Blair. Bush had talked about the dictator and the cruel regime and what a bright future Iraq would have if Saddam was taken out. Blair had talked about going the last mile for peace and about the need for the UN to stop a proliferator. Perhaps Blair still had some hope that Saddam would crack—confess his sins and promise to mend his ways—if he were faced with a unanimous Council resolution.

For France and others, the chief problem with the procedure was that once it had been endorsed by the Council, the U.S. and UK would not feel any obligation to go back to the Council for a joint appraisal of Iraq's action and a joint decision on further action, but would feel free to go to war unilaterally if they assessed the Iraqi response to be inadequate. In the view of Blair, one could not have a resolution that simply stipulated further discussions. In the view of President Jacques Chirac, Iraq did not represent an immediate threat that justified an immediate war. France would not by a vote on the resolution signal agreement with the view that the U.S. and UK had a free hand in the use of force. As France had intimated that it would vote against the resolution if it were put to the vote, France became the magnet for U.S. and UK anger. However, the French feelings were probably shared not only by Germany, Russia and China but also by a majority of the members on the Council.

Whether or not there was a difference in the hopes that Bush and Blair harbored at the Azores, the statement from the one-hour meeting was at this late stage perhaps less an ultimatum to Saddam than one to the members of the Security Council—to support the resolution or be bypassed.

The game was over. Final clarity would come on my return to the office later that Sunday afternoon. As I sat around the table with my senior staff, I got the call from John Wolf in Washington saying that it was time to withdraw our inspectors from Iraq.

I had just been asked on Swedish television if I longed for home, and I answered that I had just heard that the snow was falling up at my country cottage in Sweden. Of course I was longing for home. . . .

12

After War: Weapons of Mass Disappearance

When armed action was taken in Iraq, it was pursued swiftly and skillfully, leading to victory and occupation in less than a month's time. One of the bloodiest regimes the world has seen was eliminated. Saddam Hussein was not caught for many months, but a giant statue of him was felled in early April before the eyes of relieved Iraqis and the television cameras of the whole world. The next items the world expected to see were the dreaded weapons of mass destruction.

It had been a surprise that the Iraqi military forces had provided so little resistance. Another welcome surprise had been that they had used no chemical or biological weapons. They had used them extensively in the war with Iran in the 1980s and against their own Kurdish citizens at Halabja, but after sharp American warnings, they had not made use of them during the 1991 Gulf War. The fear this time had been that they might use them when they felt their backs were up against the wall.

The U.S. military leadership appears to have been convinced that Iraq had an ample supply of unconventional weapons. Protective suits had been distributed to their soldiers and were donned repeatedly in the first part of the military campaign. The prudence was understandable. Somewhat amazing, however, was that apparently several hundred million dollars had been budgeted for the destruction of any weapons of mass destruction that might be found. This was more than the sum of several years' UNMOVIC budgets.

Had it not made the slightest impression that the inspectors of UNMOVIC and those of the preceding UN inspection organization had searched all over Iraq for a number of years without finding any traces of chemical weapons? Their reports were certainly known to the U.S. Department of State, Department of Defense and CIA.

When, shortly before the war, President Bush and Secretary Powell had talked about the "moment of truth," they presumably meant that the occupation of Iraq would bring tangible confirmation of the existence of Iraqi weapons of mass destruction and of the brutality of the regime. In the latter respect their predictions proved right, as mass graves were opened and as detained people emerged from the Iraqi regime's horror prisons and told their stories.

However, the existence of the prohibited weapons, which had been declared to the world with such certainty and been invoked as the foremost justification of the war, was not confirmed. They were simply nowhere to be found.

There was speculation that the weapons could have been taken to Syria. However, no evidence to that effect was presented, and one wonders whether the Syrian government, under increasing U.S. pressure, would have accepted such a poisoned chalice. Further, would such transports not have been spotted by satellites or other surveillance? Another explanation advanced was that the weapons might have been destroyed by the regime just before the U.S. troops arrived. Again, no evidence was presented, and one would query whether this could have been done with inspectors circulating on the ground and much surveillance going on overhead. Other explanations, also given without evidence, were that the weapons might have been looted or buried.

Strangely, no one seemed inclined to test the thesis that the missing chemical and biological weapons had in fact been destroyed in 1991—an assertion which had been made consistently by the Iraqi side, and which the UN inspectors had sought to verify. Did it seem too absurd that weapons that had been chased for more than ten years and had now triggered war might not have existed all that time?

Dr. Amir Al Sa'adi, who had represented the Iraqi government in my dealings with it in 2002 and 2003, was the first high-level Iraqi who surrendered to the allied troops, after he learned that he was among the officials being looked for. As he gave himself up, he said to German television (which had been alerted by his German wife), "There are no weapons of mass destruction and time will bear me out." He did not say when they had been destroyed, but in discussions with me and my colleagues he had always maintained that it had been the summer of 1991, after Hussein Kamel, the son-in-law of Saddam, had ordered it. This was, indeed, also what Kamel himself had said when he defected to Amman in 1995 and talked to Rolf Ekeus, who was then the head of the first inspection organization (UNSCOM). It is also what a number of other Iraqi scientists and military officers have been saying since the occupation began.

That considerable destruction of chemical and biological weapons had taken place in the summer of 1991 had been verified much later by both UNSCOM and UNMOVIC. The problem, acknowledged by Dr. Al Sa'adi, was that the Iraqi side had no solid documentary evidence about the quantities that had been destroyed. It claimed that all documents had been destroyed along with all the chemical and biological weapons. This could all have been true, but it was also possible—and this was our concern—that documents had been hidden and quantities of chemical and biological weapons had been squirreled away. Large quantities of chemical weapons had been found by UNSCOM later than the summer of 1991 and been destroyed under its supervision. However, these quantities had not been concealed but had been found at sites that had been declared by the Iraqi side.

As far as I have been able to check, neither UNSCOM nor UNMOVIC ever found weapons on sites that had not been declared. This certainly does not allow the conclusion that there could not be such sites, but at any rate the Iraqi contention is not contradicted by evidence. Another matter is that the Iraqi side in many cases tried to conceal that installations and facilities had served in the production or storage of prohibited weapons or activities. The aim may have been to protect valuable buildings that could serve other purposes—or it could have been to retain infrastructure to facilitate a restart of weapons programs in the future. In either case, the buildings were condemned and destroyed.

At the time of finishing the manuscript of this book in early January 2004, the resumed search for weapons in Iraq has been pursued for more than a year—by UNMOVIC before the occupation and by U.S. teams, mainly the Iraq Survey Group (ISG), thereafter. While both groups have identified missile-related activities, including the production of missiles whose range contravened UN restrictions, it seems highly improbable that any significant stocks or stores of other prohibited weapons or items would have escaped discovery, had they existed. Considering the miserable economic and social situation of Iraqi scientists, military people and technical experts, the rewards promised to persons who helped to reveal any stocks should have produced leads and results.

Such rewards should also have stimulated the revelation of any low-key programs designed to maintain capabilities in the fields of chemical and biological weapons. The existence of such programs would per se appear plausible, at least to maintain a jump-start capability for some future day when Security Council restrictions would no longer apply. While UNMOVIC inspections did not find signs of such programs, the head of the Iraq Survey Group, David Kay, claimed in a statement about his interim report of October 2, 2003, that the group had discovered "dozens of WMD-related program activities and significant amounts of equipment that Iraq had concealed from the United Nations during the inspections that began in late 2002."

In the absence of any finds of prohibited weapons, the alleged existence of these programs was, not unexpectedly, highlighted by the U.S. and UK governments. Considering how many earlier contentions of this kind have disintegrated under closer scrutiny, the statement about the report of the Kay group will need to be supported by a public presentation of evidence that can be examined. Laboratories, chemicals and equipment like fermentors are said to have been found, which could have dual use—i.e., may be used both for legitimate peaceful purposes and for prohibited purposes. However, this is hardly enough for a conclusion that they *were* actually used or intended to be used for proscribed purposes. Another, more technical legal question is whether Iraq might have been required to declare them under the November 2002 resolution, if the authorities were aware of them.

Perhaps, with the capture of Saddam Hussein in mid-December 2003, reliable information can be obtained both about when the last prohibited weapons were destroyed and about any low-key programs that might have been maintained or started. We now know that while the armed operation in Iraq was successful, the main diagnosis suggesting the operation—existence of weapons of mass destruction—appears to have been wrong. It was like surgery intended to remove something malignant finding that the malignancy was not there. Moreover, the absence of prohibited items was most likely a result of the imposition of the regime of inspection, eradication and monitoring by the UN, supported by military pressure from the U.S. and the UK. The UN and the world had succeeded in disarming Iraq without knowing it. In American terminology before September 11, 2001, this had been called "keeping Saddam in his box." Colin Powell is reported to have said, "I think we ought to declare our containment policy a success. We have kept him in his box." Vice President Cheney was quoted as saying, even five days after September 11, "Saddam Hussein is bottled up." Very different lines were taken later, but the first ones were better rooted in reality.

The Mother of All Misjudgments

If we conclude that there were no stocks of prohibited weapons, it still remains to verify if, as contended by the Iraqi side, these weapons were mainly destroyed in 1991 or later. As I noted, one way to do that might be through interviews with the large number of Iraqis who were said to have taken part in the destruction. It also remains to clarify how the assessments of the U.S. and UK could go so wrong, not least about the most important category of WMD: nuclear weapons.

While nuclear weapons are routinely lumped together with biological and chemical in the omnibus expression "weapons of mass destruction," it is obvious that they are in a class by themselves. The outside world's concerns about Iraq's weapons would never have been a very big issue if it had not been for Iraqi initiatives to acquire nuclear weapon capacity, and for the level of success it had attained by 1990 in enriching uranium. It is the more disturbing, then, that categorical and key contentions about continued Iraqi nuclear efforts and attainments, made at the highest levels of the U.S. and UK governments from 2002 on, were simply wrong, and could have been avoided with a moderate dose of prudence.

I am not suggesting that Blair and Bush spoke in bad faith, but I am suggesting that it would not have taken much critical thinking on their own part or the part of their close advisers to prevent statements that misled the public. Why was it that they listened so little to and, in the cases of Mr. Cheney and Mr. Wolfowitz, seem to have had such disdain for the assessments and analyses of the IAEA?

Even if one day there were to be solid evidence that Iraq had maintained some low-key illegal programs, it would not change the conclusion that the categorical assertions about the existence of weapons of mass destruction—and the dismissal of doubts about those assertions—were plainly wrong.

Investigative journalists, particularly in the U.S. and the UK, have done a tremendous job of examining claims, uncovering errors and seeking the truth.

Reasons Why Intelligence Went Wrong

Tyrants like Saddam Hussein are not persuaded by olive branches. The UN Charter, written after the defeat of dictators, does not rule out the use of military pressure, armed force or intelligence. It does, however, prefer peaceful solutions.

Intelligence is indispensable for national defense and for combating subversion and terrorism. I have great respect for the many people I have met in that difficult profession, some of whom are living with very different risks from those which we encounter around the conference table. Yet, for all the billions of dollars spent on satellites and other overhead surveillance, on electronic eavesdropping, on export controls, on the debriefing of defectors and on human espionage, I have to conclude that the failures in the case of Iraq were monumental.

Iraq was a brutal place, and espionage on the ground must have been difficult. It seems that after the end of the Cold War, the United States (though not necessarily its allies) had reduced its network of agents in the field and did not have agents inside Iraq. Defectors appear to have played a very significant role in the U.S. dossier. Mr. Rumsfeld, for one, said that things were found by defectors, not by inspectors. Perhaps too much reliance was placed upon them.

There was in the Bush administration too little attention paid to the cautious UN inspection reports, which were based on visits to sites, interviews and close examination of records from Iraq. When the reports were used at the political level there was a tendency to misread them and use them in support of preconceived convictions. The contempt which both Vice President Cheney and the leadership in the U.S. Department of Defense appear to have held for international inspections deprived them, in effect, of a valuable source of information.

Many of the erroneous points made publicly by U.S. and UK leadership could have been avoided if they had, at the least, faithfully rendered what the inspection commissions had written in their reports, rather than distorting what was there. For instance, on January 23, 2003, Paul Wolfowitz cited figures that UNSCOM had presented in 1997 regarding quantities of various biological and chemical agents which the inspectors calculated Iraq had once produced or could have produced. The meaning he gave to these figures was very different, however, from that given by UNSCOM. In the absence of credible information about what had happened to any given quantity, UNSCOM concluded that it was "unaccounted for." This involved no assertion that the quantity still existed, nor did it exclude that possibility. However, after citing liters and tonnages from an UNSCOM report, Mr. Wolfowitz concluded, "Despite eleven years of inspections and sanctions, containment and military response, Baghdad *retains* chemical and biological weapons and is producing more (my emphasis)."

Another case: Mr. Stuart A. Cohen was acting chairman of the National Intelligence Council when the 2002 National Intelligence Estimate on Iraq's weapons of mass destruction was published. In an article that appeared on November 30, 2003, he stated that the estimate "judged with high confidence that Iraq *had* chemical and biological weapons." He then went on to say, "These were essentially the same conclusions reached by the United Nations and by a wide array of intelligence services—friendly and unfriendly alike." What Mr. Cohen said about other intelligence services may well be correct, if I can judge by my impressions from meetings with some of them. However, he provided the same misrepresentation as Mr. Wolfowitz did of the UN reports. If it is not a conscious misrepresentation, then it is even worse, because it would mean that this former high intelligence official assumed that anything "unaccounted for" existed. Preparing a national intelligence estimate with such an approach could lead to unduly ominous conclusions.

The suspicion that this is precisely what was done is strengthened by an article in the *International Herald Tribune* (November 19, 2003) which reported that a broad reappraisal of intelligence about illicit weapons programs was being made in the U.S. It cites an official explaining the need for the action by referring to the handling of the case of Iraq: "The absence of evidence that Iraq had destroyed its chemical and biological weapons appeared to have been interpreted by intelligence agencies as evidence that it still possessed them."

A few further thoughts on why intelligence failed . . .

The rock-solid conviction at the governmental level in the U.S. and UK that weapons existed, and the expectation at that level that they would be provided evidence proving this conviction correct probably had an influence on the intelligence communities, just as it did on other people and media. A former director of the strategic, proliferation and military affairs office in the U.S. Department of State, Greg Thielmann, said in July 2003 that "this administration [in the U.S.] has had a faith-based intelligence attitude [in] its top-down use of intelligence: we know the answers, give us the intelligence to support those answers."

The Economist (October 4, 2003) suggested that some of the thinking resembled that of medieval inquisitors, convinced of the existence of witches. Saddam Hussein filled perfectly the role of an evil spirit, and Iraq was a rogue state which refused to open its closets filled with pots of poison and vials of germs. Any straw in the wind was seen as evidence confirming the view that the weapons were there. In a telling *Sunday Telegraph* interview on November 23, 2003, David Kay said that being inside Iraq gave a great advantage: "We don't have to grasp at straws of evidence."

A common denominator of the failures, it appears, was *a deficit of critical thinking.* In their efforts to get at reality, courts use cross-examination to force a critical consideration of evidence. In the academic world, use is often made of a peer-group review to ensure critical scrutiny of scientific works. The assertion about Iraqi weapons of mass destruction had been so oft repeated that it was taken for granted in much of the world. The intelligence communities themselves should have provided the critical thinking but, like others, they seem to have been somewhat carried away. As I have said, intelligence agencies prefer to err on the alarmist side, because they will normally not be criticized for overstating threats but will be severely criticized for minimizing dangers or not identifying them—as happened before the 1991 Gulf War when they, like the IAEA, lacked knowledge about Iraq's nuclear weapons program.

The tragic case of David Kelly, the UK scientist and government adviser who committed suicide, I think shows how squeezed the badly needed critical thinking became under the pressures of politics. Kelly's critical scientific mind served him well when examining the Iraqi dossier. Applying the same critical sense when examining

British reports and reacting against exaggerated claims was more problematic.

Why were UNMOVIC and the IAEA not carried away? We had the advantage, compared to some of the national intelligence services, of being less exposed to pressures from the outside and from above. Our loyalty was to the Security Council, with its many member states and diverse opinions. In fairness, I must also say that despite their wishes and expectations, none of the governments involved ever suggested to us that we disregard critical thinking, whether we were examining Iraqi or other dossiers. Another advantage was the important international civil service tradition that normally prevails in the UN system. On no occasion did I find that staff members, whether of American, British, French, Russian or any other nationality, were influenced by positions that the governments of their home states had taken or could be expected to take.

UNMOVIC's exercise of independent critical judgment was, I believe, the main reason why our analyses and assessment were respected and accepted. Like most others, we at UNMOVIC certainly *suspected* that Iraq might still have hidden stocks of chemical and biological weapons. However, we were not asked by the Security Council to submit suspicions or simply to convey testimony from defectors. Assessments and judgments in our reports had to be based on evidence that would remain convincing even under critical international examination. This was why, to the despair of some government officials, our reports did not lend themselves to the categorical conclusions these officials wanted to draw. What would the reputation of international inspection be today if we had simply said "amen" to the many contentions that were claimed to be evidence, and later fell on the table like a house of cards?

Iraqi Conduct Gave Nourishment to Suspicions That It Retained Weapons of Mass Destruction

The whole world has memories about the cat-and-mouse play between Iraq and inspectors in the 1990s. The impression was that

Iraq was trying to hide prohibited weapons. That was also the impression created when Iraq kept inspectors out for about four years. If, as now seems most probable, no weapons were hidden and those that had been deemed "unaccounted for" had either never existed or been largely destroyed as early as 1991, we must look for some other reasons why the Iraqi regime allowed the impression to arise that it was keeping weapons—an impression that supported years of sanctions which crippled the country's economy and ruined its people's standard of living. In my view, the following elements may have been relevant:

- Better cooperation with the inspectors was not expected to lead to a lifting of sanctions. Saddam Hussein had heard again and again from the U.S. that only his own disappearance would achieve it. Why should he make an effort at greater cooperation?
- A sense of humiliation might have led the Iraqis to balk at giving the inspectors access in some cases, especially to various sites they associated with the sovereignty of their country. Saddam Hussein saw himself as a modern King Nebuchadnezzar, and had enormous pride in himself and in Iraq. Asked when taken prisoner why he would not let inspectors into his facilities if he had no weapons, he was reported to have said, "We didn't want them to go into the presidential areas and intrude on our privacy." If the inspectors felt it was a game of cat and mouse, perhaps to Saddam and the regime it was "sneak and peek." One of the chiefs of the chemical weapons program, Brigadier General Alaa Saeed, when asked after the war why Saddam did not help the UN resolve hundreds of unanswered questions about banned weapons, is reported to have answered, according to the *Los Angeles Times,* "I don't know. Maybe he is too proud."
- The Iraqi regime demanded that the UN should lift sanctions, claiming that Iraq had eliminated all prohibited weapons and fulfilled all obligations. Yet, like someone who

puts up a sign warning BEWARE OF DOG without having a dog, perhaps the Iraqi regime did not mind inspiring in others the thought that it had weapons of mass destruction and was still dangerous.

• The Iraqi regime may have wanted to maintain secrecy about facilities harboring conventional military forces and weapons. While such facilities were clearly subject to inspection—where should one look for weapons if not in military installations?—the close relations which existed up to the end of 1998 between some UNSCOM inspectors and the military authorities of countries that were bombing targets in Iraq might have led the regime to obstruct visits to some such sites.

The Invasion of Iraq Was about Weapons of Mass Destruction

In a now famous interview, U.S. Deputy Secretary of Defense Wolfowitz said that Iraq's weapons of mass destruction were chosen as the rationale for the war for "bureaucratic" reasons, implying that while there were many other reasons, this was the only rationale that could rally broad support in U.S. public opinion and that stood a chance at having appeal outside the U.S. and inside the United Nations.

Even with strong concerns in the world (and especially the U.S.) about the spread of WMD, it would hardly have been possible to develop a policy comprising the possibility of war on Iraq had it not been for the terror attacks of September 11, 2001. Prior to this, there had not been any serious concern in the U.S. or elsewhere about Iraq retaining a nuclear weapons program. Nor was it seriously claimed that there was any significant link between the Iraqi regime and those responsible for the terror attack. Nevertheless, there was a theoretical nexus between terrorists and weapons of mass destruction—even nuclear weapons—and there had been a factual nexus between Iraq and such weapons. This, combined with the fury caused by the terrorist attacks, appears to have led to a notion in the U.S. government that its removal of Al Qaeda and the Taliban regime in Afghanistan needed to be supplemented by an elimination of Saddam Hussein and Iraq's alleged weapons of mass destruction, as another potential source of aggression against the United States.

The general view that Iraq obstructed the UN and the world in the elimination of WMD was the obvious rationale to advance for such action. It was the only one that was presented as a justification in the United Nations, and it was by far the most important reason offered to the U.S. Congress and the American public.

Neither the U.S. nor the UK government would have been likely to get a mandate from its legislature to intervene with arms for the sole purpose of eliminating Saddam's reign of terror. It is also most unlikely that they would have got such a mandate from the Security Council.

It may be that the United Nations will one day in the not too distant future authorize armed action to free small or medium-sized countries from horrible regimes they cannot rid themselves of— a Saddam Hussein or a Pol Pot. I, for one, would find such an evolution desirable. The most important obstacle to this, however, is likely to be a reluctance to pay the cost for such action in lives and resources, rather than any restrictions in the UN Charter.

The Iraq war cannot be undone. The costs of the war and the occupation—in terms of loss of lives and property, billions of dollars spent, damage to the UN and NATO, credibility of political leaders, the fostering of hatred, and so on—are written in red. What we can do is examine if there are other things to be written in black. We must also ask if there are important lessons to be drawn.

The obvious first thing to write in big black letters is the destruction of one of the bloodiest regimes and most ruthless rulers the world has seen since World War II. This was, indeed, a welcome result of the war, but was neither the avowed aim nor the justification given for it.

The second thing to write in black is that the war might promote the emergence of democracy in Iraq and elsewhere in the Middle

East. With the capture of Saddam Hussein and the elimination of his regime, the Iraqi population is made conscious that going back to the order of yesterday is not an option. One would certainly wish that after decades of tyranny and war, the people will mobilize their own considerable intellectual resources and be given a maximum of help from the world to move toward a democracy in which the different religious and ethnic groups will learn to cooperate.

A third point would be whether terrorism was dealt a blow through the armed action. Some would write yes in black and argue that that all terrorist movements will know that after the experience of September 11, 2001, the U.S. will go after any movement that it perceives as a threat. Others will write in red that there is a risk that, especially if further mistakes are made, more states and people around the world may come to view the U.S. as a global bully, and that many Muslims and Arabs will consider the occupation of Iraq a humiliation, and that this feeling may breed hatred—and further terrorism.

There is a fourth point, which Condoleezza Rice would consider a plus, but on which I would disagree. She tried in October 2003, somewhat heroically I think, to argue that if the resolutions of the UN had "not been enforced, the credibility of the United Nations [would have] been in tatters. The effectiveness of the Security Council as an instrument of enforcing the will of the world, and of keeping the peace, would have been weakened." The Security Council did not pronounce itself against enforcement through the use of arms. The majority of the Council felt that it was too early to abandon the path of inspections, which had been followed only for three and a half months. There is something strange about the argument that the authority of the Security Council could be upheld by a minority of states in the Council ignoring the views of the majority. Can the will of the world be enforced by an action (in this case preemptive) by one or a few states, even when this action runs counter to the expressed will of the world?

Some further points have been advanced in support of the war in Iraq as a means of countering the proliferation of weapons of mass destruction, regardless of the absence of any finds of such weapons. It is suggested that the war *sent a signal* to states or movements inclined to acquire weapons of mass destruction, that in so doing they may incur more risks than they may gain security. The decision by Colonel Qaddafi in December 2003 to abandon whatever incipient mass destruction weapons programs Libya may have had may be seen as pointing in that direction.

However, it is risky to generalize. One need only think of the situations of Iran and North Korea. It might also be argued that the case of Libya shows that a successful inducement to non-proliferation is possible without armed action. We now know that Iraq under Saddam almost certainly did not have any weapons of mass destruction, and that the regime was, in fact, deterred from maintaining or reviving prohibited weapons programs by the presence of UN inspection and the U.S./UK threat supporting it. The much maligned, relatively low-cost policy of containment had worked, and the high-cost policy of counter-proliferation had not been needed.

Against that background (that in all likelihood Iraq did not possess WMD), the possibility would not seem excluded that the Iraqi regime could have done what Colonel Qaddafi did. This was, indeed, what the British urged Saddam Hussein to do in a draft Security Council resolution at about the same time that they appear to have begun their talks with Libya—just before negotiations in the Security Council broke down and the war was started in Iraq.

In an interview in December 2003, President Bush said that it made no real difference if Saddam Hussein had *had* weapons of mass destruction or only the possible *intention* of acquiring them. In either case, the world was better without him. It is.

However, one would think and hope that the first line taken by President Bush only reflects a political leader's perfectly normal unwillingness to admit that something went wrong. President Bush has correctly argued that terrorists and tyrants do not send notice before they attack; it seems certain that he would not have decided in favor of war, and asked the U.S. Congress to authorize it, if he had known that there were no weapons of mass destruction in Iraq and only some suggestions that Saddam would seek to acquire them in the future.

Indeed, presence or absence of weapons ought to make a difference as regards the response that is to be chosen. It might be argued that a clear threat of use of weapons of mass destruction within forty-five minutes—or even within four and a half months—might justify prompt preventive military action. It should be harder to hold that the possibility that such a weapon might be created in forty-five *months'* time and come to constitute what President Bush called "a gathering danger" would allow immediate military action and occupation. If, as all seem to say, force should be used only as a means of last resort, then these threats should trigger immediate countermeasures less severe than armed invasion.

It might rightly be objected that these comments start from a knowledge that was not available in March 2003. At that time, no one—the UN inspectors and myself included—could *guarantee* that Iraq was without any weapons of mass destruction. Could it have been argued that this uncertainty was intolerable and required elimination by armed action? It could, but I think it is unlikely that such an argument would have been endorsed by the legislatures of the U.S. and the UK, let alone the UN Security Council. Presumably it was an awareness of this circumstance that led the U.S. and UK governments to claim certainty that the weapons existed.

In justification of the armed action, it might be said further that being convinced—even though mistakenly—that Saddam Hussein had weapons of mass destruction and posed an imminent danger, the U.S. and UK governments had to take preemptive armed action. However, they could not have failed to notice that in March 2003 Iraq was a shadow of the military power it had been when it was defeated in the Gulf War in 1991. Moreover, if there was any one weapons area where all—including the U.S.—had felt Saddam was disarmed, it was the nuclear. It took much twisted evidence, including a forged uranium contract, to conjure up a revived Iraqi nuclear threat, even one that was somewhat distant.

It is far more probable that the governments were conscious that they were exaggerating the risks they saw in order to get the political support they would not otherwise have had. I think this is the conclusion that a large segment of the public has drawn. The consequence is a loss in credibility. It is understood and accepted that governments must simplify complex international matters in explaining them to the public in democratic states. However, they are not just vendors of merchandise but leaders from whom some sincerity should be asked when they exercise their responsibility for war and peace in the world.

The Role of Inspection in the Efforts to Prevent Proliferation of WMD and to Secure the Disarming of States

The public debate about the Iraq war has focused less on inspection than on political justifications, on unilateral preemptive action, on the role of the UN Security Council and on intelligence. Yet the role and results of inspections were at the center of the affair. To the U.S. hawks there was little problem: They knew the weapons of mass destruction were there. Secretary of Defense Rumsfeld knew that the defectors were a good source of information and the inspectors were not. To Vice President Cheney, the inspectors were useless at best. To the Germans, French, Russians, Chinese and many others, inspections were working reasonably well in March 2003 and should have been allowed to continue, at least for some time.

In the Security Council, the U.S. and the UK, like all others, expressed appreciation for what they saw as professional, independent and effective service by the inspection organizations. Yet, while the reports of the inspectors were an important factor in leading the majority of the Council to withhold authorization for a war, the governments of the U.S. and the UK trusted their own faulty intelligence more than those inspection reports, which did not confirm that weapons of mass destruction existed.

After the war, it is becoming clear that inspection and monitoring by the IAEA, UNMOVIC and its predecessor UNSCOM, backed by military, political and economic pressure, had indeed worked for years, achieving Iraqi disarmament and deterring Saddam from rearming. *Containment* had worked, in other words. It has also become clear that national intelligence organizations and government hawks, but not the inspectors, had been wrong in their assessments. Not without some pleasure, I cite a statement from July 9, 2003, by Joseph Cirincione, director of the non-proliferation project at the Carnegie Endowment in Washington:

> In the light of the past three months of fruitless searches by U.S., British, and Australian experts, the UNMOVIC inspection process in Iraq now looks much better than critics at the time claimed. It appears that the inspection process was working, and if it had been given enough time and enough resources, could have continued to work and effectively stymied and prevented any new Iraqi efforts on weapons of mass destruction. Never have so few been criticized by so many with so little justification.

This assessment is reinforced by the Carnegie study on threats from Saddam's Iraq, released in January 2004, where Cirincione and his colleagues come to the quite damning conclusion that the threats were highly exaggerated and distorted by the Bush administration.

An important question is how inspections will be shaped and used as an element in future efforts to prevent the further spread of weapons of mass destruction and to ensure disarmament. The main elements in these efforts are:

> • foreign policies that provide individual states with adequate security and thereby reduce the incentive to acquire weapons of mass destruction. They may consist of global and regional détente initiatives, protective alliances, or security guarantees;

- treaty commitments, like the Nuclear Non-Proliferation Treaty and the Chemical Weapons Convention, but also regional treaties that establish zones free of nuclear weapons;
- inspection and monitoring programs to create confidence that the commitments are being honored and that cheating is not occurring;
- export and transport controls that make it more difficult to acquire, transfer, or produce weapons of mass destruction.

These tools may be supplemented by pressures of various kinds and by positive incentives, such as economic assistance. They are designed to create confidence and containment without the use of force.

Counter-proliferation, on the other hand, consists of more active measures to prevent the further spread of weapons of mass destruction or to stop ongoing proliferation activities. Options might include targeted operations against laboratories, factories, or nuclear installations, or outright invasion and war.

In Iraq, none of the containment measures had worked before the Gulf War to stop Iraqi efforts to create nuclear weapons and other weapons of mass destruction. Foreign intelligence agencies failed to discover the Iraqi programs, and the inspection system applied by the IAEA in Iraq before the Gulf War did not detect the nuclear weapons program that was being developed. Therefore, after the Gulf War the safeguards system was replaced by the highly intrusive Security Council-mandated inspection and monitoring system under Resolutions 687, 1284, and 1441.

What was generally believed and accepted (that is, until the terrorist attacks on the United States on September 11, 2001) has now been confirmed: This system, backed up by military pressure and by sanctions that provided control of exports, did work and provided effective containment. There is much to be learned from this system and its application. The UNMOVIC experience showed that it was possible to build up a professional and effective UN inspection system that was supported but not controlled by individual governments and that, therefore, had international legitimacy.

Nevertheless, in March 2003 the policy of containment was abandoned in the case of Iraq and counter-proliferation was applied: a combined UN and IAEA inspection force of fewer than 200 inspectors costing perhaps $80 million per year was pushed out and replaced by an invasion force of some 300,000 personnel costing approximately $80 billion per year. The experience showed what a muscular counter-proliferation operation can achieve in a very short time, but it also raised troubling questions.

It was not reasonable to maintain that individual members of the Security Council had the right to take armed action to uphold decisions of the Council when a majority of the Council was not yet ready to authorize that action.

The right of self-defense if an armed attack occurs is recognized and necessary, as was the case in Iraq's attack on Kuwait in 1990. After September 11, the Bush administration maintained that in some situations a state must have the right to use armed force in anticipation of an attack—to take preemptive action. This raises the question of how one can determine that an attack is, in fact, forthcoming. In some situations such a determination might be obvious and would be generally accepted. But in other situations, especially when there does not appear to be an immediate threat, this right may be questioned and, if the intelligence is not sufficiently convincing, the state will be deemed to have abused the right of self-defense if it proceeds with the attack. The action taken against Iraq in 2003 did not strengthen the case for a right to preemptive action.

There was another option for the states that wished to take armed action against Iraq in the spring of 2003. They could have heeded the Council's requests for more time for inspection. Support by the Security Council for preemptive armed action would have given the armed action legitimacy.

Instead, a greater price was paid for this action: in the compromised legitimacy of the action, in the damaged credibility of the governments pursuing it, and in the diminished authority of the United Nations.

Index

Index

Index

Index

Index

Index

Index

Villepin, Dominique de, 94, 129, 170,
175, 180–1, 241–2
Vorontsov, Yuli, 24

weapons of mass destruction
(WMD), 6, 11, 20, 54
"cluster" document and, 226–7
counter-proliferation and, 11, 148,
266–7, 273
future of, 272–3
inspectors' search for, 12, 13, 119
intelligence misjudgment of, 260–4,
270–1
Iraq's alleged destruction of, 67,
256–7
lack of, 205, 255–60
programs related to, 258–9
U.S. claims of, 73–4, 111, 113, 169, 170,
177, 237–8, 260, 271
Weismen, Steven, 91

Welch, David, 48
Wolf, John, 6, 167, 183, 184, 189, 253
cluster document and, 190, 198,
200–2, 202–3, 212, 241
criticism of inspections by, 221,
221–2, 235
Wolfowitz, Paul, 61, 81, 83, 87, 88, 238
on aluminum tubes, 232
on inspectors vs. investigators, 152,
260
on "regime change" in Iraq, 62,
136–7
on weapons of Iraq, 261–2, 266
World Economic Forum, 233

yellowcake, 233–4

Zifferero, Maurizio, 22, 24
Zinser, Adolfo, 185
Zlauvinen, Gustavo, 81

A NOTE ON THE AUTHOR

Hans Blix was the director general of the International Atomic Energy Agency from 1981 to 1997 and was a member of Sweden's delegation to the United Nations from 1961 to 1981. From 2000 to 2003, he was the executive director of the United Nations Monitoring, Verification and Inspection Commission (UNMOVIC), supervising international inspections for weapons of mass destruction in Iraq until the inspections were suspended in March 2003. Blix has been named chairman of the newly formed International Commission on Weapons of Mass Destruction, which began its work in January 2004. He lives in Sweden.

A NOTE ON THE TYPE

This book was set in Minion, a typeface produced by the Adobe
Corporation specifically for the Macintosh personal computer,
and released in 1990. Designed by Robert Slimback, Minion com-
bines the classic characteristics of old style faces with the full com-
pliment of weights required for modern typesetting.

Composed by North Market Street Graphics,
Lancaster, Pennsylvania
Printed and bound by R. R. Donnelley & Sons,
Harrisonburg, Virginia